IRON SHARPENS IRON

Iron Sharpens Iron

*Daily Proverbs for Today's
Martial Artist*

MELINDA RANGEL

This book is dedicated to Chris,
Jenna and Jared.
Without you there would not be
a story to tell.

CONTENTS

INTRODUCTION

Why a Devotional?

All my life I have been in church. A foundational teaching was to read my Bible daily. I have not always been faithful to that teaching and my excuse often was that I did not understand it. All the "thous" and "shalts" just wasn't the language that I used every day, so it seemed a little foreign sometimes. As a child, Sunday School was the best teaching for me because I had a teacher tell me the stories of the Bible, explain the meanings, and introduce me to the people who God used to do miraculous things. In class I learned about the promises of God and the blessings that are mine as His child. Having the Bible taught to me made the words easier to understand.

As I got older, I found different versions of the Bible that also helped transform the words to apply them to my life. But the one thing that really encourages me in my walk with the Lord is a daily devotional. On the bookshelf behind me right now, I have dozens of devotional books that I have read over and over that help me grow in my understanding of what I am reading in scripture. I also enjoy finding Bible plans on my Bible app and reading them on my phone. Because I have found these tools to be a powerful and motivating factor in my life, I decided to write a devotional that might help others and give them a tool to strengthen their walk.

Why Martial Arts?

Some devotionals target specific groups of people and topics, but I have not found a devotional that speaks directly to the martial artist. For some, it's hard to imagine how martial arts and Christianity can go together, as it can seem like this sport promotes fighting and aggression. However, I have found that God will use absolutely anything to bring glory to His name and reach others if you allow Him to use the talents you've been given. I Corinthians 10:31 tells us, "So, *whether you eat or drink or whatever you do, do it all for the glory of God.*"

There are so many correlations to our walk with Christ and martial arts. Just look at how the two focus on discipline and self-control and emphasize respect and treating others kindly. Being a Christian martial artist should not be a foreign thing. In fact, the two go together beautifully.

So why write to the martial artist? For one, it's who we are in my house. My husband Chris has been in martial arts all his life, and his father and grandfather were martial artists before him. My children, Jenna and Jared, are both martial artists. We are surrounded by martial artist friends and people we train with daily who encourage us and walk beside us. It's who we are in our family and it's the people we love. Second, not only are we martial artists, but we are human beings who need Christ. Not just my family in this house, but my entire martial arts family and those we meet around the country in this sport need to know about the saving grace of God. So, I am writing to you to encourage you in your daily walk.

My Hope for You

By reading this devotional, my hope for you is:

- The Word of God comes to life for you by reading daily devotions that speak through a lens of martial arts, something you enjoy.
- God will reveal Himself to you in a new way and you will grow closer to Him.
- You are encouraged and uplifted every day by finding new truths and wisdoms that you can apply to your life.

My Hope for this Devotional

Our school, Ultimate Martial Arts, has the privilege of ministering to people in our community and our students. We sometimes travel to other places to compete and train, but our daily impact is right here within the walls of the school and in the lives of those who train here. My first hope is this devotional will minister to everyone who comes through our doors at UMA. In fact, just recently a student returned who had trained at our school as a young boy. He came not just to train, but because he was hurting. The loss of his mother, the tensions in his family, and the remarriage of his father were heavy on his heart. When Chris came home from class that night and told me this student had returned, I immediately thought, "I wish this book was done so I could give it to him."

It's not that I have anything profoundly wise to say; I simply want to walk beside you, and hope this devotional helps you draw closer to God.

My other hope is that this devotional goes beyond the walls of our school and reaches the entire martial arts community. As an individual, I hope this devotional ministers to you personally, but I also hope that it becomes a tool that you can give to someone who is hurting. I want it to be a tool that you can use to witness and help others.

Lastly, I hope that this devotional helps you find your life verse – the verse that you hold on to, that daily anchors you, that resonates clear down to your bones – and you find it because this devotional drew you closer to God by encouraging you to read His Word daily. I hope that you come back to this book, like I do with the many devotionals that are sitting behind me right now. I hope that somehow, in some way, I can say something that brings glory to God and strengthens your walk with Him.

Our School Story

Throughout the daily devotions to come, I will share with you the full story of our school Ultimate Martial Arts, but I will sum it up here so you have a sense of us and how we began. My husband, Chris, began training in taekwondo with his grandfather at the age of 3 and to this day has never lost his love for martial arts. Growing up, he would work out in the garage and practice his forms in the living room all the time. Chris's family has been in our community for years and people who know them, know that they as a family do martial arts. His grandfather taught at the local recreation center and gave lessons at his home.

One evening, a woman came to our house and knocked on the front door. Her 11-year-old son was with her and I could tell she was upset. I didn't really know her but recognized her from around town. She asked to speak to Chris, so I let her in, and we heard her story. Her son was being bullied at school. She had tried everything – talked to the principal, went to the school board, talked to parents – but nothing helped. In her frustration, she decided she would teach her boy how to defend himself and fight back. She knew Chris's family did martial arts, so that is what brought her to our door. This boy became our first student and Ultimate Martial Arts started in our basement.

Word got out and more boys started coming. Before long, there was a regular stream of students coming to and from our basement. Chris started going to more tournaments and competing, and the basement was filling up with trophies. Finally, one day I said, "Get out! We need to find a new place for your school."

Chris went to a local gymnastic studio and began renting space on their off-nights. That was a good start, but we quickly recognized that we needed our own place. A local realtor showed us an abandoned basement of a warehouse that used to serve as a chicken hatchery. He owned the building and was looking for a tenant like us who just needed a big space. I vividly remember walking into that basement 26 years ago, smelling chickens, seeing old feathers on the floor, and thinking, *This is awful!* Chris, on the other hand, was beaming with delight and exclaimed, "This is perfect!" We signed the deal that night and moved into what we now refer to nostalgically as "The Dungeon." There was a crooked, uneven stairwell that led down to the basement, no bathroom facilities and very poor lighting, but it was the best place ever if you asked Chris.

It was during this time that Chris had an encounter with Christ that changed his life. Chris was raised in a Christian home, but he was not living for God and he avoided any conversation about God or church. In fact, he purposefully held martial arts classes on Wednesday night, so he didn't have to go to church with me. However, after getting his nose seriously broken at a tournament, Chris came to know the Lord in a powerful way that changed his life and how he taught martial arts. God's timing was perfect, and He put us in this space that allowed more students to come at the same time Chris was saved and became a voice for Christ.

At every turn in our school, we have been blessed with amazing parents and families. When we moved to the chicken hatchery, our families all pitched in and cleaned up the place. Before long we did not have to walk across the street to Subway to use the bathroom, and we had new plumbing, mats, painted walls, and a decent place to train. We stayed in that location for nearly 12 years before we decided to go big-time and move to Main Street.

We bought a building just a block off Main Street and renovated it. It was much smaller than the basement, but we were excited to be in a new location. The move proved almost "too good" for us and we quickly outgrew the space. We then acquired an old shoe store on Main Street and went in half with another businessman. The former tenant had divided the building to use for a storage space and for a retail space, so we bought half and converted it into our new studio. Again, we quickly outgrew the space and began looking for a new location which landed us in the local outlet mall. They had open stores and were looking for new tenants to fill the mall occupancy. This proved to be a great location as parents loved all the parking, the ease of getting to the location, and the shopping that they could do while their children were in class.

Then a new opportunity opened in town – the local skating rink went up for auction. We did not have the capital to purchase it outright, so we leased it from a local businessman who could purchase it while we rented-to-own. It was our best and biggest space up to this point in the business. We even made some side income by having open skate nights on the weekends and birthday parties on Saturday and Sunday afternoons. The local school district contracted with us for some PE classes and we worked with homeschool families for their PE classes as well. Church youth groups also rented the skating rink for events. The extra income allowed us to purchase new equipment and really grow.

During this time at the skating rink, there was talk of a new YMCA coming to town. Eventually this talk turned into reality and the Y was built. We did not think we could compete, since with a Y membership you could get martial arts lessons plus a whole lot more. We made the decision, "If you can't beat them, join them." We closed our school and Chris went to work for the YMCA as their martial arts instructor. Chris went from a huge skating rink to a small room at the Y, but most of his students stayed with him and transitioned to becoming YMCA members.

It did not take long at the YMCA before our students and families started to complain. The space was small, and they were paying more for their membership than they did when they took classes at our place.

The YMCA decided that martial arts lessons were an additional fee, so families were paying their membership plus extra fees to take martial arts. The families came together and asked Chris to go back out on his own. They promised to follow us if we did so, and they did. Space was open again at the outlet mall and because we had a good relationship and experience there before, we moved back.

A Carter's clothing store had just closed so we moved into that space. It felt good to be back on our own, but a little scary too. Could we really compete? It did not take long for us to answer that question – the answer was a resounding "Yes!" Within a few months, we were moving again. A corner space was open in the mall that housed 10,000 square feet with office space and lots of storage areas. Our families again rose to the challenge and moved us within just a few days. We are still in this space as of now and I pray that's where we stay! We continue to grow with new families and many new classes.

Over the history of our school, I have learned a powerful lesson from God: trust. Worry does nothing to help pay the bills, but trust does. I remember when our rent for the chicken hatchery was $300 per month and we could not pay it. When we closed our school and Chris went to work at the YMCA, I worried that he would be unhappy and miss having his own place. During this time of the Covid pandemic, families have struggled to make tuition payments and I think, *Oh no, we can't pay the bills this month.* Every single time I think like this, God always comes through. Chris will come home and tell me that a new family stopped in and signed up for lessons just at the time we needed it, or God does something so unexpected and gets our school going. My human nature is quick to fall into doubt and you would think that at some point I would learn, but God is patient with me and daily I am learning to trust.

A Note from Melinda

I love to read devotionals because it fascinates me how two people can read the same passage of scripture and find different truth in it. To me, that shows how relevant the Bible is and how, if I'll let it, it will speak directly to me. Devotionals also help me better understand the Bible. Let's face it – the Bible can be hard to understand at times, so it's fun to seek out gifted, Christian authors who can help us develop a deeper, clearer understanding through their writing. I am thankful for that.

I started to write this devotional in 2006. At that time, I wrote as if I were my husband, Chris. Chris is the heart and soul of our martial arts school and he is the daily hands and feet of Christ our students see. I am the behind-the-scenes person, and I thought this devotional would be better if I wrote it from Chris's point of view. However, as I kept writing, I realized that was wrong. God was putting these words in my soul, to write from my own perspective.

But then I stopped writing. Why? I believed a lie from the devil that martial artists – the group I aim to reach with this book – would not listen to me. After all, I am not the face of our school. People know Master Chris Rangel, not his wife Melinda. I believed that Chris's name on the cover of this book would carry much more weight in the martial arts community than my name would. I also quit writing because I believed another, deeper lie: that my heart was not in the right place. I worried that I was writing for personal gain, not heavenly reward. In reality, that was just an excuse that stemmed from fear, doubt, and a lack of trust in God. Today, I am saddened because I believed those lies. Satan robbed me of fifteen years that this devotional could have ministered to at least one person.

Still, there are blessings to be found in those fifteen years that this book grew and grew inside my heart. During that time, I realized that God had been working in me and I no longer believed the lies Satan whispered in my ear. And when the Lord put this book on my heart again, in 2020, the words came flowing out of me in a river. I needed to wait to learn more lessons about his faithfulness in our school so I could share more stories with you. This book was not ready to be told in 2006 because God was still writing it within me.

My greatest hope is that this devotional ministers to you. This book was written through the lens of a martial artist, to help you in your daily walk with Christ. I picked out nuggets of truth and tried to relate them to a martial arts student and your development of this art.

Chris and I have owned Ultimate Martial Arts since 1994. It was not officially called that until a few years later, but that was the year our first student showed up to train in our basement. Martial arts is a huge part of our family and it has been the avenue for us to minister to many people throughout the years. Yes, it is a mission field unlike most, but it is the mission field God called the Rangel family to serve.

A Note from Chris

Iron Sharpens Iron has been crafted over many years. It is a continuation of a life journey that began in 1994 when our school Ultimate Martial Arts was born in our basement. Each time you pick up this book, there is an inspirational point of view that was created for you! My wife's perspective came from a daily walk in business, marriage, and the book of Proverbs.

What makes this devotional unique is that it is written from the lens of a martial arts business owner and actual martial artists. The philosophy and lessons from martial arts go hand-in-hand with powerful words from the book of Proverbs and help with your daily walk as a martial artist. These daily devotionals will help build your character on and off the mat, improve your ethical prowess at home and at work, and – most importantly of all – strengthen your relationship with Christ.

The very title of this book is dear to my heart and reminds me of what scripture has done for me and the trajectory of my life. "Iron sharpens iron" was a motto that my friend Ron and I lived by. Ron was first a student, then an instructor and ultimately our friendship turned into a brotherhood. As Ron battled cancer, we continued to support each other through prayer, reading God's word, and weekly Bible study. As I look back at our time together, I learned that by reading and applying the teaching of Proverbs, I gained a roadmap that was created to give me victory over the days when I felt defeated.

This roadmap is for you, too, and it will help you navigate through life as a Christian martial artist. *Iron Sharpens Iron* will help you deal with life when doors of opportunity close and others open, when you don't understand the direction you should take, and when life's road closures take you in a new direction. You will be blessed as you read through each chapter of Proverbs and then dig deeper into the life lessons being taught through the devotional that follows. If you diligently apply this teaching, you will find that it truly unlocks your full potential as a student, mentor, coach, and business owner.

The title of the book makes you question, "Does iron really sharpen iron?" If you do a little investigating you will learn that it does not. To sharpen iron, it takes another tool with a different texture. Proverbs 27:17 is often seen as a verse that compels us to have people in our life that are similar to us; however, it is actually a verse that compels us to find others that will challenge, correct, and confront us. It's finding a friend who will speak wisdom when the conversation is difficult or provide a new perspective when yours is limited.

Iron Sharpens Iron will challenge you to think about the teaching of Proverbs in a new way. It's the "different texture" you need to sharpen your walk as you use martial arts to impact others.

If you want a supplement to feed your mind, body and soul, dive into this book, and learn Biblical principles that will impact your journey as a martial artist and as a human being. *Iron Sharpens Iron* is designed to walk along with you as you develop yourself physically, mentally, and spiritually. Soon you will find that you have a sharpened iron that can impact the lives of others.

HOW TO READ THIS DEVOTIONAL

There are two versions of the Bible that I enjoy reading – the New International Version (NIV) and the Living Bible and I use both in this book. As you look through the devotional you will see each chapter from Proverbs followed by the daily devotional that accompanies it. Each of the 31 chapters are taken from the NIV version of the Bible.

As you read the daily devotional, you will find scripture that is taken from the Living Bible as well as from the NIV. I find that in some cases the Living Bible makes the passage easier to understand. All scriptures that are used from the Living Bible are noted as such.

My goal is that you have everything you need in one place – scripture and devotional – and can make this your one resource as you journey through the book of Proverbs.

| 1 |

Revering God

The proverbs of Solomon son of David, king of Israel:
² for gaining wisdom and instruction; for understanding words of insight;

³ for receiving instruction in prudent behavior, doing what is right and just and fair;

⁴ for giving prudence to those who are simple, knowledge and discretion to the young

⁵ let the wise listen and add to their learning, and let the discerning get guidance

⁶ for understanding proverbs and parables, the sayings and riddles of the wise.

⁷ The fear of the Lord is the beginning of knowledge, but fools despise wisdom and instruction.

⁸ Listen, my son, to your father's instruction and do not forsake your mother's teaching.

⁹ They are a garland to grace your head and a chain to adorn your neck.

¹⁰ My son, if sinful men entice you, do not give in to them.

¹¹ If they say, "Come along with us; let's lie in wait for innocent blood, let's ambush some harmless soul;

1

[12] let's swallow them alive, like the grave, and whole, like those who go down to the pit;

[13] we will get all sorts of valuable things and fill our houses with plunder;

[14] cast lots with us; we will all share the loot"

[15] my son, do not go along with them, do not set foot on their paths;

[16] for their feet rush into evil, they are swift to shed blood.

[17] How useless to spread a net where every bird can see it!

[18] These men lie in wait for their own blood; they ambush only themselves!

[19] Such are the paths of all who go after ill-gotten gain; it takes away the life of those who get it.

[20] Out in the open wisdom calls aloud, she raises her voice in the public square;

[21] on top of the wall she cries out, at the city gate she makes her speech:

[22] "How long will you who are simple love your simple ways? How long will mockers delight in mockery and fools hate knowledge?

[23] Repent at my rebuke! Then I will pour out my thoughts to you, I will make known to you my teachings.

[24] But since you refuse to listen when I call and no one pays attention when I stretch out my hand,

[25] since you disregard all my advice and do not accept my rebuke,

[26] I in turn will laugh when disaster strikes you; I will mock when calamity overtakes you

[27] when calamity overtakes you like a storm, when disaster sweeps over you like a whirlwind, when distress and trouble overwhelm you.

[28] "Then they will call to me but I will not answer; they will look for me but will not find me,

[29] since they hated knowledge and did not choose to fear the Lord.

[30] Since they would not accept my advice and spurned my rebuke,

[31] they will eat the fruit of their ways and be filled with the fruit of their schemes.

[32] For the waywardness of the simple will kill them, and the complacency of fools will destroy them;

[33] but whoever listens to me will live in safety and be at ease, without fear of harm."

Chapter 1: Daily Devotional

Proverbs has something for everyone - young, old, experienced, and novice. It outlines instructions to help us handle complex issues as well as the lesser problems that bombard us throughout our day. As we begin our journey through Proverbs, let's look at the importance of revering God and putting Him as the focus of your life.

A Manual for Living

Don't you wish there were a manual for everything we face in life? We have manuals to help assemble a new toy, perform a job to meet company expectations, and instruct us on how to operate a piece of equipment. Would it not be nice to have a manual for things like raising children, avoiding conflict with others, and making decisions to stay financially healthy? Sure, there are how-to books on all of these things, but they aren't as nice and precise as the step-by-step guide on how to put your new grill together.

A few years ago, we purchased a mixed martial arts training octagon. Chris bought it from another school in our area and hauled it in pieces to our studio. As Chris looked at it all laying on the floor he knew that he needed an assembly manual, but it did not come with one. Luckily, we had talented men in our school who could put the cage together like it was a puzzle. They picked up pieces and fit them together in such a fashion that it was like they were reading the manual in their hands. They had the talent of being able to see the finished product because of the skillsets they possess to do such work; however, they relied on each other's coaching and expertise to assemble the finished product. Just like these men relied on their knowledge and expertise, we too can rely on the manual we have been given – the Bible.

While the struggles and decisions in life are difficult at times, our manual, the Bible, helps us on our journey. There is a saying in church circles that BIBLE stands for Basic Instructions Before Leaving Earth. In other words, it's our manual for living until Christ returns. Like the manual we need to assemble a newly purchased toy, we have a manual to help us navigate the everyday challenges we face and live a life that is pleasing to God. The trick is reading and studying the manual to find how and where it instructs us on our daily living. If we just look at Proverbs to answer the first questions posed, we can quickly find help.

- raising children - *"Discipline your children, for in that there is hope;"* (Proverbs 19:18)
- avoiding conflict with others - *"A gentle answer turns away wrath, but a harsh word stirs up anger"* (Proverbs 15:1)
- making decisions to stay financially healthy - *"Dishonest money dwindles away, but whoever gathers money little by little makes it grow"* (Proverbs 13:11)

And these are just a few of the answers that I picked from Proverbs! There are answers like this along with stories that Jesus uses to help us better understand the manual. I used to have a poster of Garfield the cat in my classroom. In the poster Garfield was standing with books tied all over his body and the caption read, "I'm learning by osmosis!" It's a funny way to depict how we think we can just hold a Bible or carry it around and know what it means. The fact is in order to learn and apply the manual, it requires that you read it. As we start our new journey through Proverbs, I encourage you to read it step by step as if you were reading it with the intent of a "how-to" manual – as missing a step may cause you to put the object together wrong. If you dig in and begin studying, God will reveal to you the answers you need. They're there in the manual – it's up to you to read it.

Stay Away

So, you take martial arts? When people know this about you, they often want to see what you can do. Do any of these expressions sound familiar?

- "Let's fight."
- "Show me your stuff."
- "I've taken martial arts classes before; I can beat you!"

Don't let this challenge provoke you. As a Christian martial artist, you can use your training to make Godly decisions that will impact your life and the lives of others.

Because you are a martial artist, people may have the perception that you are "mean" or "tough." Those with evil intent will try to put you in a situation where they want you to use your martial arts training to aid them in evil. Verse 11 says that evil-minded people will say, *"Come along with us; let's lie in wait for innocent blood, let's ambush some harmless soul."*

Their cause is not to glorify God, but rather to sin. There is only one recourse for you as a Christian martial artist and that recourse is in verse 15. Stay away from this type of person. Do not make them the person you spend all your time with. Before you know it, you too will be involved in their evil plots. Simply put – stay away and find other friends.

Don't Know How?

Start with the Word. Verse 7 says to *"fear the Lord"* not man with his temporal words filled with empty promises or peer pressure from friends who choose to unwisely engage in trouble. Fear God because His promises are eternal and hold truth. Verse 19 in the Living Bible says those who live by violence will die a violent death. Fearing God, however, will help you enjoy a long life (Deuteronomy 6:2).

Wisdom to know how to walk away from evil comes from this fear of God. Psalm 111:10 repeats the same principle. *"The fear of the Lord is the beginning of wisdom..."* You need wisdom to know how to deal with people who try to lure you into their way of thinking. The first thing is to be more concerned about what God thinks of you than man. Once you begin thinking that way, saying no to the evil advances of man will become easier.

Three Steps to Walking in Wisdom

The first step to begin this walk is found in verse 7 which tells us *"the fear of the Lord is the beginning of knowledge."* Let's first define fear. Dictionary.com defines fear as "a distressing emotion aroused by impending danger, evil, pain, etc., whether the threat is real or imagined; the feeling or condition of being afraid." This definition, however, does not fit the context of verse 7. Here the word "fear" is better defined as *reverence*. Not a fear where we run and hide, but one that recognizes the awesome power of God and respects His authority. Obtaining the wisdom to know how to handle the bullies of our lives comes first by reverencing and trusting God. *"How does a man become wise? The first step is to trust and reverence the Lord!"* (Proverbs 1:7, Living Bible).

The second step is to seek wisdom. Verse 20 says that wisdom *"calls aloud."* But *who* is doing the calling? God places people in our lives to do just that and the first of these people are found right at home. They are parents. Parents instruct, tell, beg, plead, and shout, to prevent their children from making the same mistakes they did and guide them onto a better path.

I visited with a friend who has been in the military for many years and just returned from Iraq. His son is following in his footsteps and enlisting into the National Guard. My friend said he was going to advise his son how to advance quickly and avoid mistakes in his military career. He knew first-hand the avenues within the military to help his son. This is wisdom. If his son is smart, he will listen, follow his father's advice and have a prosperous military career.

Once we have obtained wisdom, we can do the third step which is to dwell safely. *"But whoever listens to me will live in safety and be at ease, without fear of harm"* (Proverbs 1:33). There are really two parts to verse 33; the first being a matter of the heart. A martial artist cannot have a prideful heart that says, "I won't listen" or "I know everything." A martial artist should always be learning and seeking knowledge and to do this, you must listen. Once you decide to listen, then the second part of the verse will follow. No matter how tough you think you are or advanced you perceive your skills to be, the promise of true peace and safety cannot be obtained through the perfection of your martial arts techniques. Only God can provide the promises of verse 33.

There is no substitute for peace and safety, but there is an opposite and it is death. A person who avoids listening to the wisdom of God will lead a life headed for destruction; however, hearing and applying God's wisdom will bring a peace that *"transcends all understanding"* (Philippians 4:7).

Points to Remember

- *Read God's Word. It's your manual for daily living.*
- *Choose friends whose motives are to glorify God.*
- *Take the first step toward wisdom by revering God in all you do.*

| 2 |

A Dedicated Commitment

My son, if you accept my words and store up my commands within you,

²turning your ear to wisdom and applying your heart to understanding

³indeed, if you call out for insight and cry aloud for understanding,

⁴and if you look for it as for silver and search for it as for hidden treasure,

⁵then you will understand the fear of the Lord and find the knowledge of God.

⁶For the Lord gives wisdom; from his mouth come knowledge and understanding.

⁷He holds success in store for the upright, he is a shield to those whose walk is blameless,

⁸for he guards the course of the just and protects the way of his faithful ones.

⁹Then you will understand what is right and just and fair—every good path.

¹⁰For wisdom will enter your heart, and knowledge will be pleasant to your soul.

¹¹Discretion will protect you, and understanding will guard you.

[12]Wisdom will save you from the ways of wicked men, from men whose words are perverse,

[13]who have left the straight paths to walk in dark ways,

[14]who delight in doing wrong and rejoice in the perverseness of evil,

[15]whose paths are crooked and who are devious in their ways.

[16]Wisdom will save you also from the adulterous woman, from the wayward woman with her seductive words,

[17]who has left the partner of her youth
and ignored the covenant she made before God.

[18]Surely her house leads down to death
and her paths to the spirits of the dead.

[19]None who go to her return or attain the paths of life.

[20]Thus you will walk in the ways of the good and keep to the paths of the righteous.

[21]For the upright will live in the land, and the blameless will remain in it;

[22]but the wicked will be cut off from the land, and the unfaithful will be torn from it.

Chapter 2: Daily Devotional

The pursuit of achieving your black belt is a dedicated commitment – one that can take many years. Some martial artists start their journey with great zeal and vigor but die out around the time they get to their purple belt. Like a New Year's resolution that fades by mid-March, so can be the dream of tying a black belt around your waist. Nonetheless, the quest always starts out with a determined resolve that propels us into starting the journey to find out more about ourselves and our capabilities.

Searching for the Treasure

Many movies are made about the quest to find hidden treasure. Pirates travel to unknown lands over uncharted waters in hopes of finding wealth. They endure battles with enemies, sickness, hardship, and even death. Their pursuit is relentless, focused, determined, and unwavering. All this for a glimmer of hope that the map they are following is indeed correct and will lead them to the treasure.

As martial artists, we too are on a quest. This quest is the pursuit of a black belt – mastery of our art. You may be a white belt beginning this journey or a brown belt ready to test for the next level. Wherever you may be along this journey, one truth remains apparent: it is not easy. It requires work, dedication, and a vision. This vision motivates us to go to a class when our bodies are tired. Proverbs 29:18 (KJV) says that *"where there is no vision, the people perish..."* We all need a goal in life or else we live day-to-day aimless and despondent, without a sense of accomplishment.

Proverbs 2:4 states that if you search for better insight and discernment as you would for lost money or hidden treasure, then wisdom will be given to you. The key here is *how* you search. How do you search for money you've lost? Earnestly! Sometimes frantically, but definitely with great intent. That lost money might be your next trip to the grocery store, your electric bill payment, or your martial arts lessons fee. Whatever that money represents, it affords you something and you desperately want and/or need to find it. So, you look hard.

Like a pirate looking for hidden treasure or like each of us looking for lost money – that is how Proverbs 2 says we are meant to search for better insight and discernment. If we do this, wisdom and the knowledge of God will follow. The important point to remember is that we must search intently. God is not hiding wisdom from us; he is hiding it *for* us.

What's in the Treasure Chest?

Open your treasure chest God has prepared for you and you'll find wisdom, good sense, protection, truth, and discernment. Need help making an important decision? The gifts God has prepared for you will show you *"how to distinguish right from wrong, how to find the right decision every time"* (Proverbs 2:9, Living Bible).

People look everywhere to find the right answers – from trusted friends to counselors, from the Internet to even alcohol and drugs. But if you want the right answers all of the time, from one you can trust, one that requires nothing of you but a heart that loves Him, then look no further than God. He knows the future and the results of every decision.

Stay on the Path

"But small is the gate and narrow the road that leads to life, and only a few find it" (Matthew 7:14).

Although it requires hard work and commitment, the godly who stay on the right path will enjoy life to the fullest. The world will try hard to pull you from the path. For example, Proverbs 2:16-19 looks at men who take the road to death and hell by falling into the flattery of a prostitute. There are roadblocks, obstacles, and detours on this narrow path, but each one can be overcome. Following Christ on the narrow road requires that you always *"guard your heart"* (Proverbs 4:23).

In the martial arts world, there are quick ways to achieve your black belt. Look for any get-rich-quick schemes that offer belt tests every other week or a sign that reads, "Obtain your black belt in three months with four easy installment payments." Taking this path may be fast, but it does not teach mastery of the martial arts. If all you want is a black belt, go to a martial arts store and buy one. But wouldn't it be better if that belt was obtained by walking the narrow path that is covered with hard work, grit, and sweat? Then that belt means more to you. No one gave it to you – you earned it. You'll enjoy and treasure your belt for-ever.

Benefits of the Path

What is this "path?" It's the daily decision we make to seek after God and draw close to Him. This decision will guide our thinking, direct our conversation, and change how we see others. The reward of walking this path is wisdom and with wisdom comes many benefits including insight, common sense, and discernment.

Verse 11 tells us that discernment, our ability to tell right from wrong, will serve as our protector. Have you ever watched Spiderman? You know how Spiderman has a "spidey-sense?" It's his extraordinary ability to sense danger. This is how I view discernment – it's that feeling I get when something just seems off.

For example, many years ago, Chris met a martial artist who created his own system of taekwondo. He patterned it off the Olympics and tried to convince schools to join his organization and claim their spot on the Olympic team. Chris got on board with his movement for a while and even attended a few tournaments with him, but I was never really sold on this guy. For one, he created a logo that *looked* like the five Olympic rings, but he altered it slightly and changed the ring colors. At a tournament in Mexico that we attended, he promoted a world-class venue that was nothing more than a hotel banquet room like we have here at home. My spidey-sense said this guy was not all he claimed to be. It was not long before his true colors showed, and his system of taekwondo is not heard about any longer. My discernment about this individual protected us from giving him control of our school and pay-ing him fees that were required for "his system." Sadly, some school owners who failed to discern the truth of this situation are no longer in business.

You might develop one of these wisdom benefits faster than an-other, or maybe one just seems to come naturally to you. If you feel like you never can get a clear picture of right or wrong, don't give up trying to develop it. Start by simply telling God that something seems weird – just like I did when my discernment was spiked about this martial artist. I couldn't put my finger on it at first, so I told God, "Something is off here." The more you do this, you'll soon learn that it's God's voice speaking to you and that spidey-sense you feel is the first step toward one of wisdom's benefits.

Wisdom is a daily decision to walk the path toward God. It's like going to the gym. You might want six-pack abs, but you won't get them in one day of exercise. You might not get them in a week or even a month! It takes time to develop physical muscles and the same is true with spiritual muscles. The trick to growing in insight, common sense and discernment is to daily seek after the wisdom of God – this consistent spiritual exercise will develop those spiritual muscles. *AND* as you are building those muscles, Proverbs 2 tells us you will:

- be protected from evil motives of men and women.
- have a life filled with joy.
- have a shield of understanding that keeps you safe.

Points to Remember

- *Seek wisdom earnestly.*
- *Open the treasure chest of God's wealth. He will provide you the map and a key.*
- *Stay on the path that leads to a full life by using what you find in the treasure chest.*
- *Go to your spiritual gym everyday to receive the benefits of wisdom.*

| 3 |

Learning Self-Defense

M y son, do not forget my teaching, but keep my commands in your heart,

²for they will prolong your life many years and bring you peace and prosperity.

³Let love and faithfulness never leave you; bind them around your neck, write them on the tablet of your heart.

⁴Then you will win favor and a good name in the sight of God and man.

⁵Trust in the Lord with all your heart and lean not on your own understanding;

⁶in all your ways submit to him, and he will make your paths straight.

⁷Do not be wise in your own eyes; fear the Lord and shun evil.

⁸This will bring health to your body and nourishment to your bones.

⁹Honor the Lord with your wealth, with the first fruits of all your crops;

¹⁰then your barns will be filled to overflowing, and your vats will brim over with new wine.

¹¹My son, do not despise the Lord's discipline, and do not resent his rebuke,

¹²because the Lord disciplines those he loves, as a father the son he delights in.

¹³Blessed are those who find wisdom, those who gain understanding,

¹⁴for she is more profitable than silver and yields better returns than gold.

¹⁵She is more precious than rubies; nothing you desire can compare with her.

¹⁶Long life is in her right hand; in her left hand are riches and honor.

¹⁷Her ways are pleasant ways, and all her paths are peace.

¹⁸She is a tree of life to those who take hold of her; those who hold her fast will be blessed.

¹⁹By wisdom the Lord laid the earth's foundations, by understanding he set the heavens in place;

²⁰by his knowledge the watery depths were divided, and the clouds let drop the dew.

²¹My son, do not let wisdom and understanding out of your sight, preserve sound judgment and discretion;

²²they will be life for you, an ornament to grace your neck.

²³Then you will go on your way in safety, and your foot will not stumble.

²⁴When you lie down, you will not be afraid; when you lie down, your sleep will be sweet.

²⁵Have no fear of sudden disaster or of the ruin that overtakes the wicked,

²⁶for the Lord will be at your side and will keep your foot from being snared.

²⁷Do not withhold good from those to whom it is due, when it is in your power to act.

²⁸Do not say to your neighbor, "Come back tomorrow and I'll give it to you" when you already have it with you.

²⁹Do not plot harm against your neighbor, who lives trustfully near you.

[30]Do not accuse anyone for no reason when they have done you no harm.

[31]Do not envy the violent or choose any of their ways.

[32]For the Lord detests the perverse but takes the upright into his confidence.

[33]The Lord's curse is on the house of the wicked, but he blesses the home of the righteous.

[34]He mocks proud mockers but shows favor to the humble and oppressed.

[35]The wise inherit honor, but fools get only shame.

Chapter 3: Daily Devotional

Many martial artists sign up for lessons to learn self-defense. In today's world this is a great idea and can provide you with necessary skills to help you in an attack. As a teenager our daughter, Jenna, taught a self-defense class called *Girl 2 Girl Self Defense*. Chris was her "ookie" and she loved to demonstrate her techniques on good 'ole Dad!

In teaching these self-defense classes, we have learned a lot about people. Some come to us because they just want to be prepared in case of an attack; others come because they have been a victim and felt helpless to defend themselves. They don't want to be caught in that situation again and want an arsenal of their own to give them power to ward off an attacker. Truly, everyone should have training to help them identify items in their surroundings as well as be equipped with the tools to defend and flee. The benefits you will receive from self-defense training are confidence, higher self-esteem, increased level of security, strategies to prevent an attack, and tactics to defend yourself.

Maintaining Quick Recall

The confidence gained from self-defense training can be fleeting if the student fails to train and practice enough for the techniques to become second nature. You need to be able to draw on your knowledge quickly and under duress. In order to do that, the techniques need to come naturally. You won't have time to think through the "4-step process" or be able to ask your attacker to grab you with the other hand because you only learned the technique "this way." No, you cannot customize the situation to match the slow, step-by-step training patterns from the dojo. The situation will be fast, and you need quick recall, which comes only from practice. These trainings need to be ingrained in your mind and heart.

Proverbs 3:1 says, *"My son, do not forget my teaching, but keep my commands in your heart."* Why? For length of days, long life, and peace. How is that for benefits?! Verse 3 goes on to say you must *know* these commandments. Study them, live them, let them be ingrained in your heart. Then when an attacker comes, you are prepared. You don't have to say, "What does the Word say about this?" You'll just know. It will come to you quickly in your time of need. Just like your self-defense training: preparedness is key.

Finding Favor

Proverbs 3:3 instructs us to continually walk and act in mercy and truth. Mercy is forgiving when you've been wronged. Oftentimes people don't want to forget past wrongs. Their thought pattern is revenge and hatred. Some will say, "I can't forgive." But, when we walk in God's wisdom, obeying his commandments, He will give us the strength to forgive. You may never forget, but you can have a different attitude of heart when you remember. Walking in God's mercy doesn't erase your memory, but it may cause the pain of those memories to fade.

What does the world see when you show mercy? Once, a friend of mine at work really turned against me with harsh words and actions.

Not only did this woman attack me, she attacked my co-workers as well. Several weeks after the incident, I suggested inviting this person to a social gathering that my co-workers were having. One of the people said, "Don't invite her after the way she treated us." However, I didn't think anything of inviting this person because she had been a friend and I was trying to walk in God's wisdom. More importantly, the world noticed. One of the others involved said, "Melinda invited her because that's how she is. She can forgive." I remember coming home and telling Chris that story because it blessed me. I wanted nothing more than to mend a friendship with no ulterior motives and I didn't realize that my words and actions were speaking greater volumes than I even intended.

Does the world notice mercy and truth? A resounding YES! Many have the stereotypical idea that martial artists have a chip on their shoulder, are arrogant or mean-spirited, and are always looking for a fight. Martial artist, break that stereotype in your life! Show mercy. Accidents happen; words are misinterpreted; mistakes are made. Forgive.

Proverbs continually gives instruction followed up with promise. In this case, the promise is favor and good understanding in the sight of God and man. Favor with God means blessings in your long life. Favor with men is just another blessing. This favor will cause you to be promoted in every area of your life. That's God's promise to you.

Accepting Correction

Getting corrected can be a hard thing to accept. How many times do you get weary when an instructor corrects your hands, yell, stance, form, or presentation? You nod your head and listen, yet in your mind you're saying, "I know, I know. Leave me alone!"

Remember: your hands are what you work with. You can build something up or tear things apart. Your yell or shout is either used to encourage or tear down. Your stance can be weak or solid, like being solidly grounded in the Lord. When God corrects our stance or how we present ourselves, we can't despise His correction, but instead we should embrace it and learn – just like the master instructor strives to mold you and make you strong. Christ yearns for us to change our stance to reflect His power in our lives.

It is often hard to accept correction. As humans we react to correction in so many ways – some with anger, resentment, or tears. Others see it in a different light and use it to improve their life or situation. Often it is how the correction is given or who the correction is given by that determines our reaction.

As a martial artist you have surely heard your instructor correct your form and while sometimes we think, "I know. I know," we should be grateful for the correction because we are likely making mistakes that we don't even realize. Advanced students are not exempt from this attitude. They have been in the art for many years and know the correct technique. Maybe tonight in class they are just tired, but maybe they're careless or have let their technique slack. Whatever the case, it is the master instructor's duty to correct them. Soon they too will be teaching others and need to understand the importance of their presentation. Their younger belts will mimic them one day.

The attitude that correction is used to improve our lives is the mindset that helps us grow. Instructors also must take correction and look to better their skills. It's important for students to see their instructor learning so they too become life-long learners. It is much easier to take correction from one who has authority and is educated in the area they are teaching. Instructors should want students to have that confidence in them; then the attitude of gratitude is more likely to come when correction is given.

Take this same principle to a spiritual level. In verses 11-12, God is the authority in all things, and we can have confidence that He knows best. There is no need to question if He knows what He's doing because He does! The Bible tells us that God goes before us. He knows tomorrow, next week and even next year. He has a plan and a purpose for us (Jeremiah 29:11). So, when He corrects us, be thankful. Know He loves you and be grateful that you are listening, and you heard Him speak.

That shows you are His child, you know His voice, and He cares enough to tell you.

I've heard many instructors say that when they stop correcting their students it's because they've given up on that student changing. The student doesn't listen, feels above correction, is hard-headed, or wants to do things his way. It seems like a waste of time and energy to correct him. The instructor will focus on other students who *do* listen.

Don't be the student who won't listen! Turn to God's correction. You are the son and daughter that He delights in. When you listen and change toward His correction, you are gaining wisdom.

The Blessings Continue

Verse 21 tells us to have two goals in life – wisdom and common sense. Common sense is the ability to make correct choices. Wisdom includes this but goes beyond common sense. Wisdom comes from listening, obeying, and applying God's truths to our lives. Again, the Word lists more benefits of wisdom.

The Living Bible tells us that wisdom and common sense will:

- Fill you with living energy (verse 22)
- Bring you honor and respect (verse 22)
- Keep you safe from defeat and disaster (verse 23)
- Keep you from stumbling from the path (verse 23)
- Let you sleep without fear (verse 24)
- Keep you from being afraid of disaster or the plots of wicked men (verse 25)
- And the greatest benefit of all is that the Lord is with you and will protect you! (verse 26)

Act Now!

Martial artists will come into your path who need help in many ways. This could be anything from finances to friendship, from lessons to love, or any number of things. God has instructed us to take care of our neighbors. Christ even compared taking care of your neighbor to loving Him in Matthew 25:40. The disciples asked the Lord, "When did we see you hungry?" and Jesus replied, *"Truly, I tell you, whatever you did for one of the least of these brothers and sisters of mine, you did for me."*

The best way to take care of your neighbor is to look in your house. What do you have? In 2 Kings 4, the woman needed oil. The prophet Elisha said to the woman, "Go into your house and look inside." She replied that she only had one jar of oil. Elisha told her, "Take your sons. Get all the pots and jars you can find. Take them inside and shut the door." As soon as the woman obeyed Elisha the oil came, and all the pots were filled. There was enough for her to pay her debt and live on the extra oil with her sons.

Look inside your house, your school, your heart, your wallet. What do you have? Don't withhold it. Give it to God. He will multiply it and it will bless others. Maybe you have a great attitude and a smile that brightens a room. Use it every day to encourage your fellow students. For some students, this is the only encouragement they receive in their life. Tell them what a great job they are doing and make a big deal over their accomplishments. Many parents have told us that martial arts has been the best thing for their child because of the rewards and accolades they receive that build their self-esteem and outlook on life.

Don't put off the good effect you can have on others. We were so blessed by our son during Easter one year. Our church gave away Blessing Boxes – boxes full of food for those in need. Our son was determined after church to get one of those boxes for his great aunt, who is disabled. He told us his idea, but we really didn't give him much mind. After church we went about our friendly greetings and left the building – without our son! He had stayed inside and found a man to help him carry this large box of food to the car. We went in to look for him and found him leading the way to our car. He was determined and took matters into his own hands. Our 11-year-old son was determined to carry this 50 lb. box to our car so he could bless someone else. He didn't wait for us, nor was he detoured by his small size in comparison with the box of food. He was going to do good. Verse 28 says don't tell your neighbor to come back tomorrow. Do it now. Don't be detoured.

Prayer is good too. When others are in need, the Bible teaches we should pray; however, this is not the first and best solution in some cases. Let me explain! If a person comes to you and needs $10 to put gas in his car so he can get to work, don't say to him, "I'll pray that you find the $10." Instead, fix the man's problem. If you have $10 in your pocket, give it to him. That is what he needs at this moment. Then pray for him in other areas of his life. But do good when it is in your power to do it.

Inherit Glory

Verse 35 sums it all up: *"The wise inherit honor."* This is the ultimate benefit that wisdom brings – an eternal home with our Lord. We are on a journey toward glory and along the way we must continually seek wisdom. When wisdom grows inside us, it's like reaching the next belt level. Throughout our training, we strive for the next belt, just like we are striving for wisdom in our walk with the Lord.

Points to Remember

- *There are many benefits to wisdom, but you have to do your part by seeking Him in everything.*
- *If you know someone in need, look at what you have and use it to help.*
- *Chastisement is a good thing. It's because He loves you so embrace the correction.*

| 4 |

Look for Wisdom

Listen, my sons, to a father's instruction; pay attention and gain understanding.

^{2}I give you sound learning, so do not forsake my teaching.

^{3}For I too was a son to my father, still tender, and cherished by my mother.

^{4}Then he taught me, and he said to me, "Take hold of my words with all your heart; keep my commands, and you will live.

^{5}Get wisdom, get understanding; do not forget my words or turn away from them.

^{6}Do not forsake wisdom, and she will protect you; love her, and she will watch over you.

^{7}The beginning of wisdom is this: Get wisdom. Though it cost all you have, get understanding.

^{8}Cherish her, and she will exalt you; embrace her, and she will honor you.

^{9}She will give you a garland to grace your head and present you with a glorious crown."

^{10}Listen, my son, accept what I say, and the years of your life will be many.

^{11}I instruct you in the way of wisdom and lead you along straight paths.

[12]When you walk, your steps will not be hampered; when you run, you will not stumble.

[13]Hold on to instruction, do not let it go; guard it well, for it is your life.

[14]Do not set foot on the path of the wicked or walk in the way of evildoers.

[15]Avoid it, do not travel on it; turn from it and go on your way.

[16]For they cannot rest until they do evil; they are robbed of sleep till they make someone stumble.

[17]They eat the bread of wickedness and drink the wine of violence.

[18]The path of the righteous is like the morning sun, shining ever brighter till the full light of day.

[19]But the way of the wicked is like deep darkness; they do not know what makes them stumble.

[20]My son, pay attention to what I say; turn your ear to my words.

[21]Do not let them out of your sight, keep them within your heart;

[22]for they are life to those who find them and health to one's whole body.

[23]Above all else, guard your heart, for everything you do flows from it.

[24]Keep your mouth free of perversity; keep corrupt talk far from your lips.

[25]Let your eyes look straight ahead; fix your gaze directly before you.

[26]Give careful thought to the paths for your feet and be steadfast in all your ways.

[27]Do not turn to the right or the left; keep your foot from evil.

Chapter 4: Daily Devotional

As a martial artist, where do you look for wisdom in your sport? Most likely you look to your senior belt instructors since they have been involved in the art the longest. You could venture to say that their once black belt that is now slightly grayed and frayed at the ends is a representation of their longevity and knowledge of their style.

I remember Chris's grandfather's black belt. It was a dingy gray, and the threads were worn. It wasn't a stiff new belt, but rather one that was soft and hung loosely. It was a belt that had been worn, tested, and tried. Its discolor and wear clearly illustrated that he had done this sport for many years. However, it wasn't just his belt that showed his experience; it was also the tone in his voice and the confidence in his step. He had been around martial arts ever since his days in the Army boxing in the Golden Gloves Division. This training carried over into his martial arts training as he developed fighters who fought and trained with the same tenacity and dedication. Chris looked to him for wisdom in martial arts training. To him, no one knew more than his grandfather.

The Instruction of a Father

Lupe, Chris's grandfather, had military experience and had trained with some of the best martial artists around. Not only did Chris look to him to teach the proper technique of a round house, but also for the split-second decision needed in a fight. Lupe's knowledge far exceeded Chris's, and his wisdom was what Chris depended on.

At the dojo, the white belt student cannot instruct anyone. They don't know anything yet. The white belt cannot teach you even basic skills like how to tie your belt. Instead, you look to the advanced students for answers to questions about etiquette in the dojo, how to fix your stance, or ways to improve your form.

Proverbs 4 starts by telling us to *"Listen, my sons, to a father's instruction; pay attention and gain understanding."* Why does verse 1 specify "a father" and not just anyone? Because a father has experience to draw from and will give you good advice. It's our job to listen, retain his words, and keep his commandments. Our reward then is life. Proverbs 4:1 doesn't say to find the next person you meet and seek wisdom. That person does not know you, does not have a relationship with you, and does not care about you like a father does. Although they may want to help or have good intentions, the experience of a father is not there. This could be an earthly father, but more importantly, it's your heavenly Father's wisdom you should ultimately seek.

Walking and Running

Let's say your martial arts class is beginning its session for the day. You start class with the basic routine of stretches, punches, and kicks. You know this routine and could do it in your sleep; it does not challenge you or teach you anything new. Still, you perform this warm-up because it prepares you for class and gets you focused on that night's lesson. This basic routine is like walking – it's the familiar, everyday part of your life. "Walking through life" is what happens to us most days of the week – our normal routine.

Now, fast forward to later in the evening; your class has progressed, and your instructor just taught you a brand-new technique that has everyone buzzing. You learn it quickly and are excited because it works with great results on your partner. This new, exciting technique is like running – the highlights of your life. These are the memories that you commemorate in scrapbooks and photo albums. Running in life is what happens to us on extraordinary days – the unusual events.

Verse 12 looks at both kinds of days; days when you are walking and days when you are running. Daily walking with God is not dull and monotonous but should be familiar and blessed. As you perform your daily chores, you can have the peace that surpasses all understanding, joy unspeakable and full of glory, and a hope that is fixed on things above. On days like this, your step will not be hampered, hindered, or strained.

Days when you run are days when something spectacular happens in your life. On these days you have extra bursts of energy and a higher level of adrenaline. This isn't your regular daily walk; this running is fast and exhilarating. Wisdom says that on these days, your foot will not stumble either.

So, no matter what kind of day it is, wisdom will lead you down the right path. This path will be clear and open, and you will not stumble.

The Right and the Wrong Path

Proverbs 4:14-19 describes the two choices of paths we have to follow. One path is like a shining light that shines bright (verse 18). The other path is full of darkness and those walking it fall because they can't see where they are going (verse 19). When the wisdom of God is living in us, our spirit pulls us to the brighter path. However, Satan will use those on the dark path to try to lure you onto the path of destruction. Verse 16 in the Living Bible says, *"They can't rest unless they cause someone to stumble and fall."* They will feel less guilty if they can get someone like you to go along with their evil schemes.

This evil can be tempting, so how do you avoid being pulled to the dark path? *"Avoid their haunts – turn away, go somewhere else"* (Proverbs 4:15, Living Bible). Do just the opposite of what Satan is pulling you to do. Tempted to fall into adultery? Call your spouse right away and talk. Tempted to cause harm or say hurtful words? Run to your car, get in, and drive away. Tempted to engage in a dishonest deal? Stop. Ask yourself what you will be losing if you do this. Recognize this sacrifice will hurt more than your gain from the deal. Here's the simple tip in verse 14: *"Don't do as the wicked do"* (Living Bible).

Once I read a commentary on how to succeed at your diet. The author wrote about purging your house of tempting foods. She advised that you should not just throw food in the trash. You need to destroy it by washing it down the sink and completely getting rid of the temptation. To avoid temptation, continue to walk down the path that is full of light and you can see where you are going. Although darkness surrounds us in this world, you can walk on a path that grows brighter and *"gives way to morning splendor"* (Proverbs 4:18, Living Bible).

Staying Healthy

During our daughter's teen years, we experienced the pains of "girl drama." This is the stuff that teenage girls experience when "this person talks about that person" or "she said, you said" and the like. Rumors get started and feelings get hurt. Our daughter Jenna was experiencing such drama one night with her friend Maddie. Her feelings were hurt, and she came to me crying and asking me to pray for her. I realized that our daughter was having a problem that she did not know how to handle, and she felt awful. She was experiencing the gnawing, achy feeling in your stomach when people are talking ill about you, or someone doesn't like you.

The best way we knew how to help her was to do what the Word tells us to do. We found the answer to our daughter's problem in Matthew 5:23-24. *"Therefore, if you are offering your gift at the altar, and there remember that your brother or sister has something against you, leave your gift there in front of the altar. First go and be reconciled to them, and then come and offer your gift."*

When I told Jenna that I was taking her to Maddie's house so we could discuss the situation, she refused to go. But, we told her what the Word says about handling a problem. It was clear that this was what we needed to do. She reluctantly agreed. We drove over to Maddie's house, knocked on the door, sat down with her and her mom, and together we all worked out the situation. The girls talked, hugged, and all was resolved. When we got back home, I asked Jenna how she felt now and she admitted that we did the right thing and she felt much better. The sick feeling had left her stomach. (Today, more than a decade later, Maddie serves as an operations pastor at a large evangelical church in our area where every Sunday we say, "God is good. All the time. And all the time. God is good.")

Verse 22 reads, *"For they are life to those who find them, And health to one's whole body."* When the Word and the wisdom of God become the focus of your life, it brings health to your body. Each of us has experienced a situation like I described with my daughter. You are familiar with that sick, uncomfortable feeling in your stomach when you have a problem with someone at work or school or even at the dojo. The Word tells us not to let the day go by without trying to resolve the problem. Matthew 5 says, *"leave what you are doing and be reconciled to your brother."*

Why is God so specific about doing it now, today? Because he knows that feeling in your stomach, if left unattended, can evolve into much worse than just a feeling, but greater health issues. He also knows that a problem left unattended grows into a bigger problem and this could lead to stress and anxiety. Taking care of the problem *now* – before it has time to grow – causes you to have better health in your body. Not only will you experience health in your physical body, but in every area of your life. Keep the Word in front of you so you can live in good health physically, mentally, and spiritually.

Tricks of the Trade

There are some lessons that you learn quickly when you begin taking martial arts. Two of those lessons are to hold on to the pads tightly and to never drop your guard. Reminders to hold on to the pads tightly is especially important for beginner students who are paired with an overzealous beginner who has not mastered any control. A wild kick will send the pad flying across the mat. Sometimes a student will get hurt because they aren't holding the pads tightly enough.

Holding on tightly will guard you and protect you – on the mat and in life. Verse 13 isn't talking about pads though, but rather instruction and wisdom. Once you gain instruction, grab on, and hold on! Not with a haphazard grip, but with a deadly grip. One that will not let go or be shaken free. Everything in this world will try to loosen your grip and pull you away from God's instruction. Work on building up your spiritual muscles so you can hold on tightly when the world tries to pull you away. You can build those muscles by reading the Word and spending time in prayer with God.

So, hold on fast to God's instruction. Know that it is life, and it will protect you from the world's blows.

The second trick you will quickly learn is to "protect your grill" and to not to drop your guard during a sparring match. If you do, the result could be ugly – as simple as a point being scored against you, or as devastating as a broken nose. Your instructor has probably barked the phrase, "Guard the grill!" as you were learning how to defend yourself in your early experiences as a fighter.

I vividly remember a time when Chris did not keep his guard up and had his nose shattered by a disgruntled opponent after the match. Chris was too busy declaring that he was "number one" and celebrating his victory. He did not notice the fist coming right for his face. Even though the fight was officially over, his opponent had enough of Chris's arrogance and punched him square in the nose.

Chris wasn't serving the Lord at that time, and as I reflect on that experience, I see how he had dropped his guard in more ways than one. First, he wasn't guarding his face; he really didn't see the need, since the fight was over. That was mistake number one. Mistake number two was his arrogance. Chris was loudly and proudly telling everyone that he was the winner. He was not guarding his character. And third, Chris was not guarding the example he set for the students from our school and the lasting impression other martial artists would have of him.

Proverbs 4:23-27 describes how to keep your guard up spiritually. Here's how:

- Watch over your heart above all else
- Put away false and dishonest speech
- Keep your eyes looking forward with a fixed purpose
- Carefully consider the path you walk
- Don't turn to the right or left; always avoid evil

Some versions of verse 23 read *"guard your heart with diligence"*; others use the word *"vigilance"*; and others state *"above all else."* Guarding your heart is an everyday requirement to finding the wisdom of God. You can't decide to do it only when it suits you, but instead you must make it part of your daily walk.

Points to Remember

- *Obtain wisdom from your Heavenly Father. It will protect you during the daily routine of your life as well as during the monumental occasions.*
- *Guard your heart by holding on tight to the wisdom of God and keeping His Word continually in your mind, ears, eyes and heart.*
- *Enjoy your daily walk with the Lord and the health benefits it provides.*

| 5 |

It's Not Okay

My son, pay attention to my wisdom, turn your ear to my words of insight,

²that you may maintain discretion and your lips may preserve knowledge.

³For the lips of the adulterous woman drip honey, and her speech is smoother than oil;

⁴but in the end she is bitter as gall, sharp as a double-edged sword.

⁵Her feet go down to death; her steps lead straight to the grave.

⁶She gives no thought to the way of life; her paths wander aimlessly, but she does not know it.

⁷Now then, my sons, listen to me; do not turn aside from what I say.

⁸Keep to a path far from her, do not go near the door of her house,

⁹lest you lose your honor to others and your dignity to one who is cruel,

¹⁰lest strangers feast on your wealth and your toil enrich the house of another.

¹¹At the end of your life you will groan, when your flesh and body are spent.

¹²You will say, "How I hated discipline! How my heart spurned correction!

¹³I would not obey my teachers or turn my ear to my instructors.

[14]And I was soon in serious trouble in the assembly of God's people."

[15]Drink water from your own cistern, running water from your own well.

[16]Should your springs overflow in the streets, your streams of water in the public squares?

[17]Let them be yours alone, never to be shared with strangers.

[18]May your fountain be blessed, and may you rejoice in the wife of your youth.

[19]A loving doe, a graceful deer may her breasts satisfy you always, may you ever be intoxicated with her love.

[20]Why, my son, be intoxicated with another man's wife? Why embrace the bosom of a wayward woman?

[21]For your ways are in full view of the Lord, and he examines all your paths.

[22]The evil deeds of the wicked ensnare them; the cords of their sins hold them fast.

[23]For lack of discipline they will die, led astray by their own great folly.

Chapter 5: Daily Devotional

The lessons taught in Proverbs 5 can be applied to many areas of life – work and school as well as the dojo. Proverbs 5 deals with an issue that is prevalent in our culture and it's one that is glorified on television, read about in books and magazines, and shown on big screens across the nation. The thought pattern is that because it is so common, it must be okay. This, however, is far from what the word of God teaches. Both Proverbs 4 and 5 start with the same directive: "Listen up! You need to understand this instruction and apply it to your life."

A Dangerous Trap

Proverbs 5 gives instruction dealing with the issue of immorality. If someone ever thought it was all right to have an adulterous affair, then they have not read this chapter. Beginning with verse 3, the Word clearly spells out the dangers of this trap. The snare can be set with something as simple as a kiss – one the Word describes as done with lips as sweet as honey. At first this may sound inviting – something sweet must be harmless, right? The problem is the person in the affair does not see the entire picture. They are only focused on the honey-comb and oil.

Chris and I taught Sunday School together for many years and I am reminded of a lesson we taught about temptation. The lesson had a picture of a mouse looking intently at a block of cheese. What the mouse did not see was the large box propped up with a stick sitting above the cheese. As soon as the mouse gave in to the temptation, the string would be pulled, the stick would fall, and the box would drop over the mouse. He had his cheese, but he was trapped in the box. Verse 3 shows how inviting it is to fall into temptation. As Christians, we too are tempted. Nowhere in God's Word does it say we are immune to it. Even Christ was tempted, but He did not sin (Hebrews 4:15).

There are temptations in the world of martial arts as well. One temptation is to never advance in your belt rank. This may sound odd, as the main goal is to earn a black belt, but some instructors and students purposefully choose to remain at a lower belt rank for several years. Why would anyone do this? For an advantage at tournaments. For example, in most cases, a student should move up from a green belt in about three months. This would mean that they also compete at the higher belt rank at tournaments. But those instructors who fall into the temptation of cheating won't advance a student – for months on end – who clearly should have been advanced, in order to win at key tournaments, bring notoriety to their school, and take home a trophy.

On the opposite end of the spectrum, a second temptation is to lie about your rank and credentials, pretending to be better or more experienced than you truly are. A martial artist in a nearby town promoted himself from an orange belt to a black belt overnight and opened his own school. He was very charismatic, and unknowing parents began signing up their children for lessons. This school owner promoted students, assigned rank, and claimed that he was teaching all they needed to know to deserve their belt rankings. He then made the mistake of taking his students to a tournament where they were beaten in every competition. The parents were concerned and started asking questions. It was quickly revealed that their instructor was a fraud and they had been cheated out of time, money, and a proper martial arts education.

Although all of us will face temptation, God has promised us a way out. The key is to do your part to make the promise happen. In the case of Proverbs 5, the answer is found in verse 8. *"Keep to a path far from her, do not go near the door of her house."* Don't go near the temptation. Get away – quickly.

The True Taste

In reality, temptations are like "wormwood." Wormwood is defined on Dictionary.com as something bitter, grievous, or extremely unpleasant. In the end, the thing that once seemed alluring and sweet will taste bitter.

Not only is the taste bad, but it leads you to death. The path in verses 5 and 6 contrast greatly with the path described in Proverbs 4:18. The path in 4:18 is shining and well-lit; it is easy to see where you are going, which is to an eternal life with Christ. The path of temptation is one that the righteous does not and should not know. It goes to hell, leads to death, and is moveable. The path of the righteous goes to heaven, leads to life, and is planted and rooted. There was an old hymn that was a favorite in my country church. The chorus said,

I shall not be, I shall not be moved.
I shall not be, I shall not be moved.
Just like a tree planted by the waters.
Oh, I shall not be moved.

Don't Be Moved

The writer of that old hymn knew the value of the words of verse 7, *"...do not turn aside from what I say."* He was saying to stay grounded in the wisdom of God when the world tries to uproot you.

Watch a martial artist who has just begun classes. As they work and train, they lose balance easily when they try to kick, miss the pads on pad drills, and yell after everyone else. This is a person who is not yet planted. They are learning and gaining instruction. Their martial arts roots are not very deep, and they are moveable because they are learning.

Now look at that same martial artist a month later. Their skills are improved, and they are more confident. Their balance is more stable, and they are not so easily knocked down. They are better because they stuck with their training and did not run off when they were scared or uncomfortable.

God is calling the righteous to be grounded too. The consequences of falling into temptation are very straightforward in verses 9-11. Instead of honoring your spouse or yourself, you've given honor to someone else, which opens the door to anger, jealousy, mistrust, lies and the like. For those who give into this temptation Hebrews 13:4 tells us God will judge them and His judgment will cast those who practice such sin into an eternal hell.

Whether you are a new student or one who has walked the righteous path for years, this instruction is so very vital for your eternal success. Beginners think they know it all and old-timers think it could never happen to them and before you know it, either one could fall into temptation. All of us need to apply God's wisdom to our very foundation, clear down to the roots. Our roots should then grow deep into the truth of God so that even when the wind blows, we will not be moved.

Love to Learn

As an instructor, the know-it-all attitude really frustrates me. Students come in who have watched every episode of WWF or every televised MMA fight and want on the first day to learn the black belt form. They don't want to listen and are "bored" learning the proper techniques. Bored – another one of my least favorite words!

What I have seen Chris do is to pair this student up with an advanced student, tell them to put on the gloves and spar. He wants the advanced student to show the beginner the value of listening and learning proper technique. Usually after a few rounds of this, the beginner concedes and listens.

It's sad to say, but we are often the same way with God. He knows what we need to learn, but we think we know it all ourselves and are ready to tackle the most difficult battles on our own. After we struggle, fail, struggle, and fail again, we realize that maybe listening to God was where we should have started all along.

Don't despise teaching. None of us know everything and we can gain valuable knowledge all around us every day. We'll never reach the point of knowing everything. Having the attitude that we know it all is simply not true. Avoid the rebellious attitude that says, "Don't tell me what to do." Instead look for the wisdom in being told what to do and learn from it.

Stay True

The final verses of Proverbs 5 speak directly to the husband and wife and the family they create. Verse 15 reads *"Drink water from your own cistern, and running water from your own well."* This says to the spouse to stay true to your spouse. Don't look elsewhere for fulfillment, but rather look at the blessing God has given you in your marriage.

God tells us when we do this, our *"fountain will be blessed"* and we will multiply and have children, thus creating the family that God intended us to have. Children are blessings *"like arrows in the hand of a warrior"*

(Psalms 127:3-5). God has set the pattern for families to be a husband and wife who together multiply and have children. God did not say to be fruitful with anyone other than your spouse.

True freedom comes when you are faithful to the person you joined in marriage. Your spouse is the one God created for you and brought to you. He has designed us to enjoy one another and live out our days together. When we do this, God will bless our marriage covenant and the generations produced from it.

Points to Remember

- *Run from temptation. Do not even consider it. It is a dangerous trap that leads to death.*
- *You are never too old to learn. All of us can learn every day. Be open to instruction.*
- *Don't be moved from what is right. Listen to the voice of wisdom that tells you to stay faithful.*

| 6 |

The Benefits of Discipline

My son, if you have put up security for your neighbor, if you have shaken hands in pledge for a stranger,

²you have been trapped by what you said, ensnared by the words of your mouth.

³So do this, my son, to free yourself, since you have fallen into your neighbor's hands: Go—to the point of exhaustion and give your neighbor no rest!

⁴Allow no sleep to your eyes, no slumber to your eyelids.

⁵Free yourself, like a gazelle from the hand of the hunter, like a bird from the snare of the fowler.

⁶Go to the ant, you sluggard; consider its ways and be wise!

⁷It has no commander, no overseer or ruler,

⁸yet it stores its provisions in summer and gathers its food at harvest.

⁹How long will you lie there, you sluggard? When will you get up from your sleep?

¹⁰A little sleep, a little slumber, a little folding of the hands to rest—

¹¹and poverty will come on you like a thief and scarcity like an armed man.

¹²A troublemaker and a villain, who goes about with a corrupt mouth,

¹³who winks maliciously with his eye, signals with his feet and motions with his fingers,

¹⁴who plots evil with deceit in his heart he always stirs up conflict.

¹⁵Therefore disaster will overtake him in an instant; he will suddenly be destroyed—without remedy.

¹⁶There are six things the Lord hates, seven that are detestable to him:

¹⁷haughty eyes, a lying tongue, hands that shed innocent blood,

¹⁸a heart that devises wicked schemes, feet that are quick to rush into evil,

¹⁹a false witness who pours out lies and a person who stirs up conflict in the community.

²⁰My son, keep your father's command and do not forsake your mother's teaching.

²¹Bind them always on your heart; fasten them around your neck.

²²When you walk, they will guide you; when you sleep, they will watch over you; when you awake, they will speak to you.

²³For this command is a lamp, this teaching is a light, and correction and instruction are the way to life,

²⁴keeping you from your neighbor's wife, from the smooth talk of a wayward woman.

²⁵Do not lust in your heart after her beauty or let her captivate you with her eyes.

²⁶For a prostitute can be had for a loaf of bread, but another man's wife preys on your very life.

²⁷Can a man scoop fire into his lap without his clothes being burned?

²⁸Can a man walk on hot coals without his feet being scorched?

²⁹So is he who sleeps with another man's wife; no one who touches her will go unpunished.

³⁰People do not despise a thief if he steals to satisfy his hunger when he is starving.

³¹Yet if he is caught, he must pay sevenfold, though it costs him all the wealth of his house.

[32]But a man who commits adultery has no sense; whoever does so destroys himself.

[33]Blows and disgrace are his lot, and his shame will never be wiped away.

[34]For jealousy arouses a husband's fury, and he will show no mercy when he takes revenge.

[35]He will not accept any compensation; he will refuse a bribe, however great it is.

Chapter 6: Daily Devotional

Proverbs 6:23 gives us an encouraging piece of knowledge. It reads, *"For this command is a lamp, this teaching is a light..."* This verse tells us that if we adhere to the teachings of God's Word it will act as a beacon to help us walk in God's wisdom rather than getting lost in the darkness of the world. *And* we learned in Proverbs 2 that walking in that wisdom brings great benefits. The second half of this verse reminds us that not only does wisdom guide us, it also corrects and disciplines us. While discipline can be uncomfortable, it should become a way of life that we embrace as disciples of Christ. Let's dig into Proverbs 6 to see what light this chapter will shed on our walk.

Don't Be the Bank

At one time or another, most of us have (or know someone who has) been asked to cosign for a loan. This loan may be as significant as a new home loan or as simple as a loan for a tank of gas. When someone doesn't repay even the smallest of loans, tension usually arises between the two parties. A tank of gas won't break you, although it can damage the relationship, but a new home – now, that's a different story! Proverbs 6:1 calls co-signing for any loan "security" – also known as surety.

The person asking for this surety may be a fellow martial arts student, a friend or a relative. No matter what the relationship, it can be a difficult response, but the only answer you should ever give is "NO!" when you are asked to secure someone else's debt. A dear friend told me a story about a time when her parents were buying their first home. Her father asked his brother for a loan and the brother refused to give him the loan. The brother did say, however, he would be happy to *give* him the money to help him purchase their new home. This experience brought the two brothers and families much closer and avoided the threat of tension due to having borrowed money between them.

Verses 1-5 tells us that if you become surety you are *"ensnared by the words of your own mouth."* You are caught in a trap that requires you to pay a debt you did not incur. If you have already done this and became the co-signer, verse 4 shows the urgency of removing yourself from the agreement. Don't let embarrassment or pride stand in the way. You may not fully know the financial situation of the person. They too may be too embarrassed or prideful to tell you the full reality of their obligations. Getting yourself released from the commitment is, as verse 5 says, compared to a deer who escapes the hunter or a bird who escapes the net. To the deer and bird, this means escaping death – and it could mean a financial death to you as well. Trust God to help you get out of the mess you are in.

Don't Be Lazy

To be a martial artist takes motivation. You must put on your uniform, gather your gear bag, drive to class, participate and do the drills, pack everything back up, and drive home. In that act of going to class, there is exercise, drive, commitment, and movement – all of which are actions God wants to see in our lives. God wants us to always be moving forward in His direction following a path He has created for us. One thing you can't be when walking this path is *lazy!* God has called us to be actively engaged in life and driven by a purpose. This purpose is the one that God has planted in you the day you were born.

People come to martial arts classes because they have a purpose. No one is pushing or dragging them to come. That purpose may be exercise, to stay in shape, to lose weight, to learn self-defense, to earn a black belt, or to just have fun! Look at the purpose of the ant in verses 6-8. They have no ruler to make them work; however, they *"labor hard all summer, gathering food for the winter"* (Proverbs 6:8, Living Bible). Their purpose is self-preservation. As we learned in Chapter 2, Proverbs 29:18 (KJV) says, *"Where there is no vision, the people perish..."* This ant has a vision!

The question in verse 9 is: *"How long will you lie there? When will you get up from your sleep?"* If you continue to sleep, poverty will overtake you and you will become poor – financially, physically, and spiritually. Laziness and slothfulness are not part of the wisdom of God. In order to seek His wisdom, you need to remove those words from your life and get moving in God's direction. Verse 10 should not be your life verse! *"A little sleep, a little slumber, a little folding of the hands to rest"* – the key word here is "little!" In other words, don't continually hit the snooze button on your life's alarm clock.

Please note here that rest is not the same thing as sleep. God commands us to take time to rest and rejuvenate our bodies and He set the example for us by resting on the seventh day of creation. Sleep, or slumber, in this context is being lazy. As we continue through Proverbs you will see a sharp contrast between the diligent and the lazy person. Here are just a few:

The Diligent vs. The Lazy

- Get rich / are soon poor. Proverbs 10:4
- Are prosperous / wastes away his time. Proverbs 12:11
- Will be a leader (ruler) / will never succeed. Proverbs 12:24
- Has an easy path / has trouble all his life. Proverbs 15:19

- Loves to give generously / wants things, but refuses to work for them. Proverbs 21:25-26

Compare this list to the students in your martial arts family and identify the leaders. They likely have a black belt or upper-level belt. Consider the work and diligence it took to earn that leadership role and belt rank. Hopefully, you are seeing some of the characteristics on the "diligent" side of this list when you envision these students. Hard work is a trait we should all desire to model, in the dojo and in every area of our lives. When we work hard, benefits are guaranteed to follow.

What Are You Sowing?

The Bible uses the term *sow* here in chapter 6, but also in other places in scripture. As early as Genesis 26:12 (Living Bible) scripture introduces sowing with, *"That year Isaac's crops were tremendous—100 times the grain he sowed."* Sowing simply means to plant. Jesus even uses sowing in a parable found in the Gospels. The seed in the parable represents the Gospel, the sower (planter) represents anyone who tells others about the Gospel, and the various soils represent how people respond to the Gospel message. When the seed is sowed (planted), it will take root and produce a harvest or it will die, depending on the type of soil and the way the ground is cultivated. Just like when you plant (sow) pumpkin seeds in June in Kansas, you can expect to harvest (reap) pumpkins in October – the same is true with anything you sow. You can expect to reap a harvest of whatever you planted at some point in the future.

So, what are you sowing? Let me tell you what not to sow – *discord!* Why? God *hates* it. Verses 16-19 tells us what God hates and the last one in the list is *"conflict in the community"* (Proverbs 6:19). In other words, don't stir up trouble and discontent.

There are adjectives in verses 12-15 that you do not want to describe you – troublemaker, villain, and corrupt. Some translations use the words liar, rebellious, and mischievous. This is so contrary to what God calls us to be in Matthew 5:9 – peacemakers.

Wisdom tells us to avoid discord. Sowing discord will produce a life with no satisfaction because it brings a life of misfortune. This misfortune will be so severe that it will leave you broken beyond repair, and that's no life at all.

So, what *are* you sowing? Let's go to Galatians 5:22-23 to see what the wisdom of God tells us to sow:

- love
- joy
- peace
- patience
- kindness
- goodness
- faithfulness
- gentleness
- self-control

These should be the words that describe you.

Warning Against Adultery

Your martial arts class begins with left and right punches, front kicks, roundhouse kicks, hook and uppercut punches, switch steps, and such. It's the same routine that starts every class. There is a reason for routine, and it is this: repetition is the essence of learning. Hearing the same instructions or repeating the same movements over and over helps embed those teachings in your mind. If you only hear something once, it usually doesn't stick with you. If you hear or do something again and again, it becomes second nature.

Proverbs is great about using repetition to make a point. In verses 20-23 we are again told to keep the commandments of our father which is the same instruction given in Proverbs 4:1. Verses 24-35 give the same instruction from Proverbs 5, which is to avoid adultery. These verses in Proverbs 6, however, are much more direct, stern, and filled with specific warnings.

Adultery can cost you your very life (verse 26). It brings death to your relationship with God, death to the blessings of God, and in some cases, even physical death. Let's look at an example of this in the Word. In 2 Samuel 11 and 12 is the recount of King David's adulterous act. He sins with Bathsheba who is married to Uriah, a man in David's army. They conceive a son together. To cover up his sin, David arranges for Uriah to be killed. Once born, the baby becomes very sick and David turns to God to save him, but the consequences of David's sin are already in motion and the infant dies. David learns there are always consequences for our sins.

David had a plan. He saw Bathsheba and lusted after her, then acted on that lust. He knew just what he was doing. In an act of desperation, he went to extreme measures to hide his sin. 2 Chronicles 16:9 says, *"For the eyes of the Lord range throughout the earth to strengthen those whose hearts are fully committed to him. You have done a foolish thing, and from now on you will be at war."*

David could not hide his sin from God. In 2 Samuel 12 God sends the prophet Nathan to tell David, "I know what you've done" and God tells him the consequences of his sin in 2 Samuel 12:11. *"...Out of your own household I am going to bring calamity on you..."* This indeed happens later, when David's son Absalom revolts against him.

Proverbs 6:27-28 says you cannot play with fire and not get burned. Adultery has lasting and far-reaching effects, and the painful ramifications can trickle down through your family. There is no other sin with such serious consequences. Even a person who steals food because he is hungry must repay sevenfold what he stole. Most people would have sympathy for the person stealing food in a situation like this, but there is still a price to pay. The price for adultery is your life (verse 26).

The story of David focuses on David's sin and his consequences, but it takes two to commit adultery. Most martial arts classes have both men and women in class. There are opportunities to be partners during drills, visit by the water fountain, sit together before class, walk to the car after class – all of which can be positive, healthy conversations. But, if one or both of you are married, guard yourself against the attack of the enemy. Don't make this friendship more than it is. Don't buy into the lie that you can let it happen once, ask for forgiveness, and everything will magically be fine.

David asked for forgiveness for his sin, but something had been put into motion that could not be stopped. David's sin resulted in the death of Uriah and the death of his infant son. Some may argue that God should not have let the son die and should have answered David's prayer. But this truly shows the justness of God. He has established His law and He is just in His punishment. The Bible says He is no respecter of persons. Even for someone that the Bible describes as *a man after God's own heart,* God is still just. We can take comfort in the fact that God is the same yesterday, today and forever (Hebrews 13:8). Heed to God's law that is so blatantly laid out before us. Verse 23 tells us that His reproofs of instruction are the way of life. Apply this wisdom to live a happy, long life in Christ.

Points to Remember

- *When someone asks you to be surety for a loan, always say no, no matter how hard it is to do so.*
- *Move forward in Christ. Don't be lazy and let life slip by you. Ask Him for the purpose He planned for you and act on it.*
- *Keep your eyes focused on God's law, not the ways of man. Guard yourself from the sins that the world thinks is "acceptable" or "commonplace."*

| 7 |

Quick Recall

My son, keep my words and store up my commands within you. ² Keep my commands and you will live; guard my teachings as the apple of your eye.

³ Bind them on your fingers; write them on the tablet of your heart.

⁴ Say to wisdom, "You are my sister," and to insight, "You are my relative."

⁵ They will keep you from the adulterous woman, from the wayward woman with her seductive words.

⁶ At the window of my house I looked down through the lattice.

⁷ I saw among the simple, I noticed among the young men, a youth who had no sense.

⁸ He was going down the street near her corner, walking along in the direction of her house

⁹ at twilight, as the day was fading, as the dark of night set in.

¹⁰ Then out came a woman to meet him, dressed like a prostitute and with crafty intent.

¹¹ (She is unruly and defiant, her feet never stay at home;

¹² now in the street, now in the squares, at every corner she lurks.)

¹³ She took hold of him and kissed him and with a brazen face she said:

¹⁴ "Today I fulfilled my vows, and I have food from my fellowship offering at home.

¹⁵ So I came out to meet you; I looked for you and have found you!

¹⁶ I have covered my bed with colored linens from Egypt.

¹⁷ I have perfumed my bed with myrrh, aloes and cinnamon.

¹⁸ Come, let's drink deeply of love till morning; let's enjoy ourselves with love!

¹⁹ My husband is not at home; he has gone on a long journey.

²⁰ He took his purse filled with money and will not be home till full moon."

²¹ With persuasive words she led him astray; she seduced him with her smooth talk.

²² All at once he followed her like an ox going to the slaughter, like a deer stepping into a noose

²³ till an arrow pierces his liver, like a bird darting into a snare, little knowing it will cost him his life.

²⁴ Now then, my sons, listen to me; pay attention to what I say.

²⁵ Do not let your heart turn to her ways or stray into her paths.

²⁶ Many are the victims she has brought down; her slain are a mighty throng.

²⁷ Her house is a highway to the grave, leading down to the chambers of death.

Chapter 7: Daily Devotional

If you regularly meditate on God's Word it will be quick to recall in times of trouble. As we study the Word, we will have confidence in knowing how to face daily problems, defeat temptation, and keep the right company. When you fail to make those daily deposits, you'll find that life will continually make withdrawals that leave your account depleted and soon could end in bankruptcy. Proverbs 7 shows us the importance of daily deposits of scripture in our life.

Deposits in the Bank

An adult female student from our school attended a business dinner in our small town. She is an executive at a local bank and is well-known and respected in our community. It was just after dark when she left for the parking lot to go home. One of the men who also attended the dinner escorted her to her car. As she opened the door to get in, he pushed her into the seat and tried to attack her. She immediately threw an elbow strike that caught him in the jaw. He pulled back and she hit him with a palm strike to the face. It gave her enough time to get up in the seat, pull the door shut and get away.

In another situation, a 13-year-old green belt student defended his mother from an abusive stepfather. The boy caught his stepfather beating his mother and decided to stop it. He kicked the man in the knee, taking his leg out from under him. The boy hit him again as he went down, giving the boy and his mother the chance to escape the house.

In both of these situations, the students said their reaction came naturally. It was just a reflex that was second-nature, and they knew exactly what to do to defend themselves. They didn't have time to think or plan what they would do. Both situations happened quickly and were over in seconds.

The reason it came so naturally was because the students practiced the defensive moves in class regularly. We worked the moves in various situations, on different sized partners, at different speeds and at different levels of fatigue.

Self-defense wasn't something these two students just *wanted* to know; they knew it. They continually made deposits into their self-defense bank by practicing the techniques. When it was time to make a withdrawal from the bank, there was money there to withdraw. My children used to say that if I had checks in my checkbook, I must have money. We all know the folly in that! You have to put money in the bank in order to write the check. Our students didn't just have checks in the checkbook when they faced their attackers. They had knowledge to draw from to write the check and protect themselves.

Study the Word

When problems arise, you want to quickly find the answer to solve it. The amazing thing about God's Word is that all the answers to your problems are there for you on the pages. One of my favorite things to do is read God's promises. I like to find books or websites that list a problem I may be facing and a scripture reference beside it to read God's answer. One I have used many times over the years is God's promise for healing.

"But he was pierced for our transgressions, he was crushed for our iniquities: the punishment that brought us peace was on him; and by His wounds we are healed" (Isaiah 53:5).

Not only does the Word promise blessings, it also provides commandments that help us live a healthy, prosperous life. For example, if you are having financial difficulties, the Word teaches us to get our finances in order. The first step in doing that is to tithe. Malachi 3:10 tells us to, *"Bring the whole tithe into the storehouse, that there may be food in My house..."*

Like the Garfield poster I described in Chapter 1, you can't just have a Bible lying on your shelf and expect the knowledge and wisdom of God to be in you. Many of us expect God to do "His part" when we haven't done ours. Our part is to study the Word. Verses 1-4 of Proverbs 7 tell us to lay up God's commandments and bind them to our fingers and heart. You are to get to know these commandments as you know your own family. Keeping them will in turn produce life (verse 2).

Facing the Problem

Once you have been studying the Word it will become forefront in your thinking and response to any situation. The first part of verse 5 tells us why studying is important.

"That they (His commandments) *may keep thee..."* The verse goes on to say *"from the adulterous woman,"* but take that part of the verse and fill in those words with ones of your own. What will His commandments keep you from? When you are facing a problem and you've been studying the Word, your response to that problem will be God-based and it will "keep you" – keep you safe, healthy, at peace and so on.

We can so easily liken our martial arts training to our spiritual training in these verses. Preparation is key to facing an attacker, whether that attacker is a person or Satan. As an old saying wisely sums it up: "If you fail to prepare, then prepare to fail."

The Temptations of Life

I think it's safe to say after reading the last three chapters of Proverbs that God means business when He says that adultery is a sin that kills. In verses 6-27 we read about a young man who is lured by a married woman into an adulterous affair. The verses go into detail about how the woman makes the temptation seem so inviting. She has tapestry, carved works, fine linen, perfume, aloes and cinnamon to entice this young man that verse 7 describes as *"a youth who had no sense."*

Temptation always makes things seem enticing and wonderful, all the while covering up its true effects. The temptation can be so great that we lose all understanding and common sense and we become so completely blind that we don't see the forest through the trees. Verses 22-23 show us how completely foolish this young man was with phrases like, *"...as an ox goes to the slaughter, or as a deer stepping into a noose"* and *"...as a bird darting into a snare."* The temptation pulled him in, and he let all wisdom go and ruined his life.

When you let your guard down in sparring class, you're going to get hit. It will probably hurt bad enough to remind you to get your hands up or you'll be lying flat on your back. You can't take a break in the middle of a fight, because your opponent is still fighting. The fight will continue until your instructor calls time. Temptation isn't going to take a break either. The lure continually tries to permeate our lives in so many ways, both outright and subtly.

During my daughter's 7th grade year, I noticed her love for hip-hop music really increased to the point it was taking over the radio station in her room and replacing songs on her iPod. She was singing the songs and "pop and locking" to the beat. Then one day in the car she proclaimed, "I really don't like hip-hop so much anymore. I listened to the words and it's really disgusting." The popular hip-hop our teenagers listen to described provocative dancing, first time experience with the opposite sex, ungodly relationships and so on. She admitted she listened to the songs because she liked the beat and sang the songs because they were popular. A subtle lure was the beat; the outright lure was the lyrics. My daughter was blindly listening and singing like the young man in verses 22-23.

But the wisdom of God inside of her said to change the radio station and she obeyed. God promises to *"...keep him in perfect peace, whose mind is stayed on You..."* (Isaiah 26:3). Peace is something we are always praying for and because of my daughter's realization that she needed to get her mind on God, He provided that peace she desired.

No One Will Know!

A popular thought-pattern is that you can do whatever you want because no one will know, and you won't get caught. The woman in Proverbs 7 told the young man that her husband was not home and would be gone for several days (verses 19-20). What she was saying was, "No one will know!"

Joseph faced a similar situation in Genesis 39:7-19. Potiphar's wife tried to seduce him when *"none of the household servants was inside"* (verse 11). No one was around and Joseph had a decision to make – to yield to the temptation or to follow the wisdom of God. Joseph's response to this temptation was just the opposite of the young man of Proverbs 7. Joseph chose wisdom and followed God's truth. God blessed him and Joseph experienced a life that could only be orchestrated by God himself. It was not by chance that Joseph was again placed in authority and was able to reconcile with his family.

"Whatever they have said in the dark shall be heard in the light, and what you have whispered in the inner rooms shall be broadcast from the housetops for all to hear" (Luke 12:3, Living Bible).

That thought-pattern of "no one will know" has gotten many people in trouble. It's amazing how things that you thought were secret can quickly become very public. Someone was watching or recording when you didn't realize it, or someone overheard your conversation, and suddenly what was done privately is being broadcast on social media. More importantly, God is always watching. *"For the eyes of the Lord search back and forth across the whole earth..."* (2 Chronicles 16:9).

Truth will always reveal itself. God is watching even when you think no one else is. Be certain your sin will be found out.

Keep Good Company

As a public school teacher, I have called many parents when their child is having problems in class. At times the conversation will change from me trying to solicit help for the student, to the parent asking me for help in parenting the student. Parents will ask who their child's friends are, who they are with in the halls, what they talk about in class, and so on. As soon as I tell the parent what behaviors I am seeing, the parent often replies, "I told him/her to stay away from that person."

Parents know that the friends their children keep have an incredibly strong influence on them. Friends have a strong influence at any age. In a report published by Fox News, the author Alicia Chang, AP Science Writer, wrote:

> *If your friends and family get fat, chances are you will too, researchers report in a startling new study that suggests obesity is "socially contagious" and can spread easily from person to person. The large, federally funded study found that to be true even if your loved ones lived far away. Social ties seemed to play a surprisingly strong role, even more than genes are known to do.*

God, too, knows the powerful influence of a friend. Although at the time the Israelites were not friends with the nations of the land God promised them, God knew they could be. So he instructed the Israelites to completely annihilate everyone of that nation. He was trying to protect them from the evil influences of these nations. But, sometimes when the Israelites went into enemy territory, they did not utterly destroy everything like God had commanded them to, and after leaving some of their influence, the Israelites began to think and act like the unbelieving people of the land.

Thinking about the students and families that have been part of our school over the years, the most challenging "company" we have had are the parents. The students typically fall in step and conform to Chris's style of teaching and class management. The parents, however, want to be sideline coaches and can stir trouble as they sit along the outside of the dojo talking to other parents. We had a father, Daryl, who tried this a few years ago. Daryl's daughter was very talented and could have likely advanced to some level of the sport; however, in his mind he knew way more than Chris did and had a more influential network of martial artists – which makes me wonder why he even enrolled his daughter at our school in the first place! During class he criticized the instruction, tried to influence parents to leave our school, and talked badly about other students. Since Chris was teaching he didn't know the full extent of this man's toxic actions until some of our parents told him. One night, it nearly became a physical altercation when one father got fed up with the negativity and verbal attacks Daryl made against his daughter. Our regular families did not want him around, did not appreciate his company, and thankfully, told him so. It didn't take long before Daryl and his daughter left our school. Our families are friends, and they talk, laugh, and enjoy each other's company. This man was not good company and was ruining the culture of the school.

God has called us to live our lives in a godly manner, not influenced by the things of this world, but rather influenced by His ways. His word says, *"For the grace of God has appeared that offers salvation to all people. It teaches us to say "No" to ungodliness and worldly passions, and to live self-controlled, upright and godly lives in this present age,"* (Titus 2:11, 12).

The problem with the man in Proverbs 7 is he did not keep good company. He ignored the instruction of verse 25 and followed the path of temptation. He let himself be influenced right down *"to the chambers of death."* God's instructions and promises never change. Your obedience will lead you down paths of righteousness and blessing.

Points to Remember

- *Make daily faith deposits into your life account by studying the Word of God.*
- *God's laws are not for yesterday. They still apply today and will continue to apply until the day He returns.*
- *Surround yourself with godly people. Remove influences that will lead you away from God's path.*

| 8 |

A Long Time

Does not wisdom call out? Does not understanding raise her voice?
² At the highest point along the way, where the paths meet, she takes her stand;

³ beside the gate leading into the city, at the entrance, she cries aloud:

⁴ "To you, O people, I call out; I raise my voice to all mankind.

⁵ You who are simple, gain prudence; you who are foolish, set your hearts on it.

⁶ Listen, for I have trustworthy things to say; I open my lips to speak what is right.

⁷ My mouth speaks what is true, for my lips detest wickedness.

⁸ All the words of my mouth are just; none of them is crooked or perverse.

⁹ To the discerning all of them are right; they are upright to those who have found knowledge.

¹⁰ Choose my instruction instead of silver, knowledge rather than choice gold,

¹¹ for wisdom is more precious than rubies, and nothing you desire can compare with her.

¹² "I, wisdom, dwell together with prudence; I possess knowledge and discretion.

¹³ To fear the Lord is to hate evil; I hate pride and arrogance, evil behavior and perverse speech.

¹⁴ Counsel and sound judgment are mine; I have insight, I have power.

¹⁵ By me kings reign and rulers issue decrees that are just;

¹⁶ by me princes govern, and nobles—all who rule on earth.

¹⁷ I love those who love me, and those who seek me find me.

¹⁸ With me are riches and honor, enduring wealth and prosperity.

¹⁹ My fruit is better than fine gold; what I yield surpasses choice silver.

²⁰ I walk in the way of righteousness, along the paths of justice,

²¹ bestowing a rich inheritance on those who love me and making their treasuries full.

²² "The Lord brought me forth as the first of his works, before his deeds of old;

²³ I was formed long ages ago, at the very beginning, when the world came to be.

²⁴ When there were no watery depths, I was given birth, when there were no springs overflowing with water;

²⁵ before the mountains were settled in place, before the hills, I was given birth,

²⁶ before he made the world or its fields or any of the dust of the earth.

²⁷ I was there when he set the heavens in place, when he marked out the horizon on the face of the deep,

²⁸ when he established the clouds above and fixed securely the fountains of the deep,

²⁹ when he gave the sea its boundary so the waters would not overstep his command,

and when he marked out the foundations of the earth.

³⁰ Then I was constantly at his side. I was filled with delight day after day, rejoicing always in his presence,

[31] rejoicing in his whole world and delighting in mankind.

[32] "Now then, my children, listen to me; blessed are those who keep my ways.

[33] Listen to my instruction and be wise; do not disregard it.

[34] Blessed are those who listen to me, watching daily at my doors, waiting at my doorway.

[35] For those who find me find life and receive favor from the Lord.

[36] But those who fail to find me harm themselves; all who hate me love death."

Chapter 8: Daily Devotional

My husband Chris has been involved with martial arts for over 45 years. That may or may not seem like a long time depending on your perspective, but my point is that he has been in the sport long enough to coach a few hundred students or so, fight in several states, compete in everything from full contact to flag, and see schools and instructors come and go. When you have been a part of something for a long time, you have insight about it that others do not. That's what wisdom is saying in this chapter: "I've been here a long time and I know what I'm talking about."

The Voice of Wisdom

Think of the times you have warned your children or your parents have warned you. What was the tone of voice of the person doing the warning? They might have been screaming, alarmed, stern, confident – all depending on the situation. I have yelled at my own children many times for the sake of protection. My voice was probably loud, panic-stricken and maybe even harsh. But my objective was to get my child's attention and to save them from trouble.

Likewise, I've seen Chris yell at his students too. Sometimes at tournaments when students are fighting, they get so engrossed in the match that he must yell to get their attention. He is trying to warn them against a technique or instruct them how to score on their opponent. The objective of both situations, parent, or instructor, is to get someone's attention and get them to listen.

Wisdom is doing the same to us in verses 1-9. In the Living Bible, the word "listen" is used three times in these verses because what wisdom has to say to us is too important to miss. Wisdom gives us understanding, common sense, and truth. Wisdom gives advice that is wholesome and good and void of lies and hatred. And what is so great about the voice of wisdom is that it is *"plain and clear to anyone with half a mind – if it is only open!"* (Proverbs 8:9, Living Bible).

Wisdom does not speak with words we cannot understand, but instead speaks at our level. It speaks clearly and directly – just like our parents talk to us or like we talk to our students when we know that what we are saying preserves life.

Better Than Rubies

"If only I had money, life would be great!" Don't many of us think that way? Yes, money does give us higher levels of material comfort and provides us with worldly luxury that we might not otherwise have. Many people today are prosperous financially even though their fruit does not show that they possess the wisdom of God.

To be very honest, we have never made enough money at our martial arts school to make a living. That's why Chris and I both work full-time jobs in addition to operating the school. It would seem foolish to some that we continue to stay in business after 26 years, but money is not our motivation. Our motivation has been speaking wisdom into the lives of others, focusing on family, and building ourselves up physically, mentally, and spiritually.

When money is the only motive for your actions, you will fall short of the many other blessings of God. Money itself is a blessing from

God and God does not want us to lack for anything. In fact, God *wants* to bless us. In Deuteronomy 28:11-13 the Lord says He will give you an abundance of good things. But God's blessings are not centered on money. He wants to bless the whole you with health, mental soundness and a peace that passes all understanding. So, if you're living for God because you want more money, you may be sorely disappointed. His Word says, *"But seek first his kingdom and his righteousness; and all these things will be given to you as well"* (Matthew 6:33).

Our purpose should be to seek the kingdom of God because we love Him, and His wisdom is *"more precious than rubies"* (verse 11). All the wealth in the world will not bring you what the wisdom of God will. God's wisdom is better than gold and anything you could desire pales in comparison (verse 19). God asked King Solomon in 2 Chronicles 1:7-12, *"Ask for whatever you want me to give you."* and Solomon replied, *"Give me wisdom and knowledge..."* Solomon knew that God's wisdom was better than anything else he could ask for. When God heard his answer, he replied to Solomon that not only would he receive wisdom, but also riches, wealth, and honor.

As we see with Solomon, when we seek Him and find Him, He will give us all we need and more (verse 21). The truth is that it's a matter of priorities. Our first priority should not be to chase money, but rather to seek after God. Prosperity is a by-product of our walk with the Lord. A strong foundation built on Godly principles is the result of daily applying God's wisdom to our lives. When we establish this strong foundation, we are putting ourselves in a position to receive from God the prosperity He has promised us. This is really the only true way to be prosperous. Setting your first priority on seeking the wisdom of God *"is far more valuable than silver or gold"* (Proverbs 8:10, Living Bible).

Wisdom Knows it All

Taekwondo is an art whose roots are from Korean fighting styles that began over 2,300 years ago. The term "taekwondo" was coined around the 1940s and 50s by various Korean martial artists that blended Korean styles with an influence of karate and Japanese martial arts. When you train in taekwondo you are advanced with belt rank, starting at white belt and moving as high as 9th degree black belt. The highest rank of black belt awarded to living people in taekwondo is the 9th degree. Some say this belt takes between 35-40 years to obtain after starting from beginner status, and most would agree that it should never be achieved in less than 30 years. The sport itself goes back centuries and to become a grandmaster, an instructor who has reached 9th degree rank, requires years of study and training. A grandmaster knows the history, growth, and development of taekwondo over the years. A grandmaster deeply knows the art, not just at a surface level, but clear down its roots. A grandmaster has trained for many years in this centuries-old sport.

Something else that has been around for years is wisdom – in fact, the Bible says it has been around for an eternity. Wisdom is not a new fad, but an eternal foundation of truth. Look at how the verses in Proverbs 8 are written – mostly in first person. It is as if the writer is wisdom, and he tells us in verse 22 that he has been around since the beginning of time. He says he was formed before the earth began (verse 23), before the oceans were created (verse 24) and before the mountains and hills were made (verse 25). Like the grandmaster who relishes and embraces taekwondo, so is wisdom's knowledge and understanding of the world. A grandmaster knows the lineage and ancestry of his style. Wisdom knows the lineage and ancestry of the world. Because the grandmaster and wisdom have this knowledge, we would be wise to follow the direction in verse 32, *"Now then, my children, listen to me."*

If we listen to wisdom he tells us we will be blessed, find life, and receive favor from the Lord. Not listening to wisdom is simply choosing a life of destruction and certain death. Just as you listen to your grandmaster because you trust in his experience, so should you trust the one who knows about all things from the beginning of time.

Can't Hardly Wait

As I walked out of class one night, I overhead a student talking to his father. The boy was so excited he was practically skipping. He said, "Dad, Mr. Rangel said I could come to class again tomorrow! Can I go?" There was such enthusiasm and excitement in his voice. He loved class so much that he couldn't wait to come again.

The anticipation of a student eagerly waiting for class to begin is how we should seek wisdom. The Living Bible describes it best in verse 34. *"Happy is the man who is so anxious to be with me that he watches for me daily at my gates or waits for me outside my home."*

Don't you know how much God is pleased when you *want* to spend time with Him? He desires to meet with us, talk with us, and be part of our lives. It's a win-win situation – God has great things in store for you. Be anxious to be in His presence, to gain wisdom, and to see what plans He has made for you.

Points to Remember

- *Listen to the voice of wisdom and receive all the benefits it provides.*
- *God's wisdom is better than any material possession you could possess.*
- *He longs to spend time with you. Take every opportunity to include Him in your day.*

| 9 |

Embrace Change

Wisdom has built her house; she has set up its seven pillars.
² She has prepared her meat and mixed her wine; she has also set her table.

³ She has sent out her servants, and she calls from the highest point of the city,

⁴ "Let all who are simple come to my house!" To those who have no sense she says,

⁵ "Come, eat my food and drink the wine I have mixed.

⁶ Leave your simple ways and you will live; walk in the way of insight."

⁷ Whoever corrects a mocker invites insults; whoever rebukes the wicked incurs abuse.

⁸ Do not rebuke mockers or they will hate you; rebuke the wise and they will love you.

⁹ Instruct the wise and they will be wiser still; teach the righteous and they will add to their learning.

¹⁰ The fear of the Lord is the beginning of wisdom, and knowledge of the Holy One is understanding.

¹¹ For through wisdom your days will be many, and years will be added to your life.

¹² If you are wise, your wisdom will reward you; if you are a mocker, you alone will suffer.

¹³ Folly is an unruly woman; she is simple and knows nothing.

¹⁴ She sits at the door of her house, on a seat at the highest point of the city,

¹⁵ calling out to those who pass by, who go straight on their way,

¹⁶ "Let all who are simple come to my house!" To those who have no sense she says,

¹⁷ "Stolen water is sweet; food eaten in secret is delicious!"

¹⁸ But little do they know that the dead are there, that her guests are deep in the realm of the dead.

Chapter 9: Daily Devotional

We have learned a lot in the last 26 years of owning a martial arts school. On the journey from the early years to the present day, we've traded boards for focus pads, concrete for spring-loaded floors, and a basement school for a storefront at the mall. Change can be difficult, but if you're going to stay competitive, change is inevitable. I am certain the school would not have the same clientele if we were still operating out of our basement. We've had to learn what does and does not work at our school and in our community.

With all this learning and changing comes two choices:

1. Refuse to change, stay exactly as you are and get offended at the suggestion of change, or
2. Embrace learning! Grow and expand and look at how suggestions can improve what you are doing.

Listen to Correction

Listening and being open-minded to suggestions is key. When I told Chris to get out of the basement and take all his martial arts stuff with him, I knew he was irritated to think I didn't support him or his fledgling martial arts school. To show his irritation, he decided to start giving lessons more nights of the week so he was away from home more. Looking back at that time, I think Chris would now admit that my suggestion to move out of our basement was exactly the push he needed to really start a school. He just did it with the wrong mindset.

When you are corrected, don't be quick to assume the worst. Many people see correction as a personal attack, when that's often not the case. Instead of responding to a suggestion like the scorner in verse 7, receive the correction with an open mind before making a judgment. Don't shut the door before you hear the person out and evaluate if it truly applies to your life and situation. And be honest with yourself. If your first response isn't anger, you might find that the advice – even unsolicited advice – is truly helpful.

My actions upset Chris and he saw things his way and only his way. That's exactly how a scorner would react. When you rebuke a scorner, the result is usually that you receive rebuke in return. A scorner is un-teachable and doesn't want to listen to anyone. The Living Bible says, *"So don't bother with him; he will only hate you for trying to help him"* (Proverbs 9:8).

We all know the type of person who is hard-headed and won't change his or her mind no matter what you say or do. They have to be right no matter what. After a while, people will stop trying to help and this person may miss out on valuable information that could bene-fit their life.

Instead, God is teaching us to stay teachable. There is always more to learn and, as hard as it may be to admit, we don't know everything! Verse 9 is a key point on our quest for wisdom. You will become wiser when you are taught. That seems pretty simple, but it is so powerful.

The element that makes it difficult is our attitude toward receiving correction.

This is true in our walk as a martial artist and in our spiritual walk with God. As a martial artist you may think a front kick has been a front kick since you were a white belt. And while that is true, there is so much more to it than just the front kick. Being a true martial artist is about perfecting your techniques, as well as your development as a whole person. The motto we use in our school is: *We build ourselves physically, mentally, and spiritually.* This is not a one-day seminar, but a continual process that requires instruction. A person not willing to listen to correction will never grow in these areas.

Receiving Instruction

The Living Bible reads in verse 7, *"If you rebuke a mocker you will only get a smart retort; yes, he will snarl at you."* The way we receive instruction will determine if we are given instruction.

One night a mother of a student called to complain about how she thought her daughter was treated in class. She felt that her daughter was unfairly disciplined and should be promoted to a higher rank. What the mother did not know was that her daughter had refused to participate in class and had been giving mediocre effort in drills. Instead of finding out the reason for the decision to not promote her daughter, the mother called to attack and criticize. She perceived the correction as unfair and undeserving.

Receiving correction is a hard thing. Being told you are wrong rarely feels good; however, you should evaluate that correction and see how it applies to your life. Parents often see their children with blinders on and teachers see a much larger picture. So, stop and listen! Hear the correction, find out the facts, evaluate how it applies and learn from the criticism. If, after investigation, the correction is unwarranted, don't be offended – simply move on and forget it. Don't have the attitude that you are above correction. Instead, remain teachable and when others see that teachable spirit, they will share more of their wisdom with you.

The same principle applies when someone gives you spiritual correction. The pastor may speak a message that you feel is right at you. That feeling is God's correction. Don't get mad at the pastor. Receive the correction from God and apply it to your life. To continue to grow in God's wisdom, we must remain teachable.

Two Descriptions

Would you like to be described as "the foolish woman?" It's not a very flattering or complimentary description. The Bible describes the foolish woman as loud, brash, and knowing nothing. She speaks her mind and gives her opinion when she really does not know what she is talking about.

Verse 17 says she tells men going by that what she is offering is sweet and pleasant. The verse also says that is done in secret. But if it's so great, why is it done in secret? Because she is hiding the fact that all who experience her offer find themselves in less than desirable situations.

The Bible describes a very different type of woman in Proverbs 31. This woman is virtuous and fears God. "*When she speaks, her words are wise, and kindness is the rule for everything she says*" (Proverbs 31:26, Living Bible).

We have had experience working with both types of people at our school who fit these descriptions. The first one would be like the foolish woman. We met this individual, Phil, about 20 years ago through a martial arts connection. He was very talented and competed both nationally and internationally. Over the years he has bounced from one school to another, getting just enough of what he wanted, and then moving on. Our paths crossed multiple times over the years and at one point we worked on a project together promoting local MMA fights. During the course of the years, Phil had lost everything and wanted very much to own his own school again. The timing seemed right and we felt like he had matured to the point where he would settle in and run our second school. We quickly learned that he had not changed; he stayed with us only until he got what he needed, and then moved on to a "new and better deal" in another city. We soon learned that the deal also fell through and he is on to his next gig. Phil talks a good game, has martial arts credentials to support his claim, and can get people to follow him. But, as he has moved from spot to spot, he has burned bridges that may come back to hurt him in the future. Like the foolish woman, Phil is hiding his true intentions and leaving trusting people in less than desirable situations.

The opposite description of the foolish person is the virtuous and God-fearing person. We have had the great fortune of working with a person who exemplifies these traits. Tony has been with our school since our days in the chicken hatchery basement. Chris has known him nearly all his life and they even went to high school together. As life would have it Tony made some poor decisions and landed himself in prison sometime after high school. Tony also struggled with abusing substances and developed a powerful addiction. After his release from prison he looked for something to fill the void of substance abuse and channel his energy into positive choices. That's when he landed at our doorstep – nearly 20 years ago. During his time with us he perfected the skill of board-breaking and then advanced into breaking cinder blocks! He holds the world record for downward elbow and downward hand breaks – you can check him out at http://www.awpba.org/. Today Tony is the kindest, most humble man you will ever meet. He teaches multiple classes at our school and is wonderful with children. His calm, methodical demeanor is quite the opposite of Chris's fast-paced instruction, but it truly resonates with the students and provides a beautiful balance of instruction at the school. He now runs our second school that the former individual left us with and has picked up the pieces to begin growing his own martial arts school. As an example of how focused Tony is on building himself up through martial arts, he even got married in his taekwondo uniform!

This is a very contrary description of two different people. You can decide which description you want to describe you. You can choose to be loud and unteachable or wise and humble. Most would agree that the latter description is more favorable. In your quest for wisdom, strive to develop yourself to honor God and be a blessing to others.

Who Will You Be?

Now that you know the two descriptions, who will you be?

A friend shared with me that her young son, Cohen, was struggling with which social group to belong to at school. There was the "cool" group that consists of the jocks and those of privilege. Then there was the "not cool" group that consisted of everyone else. Her son wanted very much to fit into the cool group, but his kind heart continually pulled him to the other group. The cool kids were often mean, foul-mouthed, and selfish, but the boys all played sports together and Cohen found himself typically with the jocks. Cohen was learning a hard lesson that trying to be someone you're not just to fit in is heart-wrenching. Cohen's feelings were hurt when he was not invited to "cool" kid parties, when he was left out in conversations, and when he was made fun of for befriending the "uncools."

Proverbs 9 has two invitations: one from wisdom and one from foolishness. Just like Cohen had a decision who he would call friend, we too have a decision who to call ourselves – either wise or foolish. Who will we befriend? The first invitation from wisdom is found in verses 1-6. Wisdom shows that she lacks nothing. Everything has been prepared for you and you simply need to accept the invitation and live a life of fulfillment.

The invitation of foolishness is found in verses 13-18. Look how this invitation differs from the first. Foolishness is described as *"simple and knows nothing."* It's empty and dark – a far cry from a life of fulfillment.

As I talked with my friend, her mom-heart was broken for her son. I encouraged her to tell Cohen to be the wise kid – follow his heart to be kind to others, stand up for the uncool crowd, and be true to who God called him to be. This is the invitation we should all accept. Take hold of the invitation to be wise and pitch the other party's invitation.

Points to Remember

- *When God speaks to you to change, listen and accept His correction. Be thankful for the correction instead of offended.*
- *Remain teachable. God's wisdom far outweighs ours. We will prosper when we receive and apply His instructions.*
- *Evaluate correction against God's Word. If it matches the Word, then change!*

| 10 |

The Choices You Make

The proverbs of Solomon:
A wise son brings joy to his father, but a foolish son brings grief to his mother.

²Ill-gotten treasures have no lasting value, but righteousness delivers from death.

³The Lord does not let the righteous go hungry, but he thwarts the craving of the wicked.

⁴Lazy hands make for poverty, but diligent hands bring wealth.

⁵He who gathers crops in summer is a prudent son, but he who sleeps during harvest is a disgraceful son.

⁶Blessings crown the head of the righteous, but violence overwhelms the mouth of the wicked.

⁷The name of the righteous is used in blessings, but the name of the wicked will rot.

⁸The wise in heart accept commands, but a chattering fool comes to ruin.

⁹Whoever walks in integrity walks securely, but whoever takes crooked paths will be found out.

¹⁰Whoever winks maliciously causes grief, and a chattering fool comes to ruin.

¹¹The mouth of the righteous is a fountain of life, but the mouth of the wicked conceals violence.

¹²Hatred stirs up conflict, but love covers over all wrongs.

¹³Wisdom is found on the lips of the discerning, but a rod is for the back of one who has no sense.

¹⁴The wise store up knowledge, but the mouth of a fool invites ruin.

¹⁵The wealth of the rich is their fortified city, but poverty is the ruin of the poor.

¹⁶The wages of the righteous is life, but the earnings of the wicked are sin and death.

¹⁷Whoever heeds discipline shows the way to life, but whoever ignores correction leads others astray.

¹⁸Whoever conceals hatred with lying lips and spreads slander is a fool.

¹⁹Sin is not ended by multiplying words, but the prudent hold their tongues.

²⁰The tongue of the righteous is choice silver, but the heart of the wicked is of little value.

²¹The lips of the righteous nourish many, but fools die for lack of sense.

²²The blessing of the Lord brings wealth, without painful toil for it.

²³A fool finds pleasure in wicked schemes, but a person of understanding delights in wisdom.

²⁴What the wicked dread will overtake them; what the righteous desire will be granted.

²⁵When the storm has swept by, the wicked are gone, but the righteous stand firm forever.

²⁶As vinegar to the teeth and smoke to the eyes, so are sluggards to those who send them.

²⁷The fear of the Lord adds length to life, but the years of the wicked are cut short.

²⁸The prospect of the righteous is joy, but the hopes of the wicked come to nothing.

[29]The way of the Lord is a refuge for the blameless, but it is the ruin of those who do evil.

[30]The righteous will never be uprooted, but the wicked will not remain in the land.

[31]From the mouth of the righteous comes the fruit of wisdom, but a perverse tongue will be silenced.

[32]The lips of the righteous know what finds favor, but the mouth of the wicked only what is perverse.

Chapter 10: Daily Devotional

Chapter 10 is written differently than the previous chapters of Proverbs. Each verse shows two contrasting results – one for the righteous and one for the unrighteous. The results are determined by how you live your life and the choices you make. The choices you make today will have lasting effects both on this earth and in eternity. There are many truths in these verses that we could focus on, but let's just look at a few and how they apply to the life of the martial artist.

Opportunity Awaits

The opportunities that await a martial artist are many. First is physical development. Taking martial arts classes develops stamina, builds strength, improves quickness and speed, increases agility and coordination, helps with flexibility, and, most people's favorite, aids in weight loss.

Next is mental development. Exercise alone improves thinking skills and alertness. Martial arts training helps build self-esteem and confidence. We have also witnessed children diagnosed with ADD and ADHD improve their attention span and ability to focus. (Many have also decreased the amount of medication they are taking, which is another physical benefit.) Respect for others, oneself and property is another mental benefit.

A third opportunity is the chance to develop yourself spiritually. Some martial arts schools take this opportunity to focus on other gods or the inner-man, but at our school we focus on our relationship with the one true God. Our students are assigned monthly Bible reading passages and then asked to write how the reading applies to their training. Younger students memorize Bible verses and students are asked to pray to start and end class as well as for each other.

Martial arts is not the only game in town with opportunities. I guess I am just biased because I have seen so many success stories over the years. Opportunities truly await us in all areas of life. Look at your martial arts training. What opportunities are there waiting for you? Getting in shape, belt advancement, head instructor, school ownership, tournament circuit, national championships, the Olympic team?

The question is, "Will you go after the opportunity before you?" Let's focus on verses 4 and 5 to see what God's Word says about hard work and moving toward your opportunity. Verse 4 says, *"diligent hands bring wealth."* Hard workers get rich; lazy workers don't. The important word here is *diligent.* This person is persistent, focused, motivated and on a mission to achieve a goal. *Rich* does not apply to only monetary wealth, but also to many other benefits of life including health, peace, strong relationships and more.

Verse 5 in the Living Bible reads, *"...what a shame to see a lad who sleeps away his hour of opportunity."* Don't let your opportunity pass you by! Go after it. As teachers, Chris and I have both seen students with great potential academically and athletically who let it slip away and do nothing to take advantage of the opportunity before them. Our response is always that of verse 5: "What a shame." God has given us many opportunities to improve ourselves; if we just walk right by or sleep right through, then the consequences are ours to bear.

Reach out and grab the opportunity God has put in your path!

Don't Be Lazy

Laziness not only hurts *you*, as we learned in Proverbs 6:6-11, but it also is despised by others. Verse 26 describes the sluggard as being like *"smoke in people's eyes or a vinegar that sets the teeth on edge"* (Living Bible). A quick way to lose your job is to be lazy, and not having a job leads to poverty. The Word compels us to work hard because hard work bene-fits us and opens the door to opportunities. If we are lazy on the job, the opportunity for advancement may pass us by. Certain martial artists in our school were not promoted because of their laziness in class. Don't let laziness rob you of the opportunities for a successful and prosperous life that awaits you.

Writing Your Dash

At a funeral I attended several years ago, the pastor's message was not focused on when the man was born or when he died, but instead on the line on the tombstone that separated the two dates. This line, the dash, represented the man's life – the things he accomplished and what he was remembered for.

The question posed at the funeral was, "What are you doing with your dash?" Long after the birth and death dates fade, people will still remember you for something you did. Verse 7 says the memory of the *"righteous is used in blessings."* When the honest man is remembered, memories of good times and laughter surface as well as feelings of thankfulness for knowing them and sadness for the emptiness without them. The good man is remembered for the positive impact they had on others and their memory lasts because people continue to talk about them, think about them, and love them.

The Living Bible says the memory of the wicked stinks. The wicked may still be talked about, but not in the light of the just. The NIV ver-sion says their names will rot. I don't want my friends and family to re-member me by saying, "I'm glad she's gone!"

How you create your dash will have a lasting impression on those around you. We should want to be a blessing to others while we are here on this earth. Proverbs 10 tells us how we can be a blessing and create a blessed memory of ourselves:

- Verse 11 – speak words of life
- Verse 12 – cover all sin with love
- Verse 31 – give godly advice

Build on your dash today by being a blessing to someone.

Your Anchor Holds

In my childhood country church, a favorite hymn of the worship leader was "In Times Like These" by Ruth Caye Jones. The song's chorus encourages the singer to cling to Jesus in all circumstances.

Disaster strikes all of us in some way. Look at the students who attend your school and list the life disasters they have experienced or are currently going through. At our school, cancer has affected many of our students. Several people have experienced the disaster of divorce and its effects on the family structure. Being a Christian does not protect you from painful life experiences. Both righteous and unrighteous will feel the pain life can inflict.

The difference between how a righteous and unrighteous person reacts to disaster is found in Verse 25. *"When the storm has swept by, the wicked are gone, but the righteous stand firm forever."* The righteous have an anchor and that anchor is fixed on Jesus and the hope of salvation that He gives (Hebrews 6:19). When disaster strikes the righteous, they may feel frightened, angry, sad or any other human emotion, but they have a peace that steadies them in the storm. They have the assurance that God is in control of everything and that His will is perfect. Whatever happens is in His perfect plan and He will work out any problems in His timing and in accordance to His will. We may not understand why the disaster is happening, but we don't need to understand. The wisdom of God is much greater than our minds can comprehend. The *"everlasting foundation"* of the righteous is their faith and hope for an eternal home.

When the wicked experience the whirlwinds of life, the Bible says they are *"whirled away."* They don't know what to grasp on to and they have no hope of salvation. What is interesting, however, is that when an unrighteous person experiences a disaster, they often find a godly person to talk to. They call the pastor of the local church they frequent on occasion, or anyone else they think has a connection with God. Many students have called us in their time of distress, wanting us to counsel them and pray for them. They want to hear that God will fix all their problems and they don't need to do anything on their part. But what we do is first tell them they need to have a relationship with God and get their lives in line with the Word of God. When they do this, then they will experience all the promises and blessings that God has promised His children.

A student in our school found out that her brother was diagnosed with cancer. That night she was on our doorstep, crying and wanting Chris and me to pray for God to heal him. We did, but also encouraged her to get involved in church and learn about living her life for Christ. She did this and really started seeking the wisdom of God by coming to weekly Bible study, helping with youth outreaches, and other acts of service. Her brother started to make a turn for the better and was later diagnosed to be in remission. God had answered her prayer. Then she stopped coming to church and lost interest in the things of God. When we encouraged her to continue her relationship and walk with God, she replied that "we should stop acting like God." Yes, we were hurt, but we were more deeply saddened by the fact that she was walking away from God. We shouldn't serve God just because of what He can do for us, but because we love Him.

The anchor that holds us during the storms of life also keeps us when life is under control. We should stay faithful during the calm times of our lives so when the storms come again, we are anchored and ready for the storm to hit.

Points to Remember

- *What opportunity is waiting for you? Ask God to show you the opportunity He has planned for you and go for it!*
- *Work hard to develop a life – a dash – that people will remember as being a blessing to others.*
- *Anchor your life in Jesus. The salvation He promises is an eternal home with Him in Heaven.*

| 11 |

Actions Have Consequences

The Lord detests dishonest scales, but accurate weights find favor with him.

²When pride comes, then comes disgrace, but with humility comes wisdom.

³The integrity of the upright guides them, but the unfaithful are destroyed by their duplicity.

⁴Wealth is worthless in the day of wrath, but righteousness delivers from death.

⁵The righteousness of the blameless makes their paths straight, but the wicked are brought down by their own wickedness.

⁶The righteousness of the upright delivers them, but the unfaithful are trapped by evil desires.

⁷Hopes placed in mortals die with them; all the promise of their power comes to nothing.

⁸The righteous person is rescued from trouble, and it falls on the wicked instead.

⁹With their mouths the godless destroy their neighbors, but through knowledge the righteous escape.

¹⁰When the righteous prosper, the city rejoices; when the wicked perish, there are shouts of joy.

¹¹Through the blessing of the upright a city is exalted, but by the mouth of the wicked it is destroyed.

¹²Whoever derides their neighbor has no sense, but the one who has understanding holds their tongue.

¹³A gossip betrays a confidence, but a trustworthy person keeps a secret.

¹⁴For lack of guidance a nation falls, but victory is won through many advisers.

¹⁵Whoever puts up security for a stranger will surely suffer, but whoever refuses to shake hands in pledge is safe.

¹⁶A kindhearted woman gains honor, but ruthless men gain only wealth.

¹⁷Those who are kind benefit themselves, but the cruel bring ruin on themselves.

¹⁸A wicked person earns deceptive wages, but the one who sows righteousness reaps a sure reward.

¹⁹Truly the righteous attain life, but whoever pursues evil finds death.

²⁰The Lord detests those whose hearts are perverse, but he delights in those whose ways are blameless.

²¹Be sure of this: The wicked will not go unpunished, but those who are righteous will go free.

²²Like a gold ring in a pig's snout is a beautiful woman who shows no discretion.

²³The desire of the righteous ends only in good, but the hope of the wicked only in wrath.

²⁴One person gives freely, yet gains even more; another withholds unduly, but comes to poverty.

²⁵A generous person will prosper; whoever refreshes others will be refreshed.

²⁶People curse the one who hoards grain, but they pray God's blessing on the one who is willing to sell.

²⁷Whoever seeks good finds favor, but evil comes to one who searches for it.

²⁸Those who trust in their riches will fall, but the righteous will thrive like a green leaf.

²⁹Whoever brings ruin on their family will inherit only wind, and the fool will be servant to the wise.

³⁰The fruit of the righteous is a tree of life, and the one who is wise saves lives.

³¹If the righteous receive their due on earth, how much more the ungodly and the sinner!

Chapter 11: Daily Devotional

Proverbs 11 is written in the same pattern as Proverbs 10. Each scripture describes consequences for our actions, both just and unjust. This shows how God takes care of His children when they walk in His wisdom and make godly choices. In every situation there is a choice to be made – the choice to do good, walk uprightly, and honor God, or the choice to do evil, walk the path of destruction, and forsake wisdom. There are many profound truths and consequences in these verses. Let's focus on a few in light of a martial artist's life.

Be Guided by Honesty

Being honest is much more than thinking, *"Thou shalt not steal"* (Exodus 20:15) in the context of robbing merchandise from a store. Being honest is more than not lying. Being honest is also about integrity and faithfulness.

What does being honest look like in the dojo? Of course, it means not stealing someone's gear from the locker room. It also means paying your tuition consistently and on time. Some people have the mindset that this isn't really "stealing" because you aren't taking a physical possession from someone else. However, it is stealing because you are stealing your instructor's time and talent. Forcing your instructor to track you down to pay your tuition is not walking in integrity; it is dishonesty.

Dishonesty for the instructor means short-changing your students with your time, energy, talent – in essence, not giving them the effort they have paid for. Not showing up for class is stealing from your students. Not having a prepared lesson plan, not having the gear in working order, and not working hard to perfect your skills are all examples of dishonesty. Advertising something you are not is another example of dishonesty.

People are dishonest for a variety of reasons, but often it is because they feel dishonesty will give them an advantage that they couldn't otherwise obtain if they were honest. Verse 1 is an example of this. *"The Lord detests dishonest scales, but accurate weights find favor with him."* The writer is referring to the scales people in the market of Jesus' day would use to weigh merchandise brought in to sell. A scale that was purposefully set out of balance would not yield the correct weight and therefore, the merchant would not receive the correct amount of money that he was due. In other words, the buyers in the market would cheat the sellers to have a monetary advantage.

God is very plain in verse 1 about how He feels toward this practice. The Living Bible says, *"The Lord hates cheating..."* If we are walking in the wisdom of God, we need to evaluate where dishonesty has permeated our walk. We need to clean out every corner where dishonesty resides – places where we justify our actions to gain an advantage. By doing this we are following the wisdom in verse 3, *"A good man is guided by his honesty;..."* (Living Bible).

The advantages the dishonest seek ultimately will profit them nothing. Verse 4 reads, *"Your riches won't help you on Judgment Day; only righteousness counts then."* The saying "Whoever dies with the most toys wins" is certainly not true in light of eternity. Whatever fleeting gain the wicked received here on earth will stay here on earth. God is calling the *"upright to be directed by their honesty"* (Proverbs 11:5, Living Bible).

When we sow honesty, integrity, and righteousness, God has promised that we will have a sure reward that lasts forever (verse 18). You don't need the advantage the world may offer for dishonesty. The reward God gives the honest far outweighs anything man provides.

A Daily Commitment of Kindness

When you describe a spouse who is faithful, you are describing a person who is committed to their marriage *all* the time. This commitment is not based on convenience or season, but rather a lifestyle of dedication to the other person. When the spouse is unfaithful just *one* time, he/she is no longer considered faithful. They are now marked as the unfaithful spouse. Notice this only requires *one* act of unfaithfulness.

Compare this to kindness. Like faithfulness, kindness should be a daily commitment. It shouldn't be an act that only occurs when we feel like it. Many people walk in "unkindness" and expect one act of kindness to change people's perception of them. Society doesn't seem to place as much emphasis on kindness as it does faithfulness. What if kindness has the same "one-strike-and-you're-out" mentality as faithfulness does? If so, I am raising my hand right now that people would consider me unkind. I have certainly, regrettably, committed acts of unkindness in my life. What about you?

Kindness is an act that should evolve into a lifestyle. Verse 17 says *"Those who are kind benefit themselves."* Think of kind acts you have done and remember how you felt afterward. Kindness brings a sense of joy and goodwill to both the giver and the receiver. In simple terms, it makes you feel good all over!

Romans 12:21 says, *"Do not be overcome by evil, but overcome evil with good."* Being kind to people who are kind to us is easy. It's not so easy to be kind to those who are mean-spirited, bitter, or antagonistic; however, cruelty will never benefit you in the long run. Verse 11 says cruelty destroys your soul and leads to death. It's easy to retaliate or want revenge when someone is mean to us, but Romans 12 tells us that is never the way to respond. When cruelty is your first response, it stirs up more strife, starts unnecessary arguments, and perpetuates unkindness.

Responding in kindness is a large part of walking in the wisdom of God. God will open doors for us to be kind to others; all we need to do is walk through. There are many ways to be kind, both in and out of the dojo. Strive to find opportunities of kindness that will be a blessing to others as well as yourself the next time you go to class.

The Good Guy Wins

The storyline of many Hollywood movies revolves around a good guy and a bad guy. The two have some dilemma that creates the plot of the movie and the good guy wins in the end. That is certainly not a picture of reality outside the movie theatre. All around us, we see the bad guy getting ahead, getting richer and advancing up life's ladder. This can be a discouraging reality for the godly who always seem to do right, but never "get ahead." The problem with the godly who feel this way is that their focus is on this world and not the eternal reward.

As children of God we have a *"sure reward"* (verse 18). That sure reward is an eternity in heaven. The Living Bible says our reward lasts forever. The reward of the unrighteous is temporal and lasts only for the moment. The promise of that reward is found in John 14:1-3. Jesus is right now preparing our place in heaven and He is coming again to take us there. Don't be discouraged when you look at what others "have"; instead, look at them through the eyes of Christ and see the true riches they are missing. When we do this, two things will happen:

1. We will be encouraged in our faith, and
2. We will have a deeper burden for the lost. That burden will compel us to win souls which verse 30 tells us makes us wise.

In the arena of martial arts schools, certain schools and instructors have flourished using deceptive or unethical practices. They have gained students by practicing unfair business strategies. Some martial arts organizations persuade schools to enlist in their group at high costs, with promises of great dividends. They line their pockets with the hard work of small business owners just trying to succeed. In many cases these types of businesses fail because people become wise to their schemes, but in other cases they continue to prosper.

Look within your school or tournament circuit at the fighter who does not fight fair and continues to win. Verse 19 tells us that, *"Truly the righteous attain life, but whoever pursues evil finds death.."* Don't let the feeling of getting ahead at any cost overcome you. Instead, continue to walk in righteousness. Verse 21 says the righteous will be delivered while the unrighteous will be punished in God's time. In this reality, the good guy will win in the end, but let God work that out. When we practice ethical standards as school owners and as martial arts students, and when we fight fair and follow the rules, we are a delight to God (verse 20). We will prosper and have life while the wicked can only expect to fall (verse 28).

Giving it Away

Verses 24-25 of the Living Bible read, *"It is possible to give away and become richer! It is also possible to hold on too tightly and lose everything. Yes, the liberal man shall be rich! By watering others, he waters himself."*

My sister and her husband were once millionaires. They owned a gas and oil company and went into business with a large fuel production corporation. Financially they were in a whole different league than Chris and I will ever imagine to be. Every time I talked to them it seemed they prospered even more – a new Hummer, a house at the lake, a Big Dog motorcycle. But the main reason my sister continued to prosper is because they gave so much away. Now, you might be thinking, that is not math that adds up! But God teaches us that the only way to truly "get rich" is to give it away.

This is what my sister and her husband did. When a missionary came to church and shared his need for a new vehicle, they bought him one. When my brother-in-law learned of young girls being sold into prostitution in India, he flew there, financially helped an orphanage, purchased girls from the prostitution ring and placed them in the orphanage where they could be fed and cared for. He then started a business called *Clear Target* that gave bird and game hunting expeditions in western Kansas. All the proceeds went to help the Indian orphanage. You can look at this story of my sister and her husband in a couple of different ways.

1. You could think, "I give at church, why don't I get this windfall from heaven?" and be jealous of their blessing; or
2. You might think, "I would give too if I had it to give."

The problem with both of these thought-patterns is they are limited to money.

Chris and I give our tithes and we also give out of our abundance. What I am so grateful for is that God knows me better than I know myself. He knows our financial struggles and hang-ups. If Chris had a dollar in his pocket, it was always burning a hole. I worry about paying the bills first before giving the tithe. God has brought us into greater things as we have grown in Him in regard to our finances. Matthew 25:21 says *"His master replied, 'Well done, good and faithful servant! You have been faithful with a few things; I will put you in charge of many things. Come and share your master's happiness!"*

As our family has been faithful in the small things, God has seen fit to give us more. So why am I not at the same financial level my sister experienced? I honestly cannot answer that and that is perfectly fine! God has placed me right here and I am not without. He has blessed me – *"pressed down, shaken together, and running over"* with blessings, more than just financial. My family and I do not lack for any needs. I cannot say, "I am not a millionaire, so I am not blessed." That would be so far from the truth! God has placed people where they are, and He knows their hearts. Instead of feeling jealous, look at what Paul writes in Romans 12:4-8. Each of us have a different function in the body of Christ. We cannot all be the feet or all be the head. We are each unique with the unique talents God has given us to advance His kingdom.

It would be easy to be jealous of others in martial arts too. You could become jealous of someone's natural athletic ability. You might be jealous that no matter how hard you train and practice, this other student always beats you at the tournament. You might be jealous of how a student leads class and gets others to follow him, or even their sense of humor. You might be jealous of another family, their possessions, or their cohesiveness. For example, we have a family in our school who spans three generations and they all train together – from grandpa clear down to the 6-year-old. We have several parent/sibling training partners and we even have a mom and son who drive 70 miles one way to train together. You might get jealous of those family bonds. You might get jealous of the woman in our school who can take amazing pictures. We could go on and on. Truthfully, you could always want what others have, but that's not who you are called to be. God has made you the _____ – fill in the blank. Maybe it's the head or the ear or the toe! Whatever it is, He has equipped you to excel in that area and He has called you to give it away.

The answer to the second reaction of "I'd give if I had it to give" is that you *do* have it! Look at the parable of the talents in Matthew 25:14-46. In the parable Christ is referring to money to make His point that we have all been given a talent to use. Each of us has a talent that can be used to glorify God – martial arts! God wants us to use the talent we have. If we don't, look at the Lord's response in Matthew 25:26, *"You wicked, lazy servant."* Matthew 25:29 says, *"For whoever has will be given more, and they will have an abundance. Whoever does not have, even what they have will be taken from them"* which brings us right back to Proverbs

11:24-25. Don't dig a hole and hide your talent. Martial arts can be the avenue you use to introduce someone to a healthier lifestyle and a relationship with Christ.

Many churches have a variety of small groups – everything from a group that changes oil, to a group that cooks meals for people in need, to a group that does scrapbooking. What would be your "small group?" That is your talent. Don't hold on to it so tightly that no one knows about it. Instead, share the kingdom of God by giving away what you have. When you do, you will become rich!

Points to Remember

- *Being dishonest to gain in this world will not afford you the blessing God will give you for being honest. The sure reward is a much better guarantee of a worldly reward.*
- *Choose today to be kind. When people describe you, "kind" should be one of the adjectives in a long list of godly words.*
- *Continue to live by the rules God has outlines for us. Look at the end of the Bible. The righteous win!*
- *You have a talent. If you know what it is, start using it today. If you think you don't have one, ask God to show you the talents He has placed in you. Then give it away and see how rich you become!*

| 12 |

Stay Focused

Whoever loves discipline loves knowledge, but whoever hates correction is stupid.

² Good people obtain favor from the Lord, but he condemns those who devise wicked schemes.

³ No one can be established through wickedness, but the righteous cannot be uprooted.

⁴ A wife of noble character is her husband's crown, but a disgraceful wife is like decay in his bones.

⁵ The plans of the righteous are just, but the advice of the wicked is deceitful.

⁶ The words of the wicked lie in wait for blood, but the speech of the upright rescues them.

⁷ The wicked are overthrown and are no more, but the house of the righteous stands firm.

⁸ A person is praised according to their prudence, and one with a warped mind is despised.

⁹ Better to be a nobody and yet have a servant than pretend to be somebody and have no food.

¹⁰ The righteous care for the needs of their animals, but the kindest acts of the wicked are cruel.

¹¹ Those who work their land will have abundant food, but those who chase fantasies have no sense.

¹² The wicked desire the stronghold of evildoers, but the root of the righteous endures.

¹³ Evildoers are trapped by their sinful talk, and so the innocent escape trouble.

¹⁴ From the fruit of their lips people are filled with good things, and the work of their hands brings them reward.

¹⁵ The way of fools seems right to them, but the wise listen to advice.

¹⁶ Fools show their annoyance at once, but the prudent overlook an insult.

¹⁷ An honest witness tells the truth, but a false witness tells lies.

¹⁸ The words of the reckless pierce like swords, but the tongue of the wise brings healing.

¹⁹ Truthful lips endure forever, but a lying tongue lasts only a moment.

²⁰ Deceit is in the hearts of those who plot evil, but those who promote peace have joy.

²¹ No harm overtakes the righteous, but the wicked have their fill of trouble.

²² The Lord detests lying lips, but he delights in people who are trustworthy.

²³ The prudent keep their knowledge to themselves, but a fool's heart blurts out folly.

²⁴ Diligent hands will rule, but laziness ends in forced labor.

²⁵ Anxiety weighs down the heart, but a kind word cheers it up.

²⁶ The righteous choose their friends carefully, but the way of the wicked leads them astray.

²⁷ The lazy do not roast any game, but the diligent feed on the riches of the hunt.

²⁸ In the way of righteousness there is life; along that path is immortality.

Chapter 12: Daily Devotional

When I was in school I don't remember kids being labeled as ADHD. From what I know now about ADHD, if Chris were in school today, he would be labeled with this diagnosis. When I read him the list of ADHD symptoms he said, "That's me!" Some of the symptoms include inattention, hyperactivity, and impulsiveness.

Just like the ADHD person gets pulled away from daily tasks, so the world tries to pull us away from God. Let's read how staying focused on Christ helps us daily grow in wisdom.

Keep Your Mind on Things Above

A struggle for many who have an entrepreneurial mind is that their thoughts wander all the time and their brain never seems to shut down, even during sleep. This describes my husband. He struggles to sit through any meeting, listen to a sermon that is more than 20 minutes long, or even hear about my day without drifting off to something else. He tries to stay engaged by tapping his pencil or clicking a pen open and closed. I can see when his eyes are glazing over and then, just like that, he's somewhere else.

The verses of Proverbs 12 are teaching us to focus. It's easy for our minds to get off focus. For Chris, long periods of sitting will send his mind to thoughts of the martial arts school, what the next workout will be, a new venture to implement – anywhere, anywhere but where he is supposed to be focused. As Christians, the world pulls at our focus 24/7. God is calling us to have a mind that is filled with His wisdom. Verse 5 tells us that, *"A good man's mind is filled with honest thoughts; an evil man's mind is crammed with lies"* (Living Bible). To keep our mind filled with honest thoughts we must stay focused on Him. This is a conscious effort in our daily walk. When the world tries to pull your mind into a web of lies, repeat the words of Paul from Philippians 4:8. This verse is a long list of things to think about other than the lies of the world. It tells us to fix our thoughts on:

- what is true and good and right
- things that are pure and lovely
- good things in others
- all you can praise God for and be glad about

This principle is like a fighter using focus pads in his/her training. The fighter keys in on the pad and makes it his focus. He is directing his energy and technique right toward that pad. He fixes his eyes on the pad, lines up his punch or kick to make contact, and with vigor delivers the strike. This process is intentful, purposeful and focused. Soon the fighter gets into a rhythm and others in the dojo don't distract him as he moves and continually strikes the focus pad.

Keeping our thoughts pure and on God requires spending time with Him and in His Word. When we fail to do this, the world will fill our minds with distractions and lies. A mind filled with the lies of the world is warped and verse 8 tells us that a man *"with a warped mind is despised."*

Every minute of every day, our minds are constantly bombarded with images, words, music, conversation, sounds, noises, and thoughts. How you handle and process this cacophony is key. It's like weeding your garden. Both weeds and flowers grow in the garden; to cultivate the flowers, you must continually pull the weeds or soon the weeds will overtake the garden. If you don't focus on keeping a mind filled with Godly thoughts, then the impure thoughts linger and grow. What is left unattended in your mind will move to your heart. Once it becomes settled in your heart, it changes your speech as noted in Matthew 12:34, *"For the mouth speaks what the heart is full of."* Proverbs 12:20 tells us, *"Deceit is in the heart of those who plot evil ..."*. The word also says *"the heart is deceitful above all things"* (Jeremiah 17:9).

See how lack of focus on your thoughts can infiltrate your body? It comes into the mind, settles in your heart, and comes out your mouth. Maintain your focus and fill your mind with honest thoughts. Avoid having "spiritual ADD."

Hard Work Pays Off

Succeeding in life requires hard work. Training for your next competition, working toward your next belt level, running your own school – all require a commitment to work. These things are not just handed to you; you have to work to obtain them. If getting a black belt was easy then everyone would do it, but they don't because it is *hard work.*

The word "work" is a bad word for some. They take a backseat to work and let opportunities pass them by. Work truly is not a bad word; it is a word that when done brings rewards (verse 14). Think of the blessing that comes from achieving your next belt level:

- joy and excitement
- a sense of accomplishment
- fulfillment of a dream or goal
- mastery of an art
- better focus and concentration
- improved mental, physical and spiritual health
- confidence and more

Blessings abound when you work hard. Stop and think about the impact of hard work in your job, in your home and in your hobbies. Hard work brings prosperity.

Working hard also means working smart. To work smart you need instruction. *"Whoever loves discipline loves knowledge, but whoever hates correction is stupid"* (Proverbs 12:1). The sooner you receive instruction about your work, you become more efficient and blessings and prosperity are soon to follow. Refusing instruction is just plain stupid!

Look what else hard work brings in verse 24 – leadership. When you work hard, others notice and will promote you as a leader. With leadership comes a higher salary, which is the prosperity mentioned in verse 11. Business owners want employees who come to work on time every day and put forth an honest, diligent effort to do their job. When employees work hard, they will be rewarded. This reward may come in the form of a raise, incentive, recognition, or promotion. Some may think, "Well, I work hard every day and no one notices." Yes, someone does notice – your heavenly Father. Nothing goes unseen with Him. God is a rewarder of those who diligently seek Him (Hebrews 11:6) and working hard when no one seems to be watching is truly seeking God and His wisdom. As Christians, we should work hard every day not just for the promotion, but because we do our work as unto the Lord, so it brings glory to Him.

Never be too proud to work. Read verse 9 again. No job should be beneath us if our very existence is on the line. It's okay to get your hands dirty – they'll wash. Look at Christ's example when he washed the disciples' feet. He was doing this to teach them to be a servant to others but imagine how dirty this job was. I really doubt Christ complained about the smell, but rather looked beyond to the real purpose of what He was doing. You certainly cannot be prideful when you're washing feet! The same is true for us in our work. Look past the tasks that seem meaningless to us and see the purpose of glorifying God in all we do. Our next meal may not be riding on this particular task, but our witness is always being scrutinized. So, work as if you are the hands and feet of Christ – without pride – and let your work be an example for others.

Your Words are Eternal

Ever try to put toothpaste back in the tube? It just won't go! Once you squeeze it out, you might as well brush your teeth with it because putting it back in is near impossible. We've all heard the phrase, "I stuck my foot in my mouth" and we've all probably said it a time or two. This figure of speech is used when you said something you shouldn't have. Once those words are out, there's no putting them back in. It would be great if we had an undo button on our mouth!

What you say can have a lasting impression on someone. This impression can be one that either builds them up or tears them down. Many martial artists in our school started taking lessons because of low self-esteem and confidence. They needed that affirmation of self-worth and thought martial arts training would be the key – and I believe it is! If this is a reason for people to begin a martial arts class, encouraging these students is essential for them to continue. As instructors we should always look for opportunities to encourage our students. One practice at our school is at the end of each class, students take a knee as Chris goes down the line and tells each one what they did well in class and things they can improve on. This process moves quickly, not dwelling on one person longer than another. Although this takes time and a concentrated effort to watch each student during class, many students express how much they appreciate that. It shows them that their instructor is paying attention to them and they are important as a student.

Encouragement need not only come from the instructor, but from fellow students also. Sometimes martial arts feels awkward as you learn the techniques and routines. Telling your fellow classmates they are doing well speaks volumes to someone who lacks confidence. This is pointed out in verse 25, *"Anxiety weighs down the heart, but a kind word cheers it up."* An "anxious heart" could be someone who is nervous, scared, intimated, uncertain or overwhelmed. Even if a new student is in the beginner class, there are other beginners who have been there longer and know the routine better. Remember the day when you first started? Now see this person through those eyes. You can make a difference in someone's class, day, or life by speaking words of encouragement.

The opposite of encouragement is discouragement. The cutting edge of discouragement can hinder someone's growth in many ways. I have seen people quit martial arts because they felt they couldn't learn the techniques and found their instructor and classmates to be impatient and unkind. We have all seen people quit something because they were discouraged. In some situations, this discouragement was done intently and other times due to simple lack of consideration. Whatever the case, discouragement is a motivation-killer and dreams and goals are left unpursued because of it.

As Christian martial artists, we can change that! Remember, *"...the words of the wise soothe and heal"* (Proverbs 12:18, Living Bible). Your words of encouragement can heal, bring life, and change the outlook of a person beaten down by discouragement. Purpose in your heart to be an encourager who looks for ways to build others up. Tell someone they did a good job in class tonight.

The Diligent Man

Diligent is a hard word – not to say, but to be. Diligence requires hard work, energy, and a never-give-up attitude. A diligent man focuses on the goal and keeps pushing forward until he reaches it. Diligence is hard because the road to the goal can be long, with many bumps and potholes along the way. The amount of diligence required depends on the goal. If your goal can be achieved in a small amount of time it may not require a lot of diligence; but if the idea, project, dream or goal is years down the road, it will definitely test your diligence.

As martial artists we see diligence demonstrated at every belt test. The short goal was to get your gold belt. Although this is very motivating for the new student, it is the first step in reaching a much larger goal of black belt. Diligence is a huge part of reaching black belt excellence. It may take three years or more before you can tie a black belt around your waist, but the day you do so will be one of the greatest accomplishments of your life.

Diligence has a price and a reward. Look at verse 24. The price is hard work; the reward is victory and leadership. Victory in what? Whatever you set your mind to. If you want to be victorious, be diligent. If you want to be defeated, be lazy and slothful and you will never succeed.

Proverbs addresses diligence again in verse 27. *"...the diligent man makes good use of everything he finds"* (Living Bible). This may or may not be physical things you can hold. It may be gifts or talents that you possess. In October 2007, God spoke to Chris that he was not being diligent with the gift he was given. The gift was his martial arts training and a desire to create a girl's self-defense video. Having a daughter of our own, Chris knew dads all across the nation would do anything to protect their daughters from an attack. They just needed the practical self-defense skills to do it. Chris had all the ideas for the video and had replayed it many times in his mind, but he was lacking the diligence to see it through. I became the "diligence enforcer."

I did some research, contacted a production company, and scheduled the initial visit. I then hired someone to create a logo, worked on a filming itinerary and typed the script. The project took ten months to complete and it took diligence to plan out film shoots, schedule times, rehearse, meet with the producers, pick music – all while working a full-time job and running the school at night. There were days when we would not have kept going with the project without the voice of diligence in our minds. This lag was not for lack of desire for the project, but lack of time and energy amidst all the other obligations in the day. But, there was always a bigger picture and this was what God had planned for us. Now, more than a decade later, this video has been used to help many women and girls learn self-defense.

Diligence not only applies to our physical being, but also to our spiritual being. When you are diligently living in the pursuit of the wisdom of God, the power of God is working on your behalf. This power is working on your behalf in regard to your job, family, marriage, finances, and anything else you experience in your life. The key is a diligent pursuit. Diligence is an intense effort, a concentrated focus, an attentive drive for the things of God. God wants us to seek Him daily and strive to know Him more. Doing so will help pattern your footsteps after His and this will transform your attitude. As we seek Him, God will impart His knowledge and understanding in small amounts. He doesn't dump it all on us at once because we couldn't handle it. Instead, as you diligently seek Him, He is faithful to be found (Matthew 7:7).

Points to Remember

- *Work to block out things from your mind that are not Christ-like. Ask Him to fill your mind with His words and thoughts.*
- *God expects us to work as if we are working for Him – regardless of the task at hand. Working hard is really a testimony of your life in Christ.*
- *Your words bring either life or death. Bring life to someone today by saying words of encouragement and showing them the Christ that lives in you.*
- *Move forward and don't get complacent. Be diligent in whatever you put your hand to do.*

| 13 |

Instruction and Correction

A wise son heeds his father's instruction, but a mocker does not respond to rebukes.

² From the fruit of their lips people enjoy good things, but the unfaithful have an appetite for violence.

³ Those who guard their lips preserve their lives, but those who speak rashly will come to ruin.

⁴ A sluggard's appetite is never filled, but the desires of the diligent are fully satisfied.

⁵ The righteous hate what is false, but the wicked make themselves a stench and bring shame on themselves.

⁶ Righteousness guards the person of integrity, but wickedness overthrows the sinner.

⁷ One person pretends to be rich, yet has nothing; another pretends to be poor, yet has great wealth.

⁸ A person's riches may ransom their life, but the poor cannot respond to threatening rebukes.

⁹ The light of the righteous shines brightly, but the lamp of the wicked is snuffed out.

¹⁰ Where there is strife, there is pride, but wisdom is found in those who take advice.

[11] Dishonest money dwindles away, but whoever gathers money little by little makes it grow.

[12] Hope deferred makes the heart sick, but a longing fulfilled is a tree of life.

[13] Whoever scorns instruction will pay for it, but whoever respects a command is rewarded.

[14] The teaching of the wise is a fountain of life, turning a person from the snares of death.

[15] Good judgment wins favor, but the way of the unfaithful leads to their destruction.

[16] All who are prude act with knowledge, but fools expose their folly.

[17] A wicked messenger falls into trouble, but a trustworthy envoy brings healing.

[18] Whoever disregards discipline comes to poverty and shame, but whoever heeds correction is honored.

[19] A longing fulfilled is sweet to the soul, but fools detest turning from evil.

[20] Walk with the wise and become wise, for a companion of fools suffers harm.

[21] Trouble pursues the sinner, but the righteous are rewarded with good things.

[22] A good person leaves an inheritance for their children's children, but a sinner's wealth is stored up for the righteous.

[23] An unplowed field produces food for the poor, but injustice sweeps it away.

[24] Whoever spares the rod hates their children, but the one who loves their children is careful to discipline them.

[25] The righteous eat to their hearts' content, but the stomach of the wicked goes hungry.

Chapter 13: Daily Devotional

As in the previous chapter, Proverbs 13 is filled with instruction and correction. It provides scriptures packed with wisdom for us to live by, as well as the admonition for us to hear our Father's wisdom and rebuke. Doing so makes us wise (verse 1), brings rewards (verse 13), and helps us avoid pitfalls (verse 14). In order to truly hear this instruction and correction, we must have an open mind and a willing heart to hear and apply what God is telling us. Let's look at a few truths from Proverbs 13 that will bring us these benefits.

Practicing Self Control

We talked in Chapter 12 about "sticking our foot in our mouths." Our mouth overrides our brain, and we blurt words out before we even think about what we are saying or the consequences of our words. This outburst might result from many different emotions: excitement, frustration, anger, or sorrow. Our words are motivated by our emotions and these emotions can overpower even common sense. This problem is not a respecter of persons – it happens to everyone when put in the right pressure cooker. So, how can you control your words and emotions so they don't bring harm to you or shame to the kingdom? The Living Bible says, *"The good man wins his case by careful argument; the evil-minded only wants to fight"* (Proverbs 13:2).

Begin with a careful argument. Anticipate the situation before it happens. If you know you already have resentment toward someone, try to not cross paths with them until you have control of the resentment. Think through your conversation before you have it.

This verse refers to the "evil-minded." That description could make us think of only people we would characterize as bad, mean, hateful and far from God. Truth be told, we are all, Christian and non-Christian, evil-minded. Even the Christian person may want to fight rather than use careful argument. To help control this emotion look at Matthew

5:23-26, a scripture we looked at in a previous chapter, which tells us to settle matters with anyone you have issue with.

Often we let ourselves get to the point of fighting because we have bottled up our anger and frustration and not talked to the person we are angry with. These verses in Matthew warn us against this. They tell us to quickly come to terms with our enemy (the person we are angry with) before it's too late. The result of "too late" could be a ruined reputation, hurt feelings, lost job, loss of income, jail time and so on.

What does this mean in the dojo? Well, if you have a problem with your instructor or someone else in the school, don't let your feelings fester and stir strife within you. Go to that person immediately and discuss the situation. Think through what you want to say before the conversation and think about *how* you will say it. Kind words will prove a much more positive result than accusing ones. Your goal isn't to "tell that person off," but rather to solve a problem in a respectful way and maintain a friendship. Remember, harsh words are like hammering nails into wood. Later you may say you're sorry, which takes one of the nails out, but there is still the hole where the nail used to be. Words are eternal and leave lasting impressions.

James 3:5 refers to the tongue as a small member of the body, but it has the capability of causing large problems. This small body part is also referenced in Proverbs 13:3 where the writer defines self-control as controlling your tongue. Don't let this small member have so much control in your life. Use God's Word to teach you how to maintain your self-control.

Don't Believe Everything You Hear

Fact checking is a term used by those in media and journalism. The idea is that they are checking sources to determine the validity of the information they are reporting. When I teach students how to find information on the Internet, one of the things I stress is that just because it is on the Internet does not mean it's true. A lot of students doing research will quote the first website they find without checking to be sure it is a reliable source. It's best to find that information on more than one website, especially if it's information the student has never heard or read before. Another test for reliability is to check who is the author of the page. To prove my point, a quick search for a famous civil rights activist shows students that a web page about this activist is authored by a white supremacy group. There are tools available on the Internet that will show you who has created the web page. This will help when determining if the information on the page is a reliable source.

Another test for reliability is simply the look and feel of the page. If the web page address is encyclopedia.com and the page looks professional, chances are good that it is accurate. If the page is hosted by a free web hosting service, has ten animated pictures, four different background colors and looks unprofessional, chances are it was done by someone who just wanted a web presence. Although those types of pages are not always inaccurate, it shoots up a red flag that the student should find the same information on multiple web pages.

The Internet today is one of our communication messengers and just like the TV, radio, or people, it can sometimes provide unreliable information. Unreliable information can cause trouble (verse 17). The lesson to be learned in this verse is to check the source – who is giving you this information and why. When you receive information, find its validity. Information passed onto you from others may be just gossip that has many errors and untruths. The old saying "consider the source" proves true here. Consider who is telling you this. Are they passing along valid information or is it just gossip? Run it through the "reliability tests" in your heart and mind. Does it sound right and feel right? If you have a gnawing feeling in your stomach about what you've been told, then don't pass it along. It's probably not true or even if it is, it shouldn't be retold.

My pastor used to always encourage us to bring our Bibles to church and read along with him as he presented scripture in his messages. He would tell us to read it for ourselves and not just take his word for it. The point is to validate what you hear.

Verse 17 says an unreliable or wicked messenger brings trouble. Consider this messenger's motive. Does this person's information bring benefit or intend harm? We all know how rumors start – often from unreliable information. The effect can damage relationships and bring unnecessary trouble. The second half of this verse, however, tells us the kind of messenger we should be as we strive for God's wisdom – trustworthy and reliable. As we apply God's wisdom to our lives, our message should change our reputation of integrity. People should expect that what we say is true and correct, and our message should build people up.

Possessing True Riches

Happiness is not determined by our financial status. Our level of comfort may be, but true happiness is not. Many people would argue that point and contend that if they only had more money, life would be perfect. While money may fix some of our problems, it does not provide the happiness, joy and peace that truly determines our wealth. If money did fix everything why do we see movie stars having mental breakdowns, the wealthy being committed to drug and alcohol rehab and divorce among the rich? These problems follow both the wealthy as well as the average-day martial artist.

Proverbs is teaching us that money is not all we need. *"Some rich people are poor, and some poor people have great wealth!"* (Proverbs 13:7, Living Bible). This mindset contrasts with the world's view of money, but we must remember we are seeking God's wisdom and His ways are much higher than mankind's. Obviously, in this verse the focus is on riches other than money to determine wealth. True wealth can then be defined as things that produce a wholeness and well-being in our body, mind and soul. The motto of our martial arts school is to "build myself up mentally, physically, and spiritually..." – and it doesn't end with "by getting rich," but instead it ends "with great character." True happiness is found by the inner joy and contentment you walk in every single day.

I Timothy 6:6 in the Living Bible asks the questions, *"Do you want to be truly rich?"* The question is answered in verses 7-10 telling us we are if we are content when our needs are met. The apostle Paul is a perfect example of a person who was rich. In the book of Philippians, he writes to the church from a jail cell – not a place you would expect a rich man to be. Philippians chapter 4 verses 6-7 and 11-13 describe the riches of Paul. He wasn't worried about how much money he was going to make or the next corporate ladder he would climb. Instead, he said he possessed greater things than the mind of man could comprehend – the peace of God, restfulness in Christ Jesus, contentment in every situation, and the strength and power of Christ. There is no price tag that can be placed on these possessions. If you strive to seek after the treasures Paul described, then the Word says you are truly rich.

Slow and Steady

Chris and I are very different in how we approach things. One year we decided to run a half marathon. We lined up at the start line together and when the gun went off, Chris took off like a wild man, sprinting through the crowd and weaving in and out of people. I, however, ran my normal slow and steady pace and found my groove in the early miles. We are like the story of the tortoise and the hare. Chris ran fast, then stopped to talk to workers, get drinks, and eat sideline snacks, before sprinting to his next stop. All the while, I just kept my steady gait. About mile 11, I saw him in the distance and he was hurting. I knew I could catch him and most likely beat him to the finish, but we decided to cruise to the finish line together and help each other through the last few miles. Like the tortoise, slow and steady won the race and I won't soon let Chris forget it!

Honestly, slow and steady does win races. Think about your retirement fund. It doesn't grow overnight but accumulates with compounding interest over the years. The same is true for your martial arts training – you don't know everything in a week. It's a process of training over time. Verse 11 shows how gradual increase is a spiritual principle and small things can make great gains. Matthew 13:32 tells us that the mustard seed *"though it is the smallest of all seeds, yet when it grows, it is the largest of garden plants and becomes a tree."* Anything in our life can start small, but if we give it attention, like water and sunshine to a plant, it will grow over time. The trick is to stay steady and not give up when the growth, answer or reward does not come quickly.

Your black belt will not come quickly. Years – not days or weeks, but *years* – will pass before you can legitimately tie it around your waist. Even when you cannot see your own growth, it is happening punch by punch, move by move, kick by kick. Even the smallest of steps are steps of forward movement that are producing gains. Your martial arts training is a marathon, not a sprint, so don't get weary in the race.

This same principle of "little by little" is true of our spiritual walk with the Lord. Every day as we walk in obedience, honoring God with our lives, we will see our spiritual walk grow stronger. Prayer by prayer, scripture by scripture we are building a foundation of faith as we strive to have a steady pursuit of the things of God.

Points to Remember

- *Follow the principles laid out in scripture to help maintain your self-control. Don't let a quick retort ruin everything.*
- *Be a reliable source of information. Don't stop the progress of God because your words cannot be trusted.*
- *Change your definition of rich from the world's perspective to God's. Rich is not defined by your bank account, but instead by your relationship with Christ.*
- *Being the tortoise is not a bad thing. Stay steady in your walk with the Lord.*

| 14 |

Reverence is Key

The wise woman builds her house, but with her own hands the foolish one tears hers down.

²Whoever fears the Lord walks uprightly, but those who despise him are devious in their ways.

³A fool's mouth lashes out with pride, but the lips of the wise protect them.

⁴Where there are no oxen, the manger is empty, but from the strength of an ox come abundant harvests.

⁵An honest witness does not deceive, but a false witness pours out lies.

⁶The mocker seeks wisdom and finds none, but knowledge comes easily to the discerning.

⁷Stay away from a fool, for you will not find knowledge on their lips.

⁸The wisdom of the prudent is to give thought to their ways, but the folly of fools is deception.

⁹Fools mock at making amends for sin, but goodwill is found among the upright.

¹⁰Each heart knows its own bitterness, and no one else can share its joy.

¹¹The house of the wicked will be destroyed, but the tent of the upright will flourish.

[12]There is a way that appears to be right, but in the end it leads to death.

[13]Even in laughter the heart may ache, and rejoicing may end in grief.

[14]The faithless will be fully repaid for their ways, and the good rewarded for theirs.

[15]The simple believe anything, but the prudent give thought to their steps.

[16]The wise fear the Lord and shun evil, but a fool is hotheaded and yet feels secure.

[17]A quick-tempered person does foolish things, and the one who devises evil schemes is hated.

[18]The simple inherit folly, but the prudent are crowned with knowledge.

[19]Evildoers will bow down in the presence of the good, and the wicked at the gates of the righteous.

[20]The poor are shunned even by their neighbors, but the rich have many friends.

[21]It is a sin to despise one's neighbor, but blessed is the one who is kind to the needy.

[22]Do not those who plot evil go astray? But those who plan what is good find love and faithfulness.

[23]All hard work brings a profit, but mere talk leads only to poverty.

[24]The wealth of the wise is their crown, but the folly of fools yields folly.

[25]A truthful witness saves lives, but a false witness is deceitful.

[26]Whoever fears the Lord has a secure fortress, and for their children it will be a refuge.

[27]The fear of the Lord is a fountain of life, turning a person from the snares of death.

[28]A large population is a king's glory, but without subjects a prince is ruined.

[29]Whoever is patient has great understanding, but one who is quick-tempered displays folly.

[30]A heart at peace gives life to the body, but envy rots the bones.

[31]Whoever oppresses the poor shows contempt for their Maker, but whoever is kind to the needy honors God.

[32]When calamity comes, the wicked are brought down, but even in death the righteous seek refuge in God.

[33]Wisdom reposes in the heart of the discerning and even among fools she lets herself be known.

[34]Righteousness exalts a nation, but sin condemns any people.

[35]A king delights in a wise servant, but a shameful servant arouses his fury.

Chapter 14: Daily Devotional

Reverence is a mindset that is diminishing in our culture. As a high school teacher, students have said things to me or in my presence that I would never have thought of saying to my teacher and they think nothing of it. This lack of reverence seems to permeate our society. Reverence has application in our martial arts school and in our spiritual walk. Let's look at how reverence is part of the "real living" described in Chapter 14. It's shown in how we speak to instructors, treat those in authority, and live in obedience to God's instructions.

Reverence for God

Look at the word that starts both verses 26 and 27 in the Living Bible. That word is *reverence*. In the martial arts world, we give reverence to the black belts and senior instructors in the school. This is typically shown by bowing to them and using the title "Sir" or "Ma'am" to address them. Showing this respect establishes a sense of order and discipline in the school. Words like *discipline, respect* and *order* are adjectives that are (or should be) used to describe martial arts. Many parents have brought their children to our school to learn discipline in hopes that it will carry over into other areas of the child's life, and in many cases it has.

Reverence means being humble and thinking of someone else more highly than yourself. It means listening and obeying and responding with respect. As a martial artist, it is important to respect those who have studied longer, who have accomplished more in the art, and who have achieved greater rank. By giving them reverence, you art will improve, and your character will develop.

A reverent spiritual attitude has its own benefits as well. It gives a person:

- strong confidence
- a place of refuge and security for his or her children
- a fountain of life
- a rescue from death

Wow – all that for giving God the reverence He is due (verses 26-27). Humbling ourselves before God means we recognize His great and awesome power in our lives. We are saying we cannot live in our own strength, but instead need the strength only He provides. Like the martial artist, reverence to God means listening, obeying, and responding with respect.

Reverence for the Lord may require an attitude adjustment in our own lives. Deliverance from a haughty attitude is one step toward changing your mindset that you are in control. The truth is God is in control, and when we recognize this and submit ourselves to His control, the fountain of life within us really comes to life.

This fountain of life begins when we put God first in our lives, in our home and in all we do. Our children will then benefit from our reverent attitude and learn that there is refuge and security in Christ. Read the latter part of verse 26 again. The verse says "his children." Put yourself as the child of God in this verse. As you do that, you become the recipient of the benefits that follow. Read it again as *your* children are the recipients. When you do this, it creates a generational blessing.

Many parents at our martial arts school have shared their heartache over their children. From rebellious attitudes to kids lost with no direction in life, families have grieved over what they did wrong in their parenting. These two verses in Proverbs 14 show us a key element to instill in our children, which is reverence for God. When God is revered, reverence for others and authority will follow. Children will learn to listen, obey, and respond with respect.

Strong Confidence

A man at our school sent us this message about his two children:

My kids went from quiet kids who would stay in the corner to team leaders confident in themselves and members of a great team. In just six months they were facing opponents multiple levels/belts above them and winning. Winning was great, but the fact they had the confidence to step up to the challenge was a win by itself.

This father very accurately described his two children – they were extremely shy and reserved when they started training with Chris. Today you would never believe it. They lead class, help with instruction, and work in the dojo. The transformation is uncanny. Over the years, many parents have brought children to our school to help them build confidence. Chris has a way of teaching that encourages all students to participate; he does not let them sit on the sidelines. Every one of every age learns and trains together. He has a knack for pushing students in such a way that they will at least try! And when they do, the whole dojo celebrates. It's a huge confidence builder and students quickly begin to demonstrate our motto that promotes mental growth.

Gaining strong confidence is another of the many benefits afforded to us as Christians who walk in wisdom. We have the confidence that whatever God promises will happen. With confidence, we can believe for prosperity, healing, and favor because God has promised it to His children. When you are living for God, you can boldly go into God's presence with an assurance that He hears and answers. If you're walking in disobedience, then you don't have the same confidence. This strong confidence comes to believers who are living for God.

A Matter of Life or Death

Define "real living." What does that mean to you? Thoughts of expensive homes, luxurious vacations, and servants to meet every need may come to mind. Proverbs frequently talks about life and death. According to Proverbs, wise living tends to allow you to live longer, whereas foolish living leads to an early grave.

If you take this at face value, then there is a problem. We all know people who have lived foolish lives but survive into an old age. For example, take a person who has smoked nearly all his life and is living into his 80's, while a healthy runner dies of a sudden heart attack. This seems contrary to the teachings of wisdom found in Proverbs.

Because of this, it makes you wonder what kind of life and death Proverbs is talking about. "Real living" according to the wisdom of God is nothing money can buy. Instead it is a life full of joy, peace, and wisdom. Look at verses 27 and 30 to see examples of real living. Verse 27 says that fearing God brings a *"fountain of life."* The word "fountain" implies a continual outpouring and constant refreshing. This fountain brings life *and* keeps a man from death. To live well, you must avoid death and you can do this by giving God the honor He is due. Real death means a spiritual as well as physical decay. A person may be walking this earth, but if he has missed the wisdom of God, he is like a dead man walking.

Verse 12 talks about the wide road that lies before all of us. Those choosing this road will find that it is easy and well-traveled. The perception of those walking this road is that, *If so many are headed that way it must be right; therefore, I'll just follow along.* The Living Bible calls this path the highway to hell in Matthew 7:13. The problem with this perception is that those following don't check the map to see where the road is taking them. If they would stop and read the map of God's Word, they would find the destination stated in plain English – a wide and pleasant road that seems right but ends in death. The ending point on this path is an eternity separated from the presence of God. This is real death.

"Real Living" Benefits

Look again at God's definition of real living in verse 30. It is a life that walks in His wisdom and is filled with joy and peace. This verse points out two great benefits of this "real living" existence.

The first benefit is a "relaxed attitude" (Living Bible). This benefit is not only spiritual, but physical as well. When your heart is not at peace you have stress and tension, which can lead to numerous physical ailments and affect many parts of your body. Stress can settle in your neck and shoulders, causing tight muscles and headaches; stress can result in high blood pressure, heart problems, obesity, and others. All of these affect your ability as a martial artist to exercise and compete. A relaxed attitude can improve health in all areas of your body. Your relaxed attitude is a direct result of walking in God's wisdom which produces real living.

The second benefit which has a direct correlation to the first is "a longer life." It makes sense to think if you have less stress and fewer worries, you will live longer. When you visit a doctor because you are experiencing chest pain, what kind of test does he perform? A stress test! And often the advice from the doctor is to reduce the stress in your life. The doctor knows the effects of an attitude that is not relaxed can lead to many illnesses or death.

Some martial arts schools look to meditation or the inner-self to find the "relaxed attitude" verse 30 is referring to. This practice will only leave a God-shaped hole within your heart and soul. You alone do not have the power to walk this life in a state of true "real living" without God. The best practice is to replace meditation with prayer and seek

God, rather than the inward man, for wisdom. When you do this, real living begins.

Points to Remember

- *Give God the glory, honor and respect He is due. Reverence Him in your daily walk and watch how He takes care of you.*
- *Real living is not man-made. It is walking in the peace, love and joy of the Lord.*
- *Real living comes with its own price tag, but its benefits of a sound mind and healthy body far outweigh any cost. A man that has wealth, but no health, has nothing.*

| 15 |

Generational Sin

A gentle answer turns away wrath, but a harsh word stirs up anger.
² The tongue of the wise adorns knowledge, but the mouth of the fool gushes folly.

³ The eyes of the LORD are everywhere, keeping watch on the wicked and the good.

⁴ The soothing tongue is a tree of life, but a perverse tongue crushes the spirit.

⁵ A fool spurns a parent's discipline, but whoever heeds correction shows prudence.

⁶ The house of the righteous contains great treasure, but the income of the wicked brings ruin.

⁷ The lips of the wise spread knowledge, but the hearts of fools are not upright.

⁸ The LORD detests the sacrifice of the wicked, but the prayer of the upright pleases him.

⁹ The LORD detests the way of the wicked, but he loves those who pursue righteousness.

¹⁰ Stern discipline awaits anyone who leaves the path;the one who hates correction will die.

¹¹ Death and Destruction lie open before the LORD—how much more do human hearts!

¹² Mockers resent correction, so they avoid the wise.

¹³ A happy heart makes the face cheerful, but heartache crushes the spirit.

¹⁴ The discerning heart seeks knowledge, but the mouth of a fool feeds on folly.

¹⁵ All the days of the oppressed are wretched, but the cheerful heart has a continual feast.

¹⁶ Better a little with the fear of the LORD than great wealth with turmoil.

¹⁷ Better a small serving of vegetables with love than a fattened calf with hatred.

¹⁸ A hot-tempered person stirs up conflict, but the one who is patient calms a quarrel.

¹⁹ The way of the sluggard is blocked with thorns, but the path of the upright is a highway.

²⁰ A wise son brings joy to his father, but a foolish man despises his mother.

²¹ Folly brings joy to one who has no sense, but whoever has understanding keeps a straight course.

²² Plans fail for lack of counsel, but with many advisers they succeed.

²³ A person finds joy in giving an apt reply and how good is a timely word!

²⁴ The path of life leads upward for the prudent to keep them from going down to the realm of the dead.

²⁵ The LORD tears down the house of the proud, but he sets the widow's boundary stones in place.

²⁶ The LORD detests the thoughts of the wicked, but gracious words are pure in his sight.

²⁷ The greedy bring ruin to their households, but the one who hates bribes will live.

²⁸ The heart of the righteous weighs its answers, but the mouth of the wicked gushes evil.

²⁹ The LORD is far from the wicked, but he hears the prayer of the righteous.

³⁰ Light in a messenger's eyes brings joy to the heart, and good news gives health to the bones.

³¹ Whoever heeds life-giving correction will be at home among the wise.

³² Those who disregard discipline despise themselves, but the one who heeds correction gains understanding.

³³ Wisdom's instruction is to fear the LORD, and humility comes before honor.

Chapter 15: Daily Devotional

"I just can't help myself! I was born this way." Have you ever heard someone say these words? This excuse is for those who grew up watching and learning a generational sin that is now affecting their lives. A generational sin is an action, behavior or thought pattern that is handed down through a parent or family member and continues to plague family members repeatedly. Generational sin may be a learned behavior but is it one that can be changed. It's important to know that you cannot blame your sin on generational sin. Ezekiel 18:30 tells us that God will judge each of us according to our own actions. Because we have to own our own sin, let's dive in and learn how to break sin's generational curse.

Breaking Anger

Proverbs 15 deals with the generational sin of anger. My grandfather struggled with a bad temper that was accelerated by his use of alcohol. This temper often turned into violence and abuse and was observed by two children in their home. His temper was passed on to his daughter, who then passed it on to me. My mom tells of how at an early age I would get so mad that I would jump out of my crib when someone would not come quickly enough to get me. How does a young child learn to have such a temper? The answer is by observing a generational sin that has not been dealt with.

The wisdom of God tells us how to avoid anger in Proverbs 15:1. *"A gentle answer turns away wrath, but a harsh word stirs up anger."* A person who is slow to anger also avoids conflict. *"A quick-tempered man starts fights; a cool-tempered man tries to stop them"* (Proverbs 15:18, Living Bible). Having a soft answer and a cool temper are the two key elements to breaking anger and discord in your life.

An angry man's answer can be found in the first part of Chapter 15. Verse 2 in the Living Bible says the *"rebellious teacher spouts foolishness"* followed by *"griping brings discouragement"* in verse 4. Words can either bring blessing or curse and verses 2 and 4 show both. The blessings of joy, life and health are followed by the curses of foolishness and discouragement.

As martial artists we have a responsibility to think about what we say before we say it. We need to be in control of our tongue, thoughts, and actions. *"A good man thinks before he speaks; the evil man pours out his evil words without a thought"* (Proverbs 15:28, Living Bible). If we don't have control we will spout out evil words that cause harm without giving thought to the consequences. Our goal should be to bless others with words that are encouraging, kind, motivational and full of love. When we speak to each other this way it builds friendships, encourages other martial artists to try something they never thought they could do and creates an overall better martial artist both in you and those you encourage.

Don't believe the lie of the devil that anger or any other sin cannot be broken in your life. I once heard a pastor who was describing a woman in his church who battled anger and a bad temper. Her excuse to him was, "I am Irish. I cannot help myself." The pastor's response was, "God trumps Ireland." Do you catch yourself saying things or making excuses like this woman to cover your behavior? That is essentially declaring that God has no place in your life. We were all born sinners, but Christ covered all our sins when he shed His blood for us. He trumps every sin. You've been recreated in Christ and you are a new creature. Christ has given you the power to remove the attachments of anger from your life.

Look at Romans 6:10 where Paul tells us that Christ died for all of us to end sin's power. Because of Christ's death and resurrection, sin holds nothing on us. In verses 12-13 of Romans 6, Paul admonishes us to not let sin control our lives so that we may be used by God for His purposes. He goes on in verse 14 to say, *"For sin shall no longer be your master, because you are not under the law, but under grace."*

Proverbs 15 addresses anger, evil words and thoughts, griping, quick tempers, and pride. These sins – and any other sin that grips your life – never has to have a hold on you again. Christ broke the curse when he died and rose from the grave. When you give your life to Christ, you become a new man according to II Corinthians 5:17. As a new person in Christ, you have the power to break sin's hold on your life. This will not only end the bondage in your life, but it will carry on to your family and stop the generational sins that have existed for years.

However, this stubborn sin will not quickly give up its hold on you. You must identify the kind of evil spirit to watch out for in your life and guard yourself against it. Suppose you were once an alcoholic but have now given your heart to the Lord. The same sin of alcoholism may try to tempt you in your spiritual walk. It may be that you have been a Christian for many years before this temptation tries to make you stumble again. If sinful tendencies try to reestablish a foothold in your life, refuse to let them in. Remember you are no longer a slave to that sin. You are free under God's mercy. In the name of Jesus and by the power in His blood, you can stop this sin that tempts you.

How? Simply determine that sin no longer has a hold on you and stop it from moving down your family tree. As a believer in Christ, you have all the tools to act as the guardsman and keep out generational sin. If you ever feel like you are being defeated in this battle, read John

16:33. *"I have told you these things, so that in me you may have peace. In this world you will have trouble. But take heart! I have over come the world."* As His child *you* can overcome the attack of the enemy in your life.

Spiritual Laws will Prevail

We talked in Chapter 7 about the problem of using the excuse, "No one will know." Proverbs 15:3 tells us that this thinking is completely wrong because God knows. *"The eyes of the Lord are everywhere, Keeping watch on the wicked and the good."* Sin does not go unnoticed and neither does the good you do. Some may think God sits in Heaven watching us only to catch us doing wrong. Quite the contrary is true. God does not delight in punishing us for our sin. What God has done is set spiritual principles in place that apply to all of us and are set in motion by our actions and choices (Proverbs 1:31).

The contrast between those who forsake sin and those who embrace it is found in verse 6. *"The house of the righteous contains great treasure, but the income of the wicked brings ruin."* Walking in wisdom is taking the road that leads upward (verse 24). This path sets spiritual laws into motion that bring prosperity and blessing. Verse 6 shows us that spiritual laws are also set in motion for those who embrace sin – trouble is always at their doorstep, drama is prevalent in their home and unrest becomes a regular state of life. The Living Bible says *"trouble dogs the wicked."* Like a bird dog after its catch, it is relentless in the pursuit.

In martial arts, if students are not taught the correct style of forms for a competition, you can expect the outcome to be that they do not score well. The instructor needed to do his homework and find out the rules of the tournament. The instructor is accountable to the students to train them properly. When we go to the tournament, it is irresponsible for the instructor to say, "My students made me teach this way" or "They liked this form better than that one." The judges are not sitting at the table giving us low scores simply because they don't like my student or the color of their uniform or the way they tied their shoes, but rather because they are unprepared to compete and do not know the required form. The low score is the consequence of a poor performance and lack of preparation.

Such is the same with the spiritual laws that God has established. Your actions result in a consequence. That consequence is either favorable or it is not. If we walk in the wisdom of God, His provision will follow us because the Lord loves those who try to be good (verse 9). God does not change His spiritual laws for the person or situation – as neither does the judge change the grading scale for each competitor.

The life of David is a perfect example of this. David committed adultery and ordered a murder. This is the same man that God chose to be king and was described as a man after God's own heart. The spiritual laws were not changed even for him. The child that was conceived from David's adulterous affair died even though David prayed, begging the Lord to spare the child. God loves us just as He loved David, but contrary to popular belief, there are consequences for our actions. God did not set the spiritual laws into motion against David. David's actions did that. It is *man's* actions, not God that bring the consequence of sin into our lives. We are quick to blame God, but we need to ask ourselves what steps we took that put us on the path we are on.

I'd Rather Have Jesus

I grew up in a country church where our worship leader was a dear, elderly gentleman who loved God. As I read Proverbs, I am reminded of the old hymns he led us in on Sundays and Wednesday nights. Verse 16 is one of those reminders. The song is "I'd Rather Have Jesus." Written in the early 1900's by Rhea Miller, the first verse reads:

I'd rather have Jesus than silver or gold;

I'd rather be His than have riches untold;

I'd rather have Jesus than houses or lands.

I'd rather be led by His nail-pierced hand.

There is no greater treasure than having a relationship with Christ. For me, the greatest nugget in this treasure box is peace. Philippians 4:7 tells me that I have *"the peace of God, which surpasses all understanding"* and this peace will *"guard [my] heart and mind through Christ Jesus."* Because of His peace, I sleep soundly at night, don't worry about my kids, and am not afraid of what tomorrow will bring. When there are conflicts that arise in my life, I have learned to tell Him about it and when I do, He begins to restore the peace that the world is trying to steal.

Verse 17 describes another piece of treasure – love. It tells us to have a little in love is better than a lot filled with hatred. I Corinthians 13:13 reads, *"And now these three remain: faith, hope, and love. But the greatest of these is love."* Love allows us to overlook many faults. Love helps us to be patient, kind, and caring. What is it about your relationship with God that you say is better *"than silver or gold"?*

My prayer for our martial arts school is that we can be a small nugget in the box and that because of your relationship with Christ, you will be blessed by your interaction with us. For example, a mom messaged Chris and said, *"You just have no idea what an impact you have on our family."* Without the hand of God on our lives and our school, we would not have that same impact. As a martial artist, consider how your art is a piece of your treasure chest and how claiming that you would *"rather have Jesus"* impacts you, your school, and your training.

Points to Remember

- *God trumps all generational sin and He gives you the power to trump it too. No matter how far reaching the sin is, God is greater.*
- *Your actions put spiritual laws into motion. Resist the temptation of sin and prosperity will follow.*
- *You can have this treasure box that comes with having a relationship with Christ. The first step is inviting Him into your heart.*

| 16 |

Things Happen

To humans belong the plans of the heart, but from the Lord comes the proper answer of the tongue.

²All a person's ways seem pure to them, but motives are weighed by the Lord.

³Commit to the Lord whatever you do, and he will establish your plans.

⁴The Lord works out everything to its proper end even the wicked for a day of disaster.

⁵The Lord detests all the proud of heart. Be sure of this: They will not go unpunished.

⁶Through love and faithfulness sin is atoned for; through the fear of the Lord evil is avoided.

⁷When the Lord takes pleasure in anyone's way, he causes their enemies to make peace with them.

⁸Better a little with righteousness than much gain with injustice.

⁹In their hearts humans plan their course, but the Lord establishes their steps.

¹⁰The lips of a king speak as an oracle, and his mouth does not betray justice.

¹¹Honest scales and balances belong to the Lord; all the weights in the bag are of his making.

[12]Kings detest wrongdoing, for a throne is established through righteousness.

[13]Kings take pleasure in honest lips; they value the one who speaks what is right.

[14]A king's wrath is a messenger of death, but the wise will appease it.

[15]When a king's face brightens, it means life; his favor is like a rain cloud in spring.

[16]How much better to get wisdom than gold, to get insight rather than silver!

[17]The highway of the upright avoids evil; those who guard their ways preserve their lives.

[18]Pride goes before destruction, a haughty spirit before a fall.

[19]Better to be lowly in spirit along with the oppressed than to share plunder with the proud.

[20]Whoever gives heed to instruction prospers, and blessed is the one who trusts in the Lord.

[21]The wise in heart are called discerning, and gracious words promote instruction.

[22]Prudence is a fountain of life to the prudent, but folly brings punishment to fools.

[23]The hearts of the wise make their mouths prudent, and their lips promote instruction.

[24]Gracious words are a honeycomb, sweet to the soul and healing to the bones.

[25]There is a way that appears to be right, but in the end it leads to death.

[26]The appetite of laborers works for them; their hunger drives them on.

[27]A scoundrel plots evil, and on their lips it is like a scorching fire.

[28]A perverse person stirs up conflict, and a gossip separates close friends.

[29]A violent person entices their neighbor and leads them down a path that is not good.

30Whoever winks with their eye is plotting perversity; whoever purses their lips is bent on evil.

31Gray hair is a crown of splendor; it is attained in the way of righteousness.

32Better a patient person than a warrior, one with self-control than one who takes a city.

33The lot is cast into the lap, but its every decision is from the Lord.

Chapter 16: Daily Devotional

We have all wondered at times why certain things happen in our lives. This doesn't mean just bad things, but also things that surprise you, benefit you, or bring you joy. The question we tend to ask is, "Why did that happen?" – especially if the circumstance is painful, but even if it's not, we wonder "why" or "how." So many times in church I've heard pastors say that we may never know how our lives have impacted others until we reach eternity. Things happen because God has a greater plan than what you and I can see. He knows what will happen to us in the next hour, day, week or month. His plan for our lives extends to the end of our lives. Knowing this, we step into the wisdom of Proverbs 16.

Commit Your Works

The first step in realizing God's plan for our lives is to relinquish control. We want to hold on tightly to our plan for our life, when instead we should release our grip and let God's plan be our guide. When our carefully made plans fail us, we wonder why life didn't all go like we thought it should. It's because we are near-sighted and cannot see the far-reaching impact of our choices. A better way to plan your life is to follow verse 3 in the Living Bible which reads, *"Commit your work to the Lord, then it will succeed."*

Because our human nature is stubborn, committing to the Lord can be a hard thing. Many years ago we had a boy in our school that did anything for attention and liked to play the victim – nothing was ever his fault. We tried to change his mindset and attitude about life both in and out of the school. Through our martial arts connections in town we were able to find people outside of the school to be positive role models for him – my dad coached him in flag football, a man at our Christian school coached him in basketball, others took him to church. As life would have it this young man ended up in prison. He's now in his twenties, released from prison, and living in our community. Life circumstances have changed him and his outlook on life and so he came to the school to tell Chris about his realization of the impact our school family had on him in his early years. With the scars of many bad choices, he asked to rejoin our school by saying:

> *I can't tell you how much this means to me. I have always looked at the wrong way of life,.... God gave me the knowledge and strength to see. I am so thankful for you and my Ultimate Martial Arts family. You've always been a good father figure to me in my life. I chose to steer down the wrong path..., but God gave me the chance to see what was right in the life that I need and want to live with my wife and children.*

It's taken years, but this young man has finally started the processing of relinquishing control and letting God take the reins.

Now, let's clarify one thing here. Planning is a good thing. We don't want to live life by waking up every day and saying, "What should I do today?" Remember Proverbs 29:18 (KJV)? *"Without a vision, the people perish."* The key to planning is in verse 9: *"In their hearts humans plan their course, but the Lord establishes their steps."*

Committing your work to God means to rely on the Lord to help you make decisions in your life. When we make the decision to include

God in our planning, we become a two-person team with God as team captain. Your planning should work like this:

1. Tell God what you want, the desires of your heart, your dreams, and your hopes for the future.
2. Wait for Him to confirm if your plans match His will for your life.
3. God will then give you one of three answers: *yes, no or wait.*

This is the commitment needed for a successful life plan.

Tell Him Your Desires

God's intent is to give you the desires of your heart (Psalms 37:4) When you talk to God, tell Him what you want and need. He longs to talk to His children and work on their behalf. You will soon find that God's will for your life matches the desires of your heart. He didn't put those dreams inside of you just to keep you from them. He made you for that purpose and has put within you the skills and abilities to fulfill that purpose. He has designed you with those desires and He works within you to help you follow His plan and obey Him (Philippians 2:13).

So, when you commit your works to God, your desires will naturally flow with His plan. Your plans will succeed because it was God who put everything together in the first place. He will even show you an improved version of your plans, and you will be amazed that you have never seen it like that before.

Martial artist, step back and ask yourself what plans you have for your life; what desires motivate you every day. For Chris it was to operate his own school and to impact the lives of his students. I had no background in martial arts so this was not a life goal for me, but God put a desire within me to support Chris and come alongside him in this endeavor. Once we shared this with the Lord and committed our plans to Him, door after door opened that allowed us to pursue this desire. He put people in our life, provided finances and gave us favor in business decisions that made these dreams a reality. God will do the same for you, but the first step is yours to take.

Waiting for the Answer

The next step in this process is waiting for God to answer... and waiting is not a trait many of us do well. We want an answer *yesterday*! During this time of waiting, we must go back to step one where we decided to commit to the fact that God has a plan that spans our lifetime.

I can distinctly remember a time when Chris and I got ahead of God. We were relocating our martial arts school and wanted a place on Main Street. There were a few places to rent, but one was closer to the size we wanted. The building formerly housed a restaurant and the owner had moved to a larger location. Immediately, Chris was excited about the exposure of being on Main Street and the expansion of class offerings with all the floor space. Two days after seeing the building, we called the realtor to make an offer. On the way to do another walk-thru, a friend who I seldom talked to called. He said he had been praying for us and God spoke to him that we shouldn't get this building. Instantly an unsettling nervousness developed inside us. It was the voice of God speaking through my friend. We had gotten so excited about the possibilities for the school that we didn't even talk to the Lord about it. In all the excitement, we nearly agreed to take the building without taking necessary precautions and inspections. The week after we backed out of the deal, a big white sign appeared on the building's front door – the city had condemned the building. Thank the Lord for godly friends who obey the voice of God!

First, remember that you committed your works to the Lord. Then, your second step is to wait for direction. Many times in the Word, God directs us to wait on Him. The Psalmist David writes in Psalm 27:14, *"Wait on the Lord..."* Again he writes in Psalm 37:7, *"Be still before the Lord and wait patiently for him."* The solution is for us to stay focused on God, believe He has the answer and He will answer, and to not get discouraged in the wait. You will know when it's time to move. God will give you peace in your heart. In my everyday walk, I expect God to make my thoughts agree with His plan. I expect Him to direct me in my decisions. When I feel His peace, I know I have the answer and the wait is over.

Living in the Wait

Since we all know we must wait on God to answer and we know waiting can be hard to do, we need to find ways to help us through this time. A key element in the wait is letting peace rule your life. A scripture that helps to follow the Lord's direction in regard to peace is Colossians 3:15 of the Living Bible. *"Let the peace of heart which comes from Christ be always present in your hearts and lives, for this is your responsibility and privilege as a member of his body. And always be thankful."*

Peace should act as your mind's referee. When you are faced with a decision, the referee inside you will help you make the right choice. If you are not sure of God's will, take time to pray about it and bring it to the Lord. Don't act until you pray. God will speak to you and you'll experience the peace in your decision. When God speaks, it most likely will not be in an audible voice, but more likely will be an inward voice that you must watch and listen for. We will have to look inside our hearts and see what the spirit is telling us to do.

During your time of waiting, continue to bring the situation before God, asking Him to help you let peace rule your life. Remind yourself that God has a bigger plan and continue to place your confidence in knowing He is working on your behalf. This alone can bring you peace.

A second element you need in the wait is a thankful heart. A thankful heart helps you maintain peace. The last part of Colossians 3:15 says, *"And always give thanks."* Thank God daily for the wait and the plan He has that is so much bigger than what you had in mind. Focus on all the good He has done for you rather than all the frustrations in your life – and there can be many frustrations! Thanking God keeps your mind fixed on Him. A mind fixed on the blessings of God will continue in peace when the world tries to steal it from you.

You can either start the day with "Good Lord, it's morning" or "Good morning, Lord." This second attitude sets you up to maintain a grateful heart throughout your day. Focus your day on all He does for you and all He continues to do. Fighting for your peace is a daily battle. Your job, your family, even your martial arts can try to steal your peace. You can fight back by thanking God for your job, your family and even your martial arts instructor who is yelling at you to correct your stance!

Points to Remember

- *Commit every situation to the Lord and don't look back. Trust Him with all you have and all you are.*
- *Ask God for direction on every major decision, then wait for His answer. Be patient -- God's got this!*
- *Thank God for the wait. He's working on your behalf.*

| 17 |

Avoid the Drama

Better a dry crust with peace and quiet than a house full of feasting, with strife.

²A prudent servant will rule over a disgraceful son and will share the inheritance as one of the family.

³The crucible for silver and the furnace for gold, but the Lord tests the heart.

⁴A wicked person listens to deceitful lips; a liar pays attention to a destructive tongue.

⁵Whoever mocks the poor shows contempt for their Maker; whoever gloats over disaster will not go unpunished.

⁶Children's children are a crown to the aged, and parents are the pride of their children.

⁷Eloquent lips are unsuited to a godless fool how much worse lying lips to a ruler!

⁸A bribe is seen as a charm by the one who gives it; they think success will come at every turn.

⁹Whoever would foster love covers over an offense, but whoever repeats the matter separates close friends.

¹⁰A rebuke impresses a discerning person more than a hundred lashes a fool.

[11]Evildoers foster rebellion against God; the messenger of death will be sent against them.

[12]Better to meet a bear robbed of her cubs than a fool bent on folly.

[13]Evil will never leave the house of one who pays back evil for good.

[14]Starting a quarrel is like breaching a dam; so drop the matter before a dispute breaks out.

[15]Acquitting the guilty and condemning the innocent the Lord detests them both.

[16]Why should fools have money in hand to buy wisdom, when they are not able to understand it?

[17]A friend loves at all times, and a brother is born for a time of adversity.

[18]One who has no sense shakes hands in pledge and puts up security for a neighbor.

[19]Whoever loves a quarrel loves sin; whoever builds a high gate invites destruction.

[20]One whose heart is corrupt does not prosper; one whose tongue is perverse falls into trouble.

[21]To have a fool for a child brings grief; there is no joy for the parent of a godless fool.

[22]A cheerful heart is good medicine, but a crushed spirit dries up the bones.

[23]The wicked accept bribes in secret to pervert the course of justice.

[24]A discerning person keeps wisdom in view, but a fool's eyes wander to the ends of the earth.

[25]A foolish son brings grief to his father and bitterness to the mother who bore him.

[26]If imposing a fine on the innocent is not good, surely to flog honest officials is not right.

[27]The one who has knowledge uses words with restraint, and whoever has understanding is even-tempered.

[28]Even fools are thought wise if they keep silent, and discerning if they hold their tongues.

Chapter 17: Daily Devotional

There are some people who constantly live in drama. It's like they need it to survive so they stir up discord by talking about others, saying half-truths, or sharing information that was said in confidence. Chapter 17 calls this "strife" and it is a divider of families, friendships, and fortunes. Strife is a tool of the devil and it's one that we allow to be effective when we continually stir it up. Not one positive thing comes from this drama so make it stop! Proverbs 17 can help us break this divisive tool and live in the way God has called us to.

Strife at Home

If the devil can bring conflict into your home you won't be as effective anywhere else. Proverbs 17:1 says, *"Better is a dry crust with peace and quiet, than a house full of feasting, with strife."* Whatever strife happens at home carries with you right out the front door and inhibits your relationships with others.

The home is Satan's prime target. Just look at the world today. The divorce rate is high, leaving couples hurt and angry and children living in separate homes. Movies and television idolize adulterous affairs and unfaithful marriages. Children bring strife with ungrateful attitudes and rebellious spirits. If Satan can stir this pot and open the door to strike at home, your family cannot be the powerful tool God has called you to be.

Home is where you let your guard down and take off the mask of everyday life to just be yourself. At home you can relax and unwind, letting go of the stress you experience outside its doors. With this relaxation of the workday self comes the freedom to say or do whatever you want. Home should be the safe place for you to be you. What you need to remember is that in order to keep this safe haven, you cannot take out all your anger and frustrations on the others who live with you. We are all guilty of doing this at times because we're comfortable at home.

Your family are the people who love you the most, so they are the ones you should treat the best. Instead of blowing up at home or numbing out after a stressful day, talk to your family about your day. Share your disappointments and your successes with them. They know you best and can provide understanding and a different perspective.

Protect your relationships at home. It *does* matter how you act and treat those you live with. It's a reflection of your testimony of Christ when the world looks at your home. If the world sees strife in our Christian homes, we are no better example than a family who does not know the Lord.

Strife Moves to Another Place

If Satan cannot get an active amount of strife at home, he won't stop there and say, "Oh well, that didn't work." He'll look for another avenue that hurts the testimony of Christ and that place is in the body of Christ. Starting strife in the church is a dangerous thing and one God warns us that He hates. Read Proverbs 6:16-19 again. Notice number seven in the list – "*sowing discord among brothers.*" This is strife and God ranks that right up there with murder. That alone is enough to make me seriously consider how important it is to spread that juicy piece of gossip.

Because this scripture uses the word "brothers" it's often translated to mean "the church." When we say "church" we often think of the physical building itself; however, that building is simply the location we go to worship. *You and I* are actually the church. Christ is not limited to a building on Main Street, but rather He moves and lives within us wherever we go. Since we are the church, we can extend this to meaning the dojo. At the martial arts school, we are the body of Christ and causing strife here is *"sowing discord among brothers."* While stopping Satan at the doorstep of your home is important, it is also important to stop him at the door of the dojo.

When you stop to compare spreading strife and having God's favor, there is no comparison. Those feelings stirring within you to right a wrong, get someone back, criticize your fellow teammates comes from our sinful nature. So, before you let those words come out of your mouth, get away from the situation and avoid the urge to spread strife. The second step after you remove yourself from the situation, is to forgive because if you can't forgive it's harder to let strife go. Verse 9 reads, *"Whoever would foster love covers an offense, but whoever repeats the matter separates close friends."* The Living Bible reads, *"Love forgets mistakes; nagging about them parts the best of friends."* That word "nagging" means complaining, griping, and gossiping. You are simply not letting the strife go, but rather holding on to it until it ruins the friendship. In the words of a popular movie, just "let it go!"

Work hard to stay away from strife. If you have entered into strife, ask God to reveal it to you and help you stop it. Repent and make a conscious decision to avoid it in the future. Walking in God's favor is a much better path.

Avoid the Drama

Most teenagers would define strife as "drama." Drama can happen anywhere – one person saying something about another is enough to start the angry words, gossip, and contention. Proverbs 17 instructs us to talk about this in our home.

When my daughter came home from school one day upset about the drama of the day, I wrote her a note to help encourage and educate her. It simply read, "Read Proverbs 17. It applied to last week and shows you did the right thing." I wanted her to see in scripture that God was pleased by her decision to avoid conflict. Once you get caught up in drama, it's hard to shut it off. Verse 14 tells us that even slightly opening the door to any type of quarreling, conflict or strife is like a small crack in the dam. Water will continue to push against that crack until it breaks wide open. Just like the push of the water on the dam, so is drama, or strife as scripture calls it, pushing us into a life of contention, discord, and friction. If we do not fix the crack in the dam, it will break, just as we will be engulfed in a life saturated with unrest if we fail to avoid the drama.

Strife can easily start at the martial arts school. Maybe someone was promoted over you and you were jealous. Maybe your instructor told you your form was sloppy today and you were offended. Maybe a teammate took a cheap shot and left you with a black eye and you were angry. Whatever the situation, you must choose not to yield to strife. Avoid being described as the person in Verse 19, *"Whoever loves a quarrel loves sin..."* It is easy to start drama when you are angry or jealous. So, when you sense those feelings rising in you, decide to avoid the drama that you feel you might want to engage in.

For some people, a life of drama has become a habit. Habits can be hard to break, so don't give up when you find that you yielded to strife. Many psychologists suggest that it can take up to 21 days to create a new habit and up to 90 days to break an existing habit. Some experts say it takes 66 days for a behavior to become automatic. Regardless of what the magic number is, the bottom line is it takes time and a conscious, consistent effort for habits to be broken. Repent and make the decision to not do it next time. Strife can happen every day if you let it, so there will be ample opportunity for practicing your new habit. Soon you'll find that you don't like to be in the middle of the drama and walking away from it will be easy and freeing.

Why Avoid Strife?

Read verse 9 again. God has instructed us to walk in love (John 15:12). When strife is present, love becomes absent and we fail to maintain this commandment of loving others. Strife separates the best of friends as noted in verse 9, but we don't always see it as a separator, but rather a connector. People will use drama or gossip to connect with one friend at the expense of someone else. One reason gossip can be so hard to resist is that it makes us feel "closer" to the person we are sharing the gossip with, for that moment in time. However, it is at the expense of someone else, and this closeness we feel is a false closeness that doesn't last – a friendship tower built on sinking sand rather than a solid foundation. This does not align with loving others at all. Verse 17 says, *"A friend loves at all times..."* If your life is full of contention and conflict, drama and gossip, love becomes a difficult thing. We must avoid strife so the world will know we are Christians by our love.

Points to Remember

- *Stop strife at your doorstep – don't let it enter your home, dojo, workplace or school.*
- *Strife stops the flow of love in our lives. Be quick to overlook the offense so strife cannot gain a foothold.*
- *Refuse to live in strife! Tell the drama it has to go.*

| 18 |

The Power of Words

An unfriendly person pursues selfish ends and against all sound judgment starts quarrels.

²Fools find no pleasure in understanding but delight in airing their own opinions.

³When wickedness comes, so does contempt, and with shame comes reproach.

⁴The words of the mouth are deep waters, but the fountain of wisdom is a rushing stream.

⁵It is not good to be partial to the wicked and so deprive the innocent of justice.

⁶The lips of fools bring them strife, and their mouths invite a beating.

⁷The mouths of fools are their undoing, and their lips are a snare to their very lives.

⁸The words of a gossip are like choice morsels; they go down to the inmost parts.

⁹One who is slack in his work is brother to one who destroys.

¹⁰The name of the Lord is a fortified tower; the righteous run to it and are safe.

¹¹The wealth of the rich is their fortified city; they imagine it a wall too high to scale.

[12]Before a downfall the heart is haughty, but humility comes before honor.

[13]To answer before listening that is folly and shame.

[14]The human spirit can endure in sickness, but a crushed spirit who can bear?

[15]The heart of the discerning acquires knowledge, for the ears of the wise seek it out.

[16]A gift opens the way and ushers the giver into the presence of the great.

[17]In a lawsuit the first to speak seems right, until someone comes forward and cross-examines.

[18]Casting the lot settles disputes and keeps strong opponents apart.

[19]A brother wronged is more unyielding than a fortified city; disputes are like the barred gates of a citadel.

[20]From the fruit of their mouth a person's stomach is filled; with the harvest of their lips they are satisfied.

[21]The tongue has the power of life and death, and those who love it will eat its fruit.

[22]He who finds a wife finds what is good and receives favor from the Lord.

[23]The poor plead for mercy, but the rich answer harshly.

[24]One who has unreliable friends soon comes to ruin, but there is a friend who sticks closer than a brother.

Chapter 18: Daily Devotional

The Bible talks about the power of words in many places. In fact, we've already seen this principle repeated several times in our study of Proverbs and it's repeated in verse 21 of this chapter – *"The tongue has the power of life and death, and those who love it will eat its fruit."* This small body part that the Bible compares to a rudder on a ship, or a small spark that starts a forest fire, can change the course of your life or someone else's depending on how you control it. In this chapter, we are again admonished to be careful in our choice of words, but to also listen closely to the words that are spoken to us.

Hear the Whole Story

We've all heard the expression, "There are two sides to every story." Each person has their own perception of how an event or conversation played out. In all roles of our lives – teacher, parent, coach, friend, coworker, employer – conflict will arise where the two parties involved don't have the same version of events. Verses 13 and 17 tell us to hear both sides of the story before passing judgement. Often, after hearing both sides, you'll find the truth lies somewhere in the middle. Both parties are right to some degree. They have most of the facts right, but we all have our own filters and experiences that impact the true meaning of the situation.

Think about a time when you have acted as the judge in a situation. Did you follow the advice given in verses 13 and 17? It's easy to hear the first person's account and agree with it. It likely sounds logical and accurate and you trust that person to be truthful; however, we are told in these verses that forming an opinion or making a judgement without hearing the other side of the story is foolish.

One area I've seen this play out is in dealing with parents. As a parent, I am the first to admit that I will do whatever I can to defend my children. I want what's best for them and I believe the best of them. Like most, I want my kids to have every opportunity and to be given a fair shake. What can be difficult is taking the blinders off and seeing that my kid isn't always perfect.

As teachers and school owners, Chris and I have dealt with parents who have no martial arts training and don't understand the system at our school, but who have a strong opinion of how their child is performing. This opinion *can* be part of a healthy conversation – it's great when parents are involved in their child's interests. What's difficult is when parents can't take their blinders off and objectively see how their child is training. Once a family moved into our community and signed their child up for lessons. They had trained at another school and the boy came in wearing a brown belt – the belt just below black belt. As the child started participating in class, it quickly became apparent that he was not skilled enough to be wearing that belt level. Chris got ready to have what he thought would be a difficult conversation with the parents; however, just the opposite happened. The parents had been involved in their child's training and, seeing our style, easily saw the differences between our school and their former one. Because the conversation went so well, the family was appreciative of their new training and Chris allowed the student to work one-on-one with an advanced student to help bring his skill level to match his belt. This family was open to "hear the whole story" and not have blinders on about the abilities of their child.

What's especially difficult is when a parent drops their child off for class, returns an hour later to pick them up, and listens to their child's account of training without even talking to the instructor to clarify. If the child is mad, feels cheated, has hurt feelings, or maybe got injured in class, it's our nature as parents to defend the child – and rightfully so. But, while it may be hard for some parents to believe, our kids don't always tell us the truth. They may get part of the truth, but after it runs through their filter it might be a little "off." This change of truth may be done intentionally or unintentionally, but regardless it is the parent's responsibility to hear the whole story and gain a better understanding of the situation before passing judgement. I have heard parents say, "I know my kid and he would never lie." I have two great kids myself, but I would be foolish to believe they have never twisted the truth for their own gain.

Our son, Jared, played soccer from an early age clear through college. During his high school years, he typically started and played every game, so we were quite surprised when one game he did not start and played very little. At first, the parents in us wanted to defend Jared and call out the coach, but after reflection we realized there must be a reason for this change. We waited for the coach after the game to check in with him. He was immediately taken aback because he thought we were there to attack him. Our intent was to understand the situation and learn if our son had done something that would require consequences at home as well. This approach saved our relationship with the coach, benefitted Jared in the long run because his coach knew he could talk to us, and showed support for both the coach and our son.

Regardless of the role or arena, whether you are acting as a parent, co-worker, or employer, the Bible tells us that it is *"folly and shame"* to not hear the entire story before answering. Talk to both parties involved and examine the information with an open mind, gather answers for yourself and not from hearsay, and then make a judgement on where the truth lies.

You Know the Story

After you have followed the advice of verses 13 and 17 and heard all sides of the situation before forming your opinion, it is time to talk to all parties. You may find that "agreeing to disagree" happens before the conversation really starts. Verses 20 and 21 give us some insight on how the conversation should go. The Living Bible puts it like this: *"Ability to give wise advice satisfies like a good meal!"* If you are the mediator in the conflict, your role is to offer wise advice so that both parties learn from the situation, leave with a better understanding of both perceptions, and hopefully save their friendship or relationship.

As the parent, you may even have good advice for the instructor. For example, what if the child gets embarrassed when told he is wrong, and this impacts his performance. The instructor might think the child is quitting without even trying, but rather the student is just overwhelmed! Maybe there is a health or medical issue the instructor is not aware of or a family situation that is impacting how the student is training. The instructor does not know what he does not know. Communication is key and offering advice like, "It might be best to put Zach in the front row because his vision is impaired and he can't see well from the back when you demonstrate" benefits everyone.

For years, we had a student who attended classes on and off. He would come regularly for a period of time when his life was going well. During those high points, he would work at the school and we would trade out fees for his work. He would regularly call to see if he could help in any way and was dependable and responsible. Then he would hit a bout of depression and everything in his life would take a turn for the worse. On top of fighting depression, he also fought obesity and weighed well over 400 pounds. When life was going well, the weight came off, but it always went back up during his low times. He was in a perpetual cycle and couldn't get off the hamster wheel. Once a student made a video of our school and decided to focus on this student. For the video Chris interviewed Big Jim, as he was affectionately called, talked to other students in the school about his impact on the school and their training, and added some of his own commentary on Jim's life. One of the 6-year-olds who was interviewed said, "I like how he yells!" A parent said, "Jim is an inspiration to all the students on how to overcome difficulties in our lives." Chris echoed those same sentiments and talked about Jim's journey from white belt to black belt and the determination he had invested in his nearly 20 years of training.

When Big Jim watched the video he said, "I didn't know people thought that way about me!" What a positive impact those words had on him. Jim continues to fight his personal battles, but he can reflect on those words as encouragement to bring himself up when he is low. Verse 21 says, "*The tongue has the power of life and death...*" Imagine the life these words brought to a man who has battled depression, self-worth and poverty all of his life.

It never ceases to amaze me, however, that as soon as we experience good things the devil tries to destroy that progress and keep us defeated. Jim was getting ready to test for his black belt just weeks after watching the video, but then he started to slide downhill. He called in a panic and said he needed to be committed to a mental facility because he was losing his mind. When Chris talked to him, Chris told Jim that the devil was not going to win this battle of the mind and really scolded Jim for thinking this way. The truth was not that he was losing his mind, it was that he was nervous about his belt test and thought he was going to let everyone down if he did not pass. After Chris reassured him that he would not test if he was not ready and that everyone was pulling for him, Big Jim agreed to test and did a fantastic job. The whole school cheered and encouraged him, and he proudly tied on his black belt that day.

At the martial arts school, at your work, at the grocery store, at home – *anywhere* you are present – the Bible tells us to be an encourager. You never know what greatness the person you are encouraging is made for. In Deuteronomy 1, Moses is talking to the Israelites and telling them that only Caleb and Joshua will enter the Promised Land. In verse 38 Moses instructs the Israelites, *"Encourage him, because he will lead Israel to inherit it."* The next book of the Bible is titled, "Joshua!" The entire chapter is dedicated to Joshua's life and the greatness God had planned for him as he led Israel. Your encouragement might be impacting the next Joshua.

Closer Than A Brother

In 2002 Chris met a man that I would later consider Chris's brother. Ron Ornelas came to our church on an invitation from our Pastor. Pastor and Ron met while sitting and waiting on their wives who were shopping at the mall. At their first meeting at church, Ron and Chris immediately hit it off as they both had an interest in martial arts. Ron started coming to the school and the two trained together constantly. Ron eventually earned his black belt and taught beginner classes. The two guys talked so much on the phone that Ron regularly used up the minutes on his family plan, so his wife changed cell phone carriers to the one we used! Ron and Chris attended morning Bible study together, started a new kickboxing class that is still taught today, shared struggles with family and children, and laughed and joked like they were kids.

In his early years before giving his heart to the Lord, Ron had been an alcoholic and drug user. His abuse later manifested as Hepatitis B and this disease was the start of the decline in his health that eventually took his life. For Chris, there has never been and never will be another friend like Ron Ornelas. He was a friend that stuck closer than a brother.

The key to their friendship was that they adhered verse 24 which says, *"One who has unreliable friends soon comes to ruin, but there is a friend who sticks closer than a brother."* In order to have friends, you must exert the effort to first be kind. In the case with Ron, he was new to our church and we simply started talking at a church dinner the first Sunday his family visited. His wife, Karen, and I were involved in our own conversation and the four of us became friends. This conversation later turned into Friday night card games and Super Bowl Sundays where we just hung out as families.

In looking at this example, the first step at class for you might be to talk to the new student or partner with someone you have never worked out with before. You never know what things you might have in common and thus a friendship may develop.

One thing that many people lack these days is time. We are so busy with our lives and the things we need to get done, that it can seem like we simply don't have time to be friendly. Look at everyone as they quickly pack up their gear and scurry out to the next event waiting for them. However, being friendly and striking up a conversation does not need to take up hours of your life. Rather, you can simply ask how someone is doing and talk for a minute.

Another barrier to speaking words of life is our phone. When our children were still living at home the rule was "no phones at the dinner table." It's important to have conversation and engage with each other in a face-to-face dialog. The next time you go to a restaurant, to the park, or to the mall look at everyone on their phones. Faces are buried in the next social media post and people are not talking to each other.

While phones can be a way of connecting with others – like Chris and Ron's daily calls – they also can be walls that we unintentionally put up that prevent us from meaningfully connecting with others. It's like a sign that says to others, "Keep out! Stay away! I'm busy!"

I cannot begin to express the joy Chris experienced from having a brother in Ron. When times are tough or when you just want someone who will experience life with you, it is important that you have taken time to develop friendships that are more than surface friends. You need friends who are there for you no matter the situation, and friendships that develop more and more as you talk and spend time together.

I am fortunate to also have wonderful, strong women in my life who I can call anytime. One group of friends are women that I taught high school with. We have regular "board meetings" as we call them for every birthday, Christmas, or life celebration. This group of women has done life together for over 20 years – we have attended funerals of each other's parents and siblings, celebrated over the birth of children and grandchildren, and shared countless stories of life in the classroom and life at home. Our board meetings are full of laughter, smiles, hugs and sometimes tears, but we always speak life into each other.

Who are you having "board meetings" with? Who speaks life into your life? We all need someone who listens and will be a *friend who sticks closer than a brother."*

Points to Remember

- *Find out both sides of the story before making a judgement. The first side you hear might not be the right one.*
- *Use your words to encourage others, mend friendships and correct wrongs.*
- *Be a friend to someone today. That person may become the next "Ron" in your life.*

| 19 |

Accepting Instruction

Better the poor whose walk is blameless than a fool whose lips are perverse.

²Desire without knowledge is not good how much more will hasty feet miss the way!

³A person's own folly leads to their ruin, yet their heart rages against the Lord.

⁴Wealth attracts many friends, but even the closest friend of the poor person deserts them.

⁵A false witness will not go unpunished, and whoever pours out lies will not go free.

⁶Many curry favor with a ruler, and everyone is the friend of one who gives gifts.

⁷The poor are shunned by all their relatives how much more do their friends avoid them!

Though the poor pursue them with pleading, they are nowhere to be found.

⁸The one who gets wisdom loves life; the one who cherishes understanding will soon prosper.

⁹A false witness will not go unpunished, and whoever pours out lies will perish.

[10]It is not fitting for a fool to live in luxury how much worse for a slave to rule over princes!

[11]A person's wisdom yields patience; it is to one's glory to overlook an offense.

[12]A king's rage is like the roar of a lion, but his favor is like dew on the grass.

[13]A foolish child is a father's ruin, and a quarrelsome wife is like the constant dripping of a leaky roof.

[14]Houses and wealth are inherited from parents, but a prudent wife is from the Lord.

[15]Laziness brings on deep sleep, and the shiftless go hungry.

[16]Whoever keeps commandments keeps their life, but whoever shows contempt for their ways will die.

[17]Whoever is kind to the poor lends to the Lord, and he will reward them for what they have done.

[18]Discipline your children, for in that there is hope; do not be a willing party to their death.

[19]A hot-tempered person must pay the penalty; rescue them, and you will have to do it again.

[20]Listen to advice and accept discipline, and at the end you will be counted among the wise.

[21]Many are the plans in a person's heart, but it is the Lord's purpose that prevails.

[22]What a person desires is unfailing love; better to be poor than a liar.

[23]The fear of the Lord leads to life; then one rests content, untouched by trouble.

[24]A sluggard buries his hand in the dish; he will not even bring it back to his mouth!

[25]Flog a mocker, and the simple will learn prudence; rebuke the discerning, and they will gain knowledge.

[26]Whoever robs their father and drives out their mother is a child who brings shame and disgrace.

[27]Stop listening to instruction, my son, and you will stray from the words of knowledge.

[28]A corrupt witness mocks at justice, and the mouth of the wicked gulps down evil.

[29]Penalties are prepared for mockers, and beatings for the backs of fools.

Chapter 19: Daily Devotional

Learning martial arts can be hard. You must listen to instruction, learn new techniques, and perform in front of your instructor and others. There is constant correction happening in class on how to better your stance, improve the power in your strike, or increase the strength of your performance. To become a skilled martial artist, you have to be willing to accept this instruction. Instruction is what makes us better, but it can be hard to receive at times. Proverbs talks many times about the importance of receiving instruction and applying it to our lives. Again, we are admonished to seek wisdom so that we can understand the principles of God and pass this wisdom on to our children, students, and others we interact with in our lives.

Don't Blame God

When things go wrong in our lives, many times we look for someone else to blame. We decide that our circumstances surely cannot be *our* fault or the result of choices *we* made. Often the most popular person to blame is God. I'm sure we have all heard – or maybe we ourselves have said – expressions like:

- "If God is so loving, how could He let this happen to me?"
- "Where is God? I thought He was supposed to protect me."
- "This is God's fault!"

There are two distinct personality traits of God displayed in the Bible. The first is a loving God who sent his only son Jesus to die on a cross to save us from our sins. This loving God has made many promises and provisions on our behalf to ensure that we can spend eternity with Him. He forgives us daily and longs to be part of our lives. There are too many gifts he gives us beyond salvation to mention, but my favorite two are peace and health.

So if this loving God has promised health and healing, why do people get sick? Isaiah 58:8 in the Living Bible reads, *"...God will shed his glorious light upon you. He will heal you..."* Another verse is Jeremiah 30:17 where God says, *"But I will restore you to health and heal your wounds..."* It's easy to pick verses like these out of the Bible and believe that God will heal every sickness. I could say that God is a liar since I know this does not happen; however, I also believe in the second personality trait of God and that is justice.

Our good friend Ron that I introduced in the last chapter died of Hepatitis and other diseases. I prayed for Ron, as did our entire church family, his wife and his four children; however, God did not heal Ron. I could blame God and say, "How could he let this happen?" But I have to believe that God has a bigger plan, sees things that I cannot see, and that He ultimately is just. Ron himself would tell you that his disease was primarily the result of poor choices he made early in his life, and there are consequences to our actions. Rather than being angry at God for these consequences, it brings us more peace to be grateful for the memories we have of Ron. Even today, we still laugh when we remember the jokes Chris and Ron played on each other, the times they got lost going to martial arts tournaments, or the crazy work-out plans they challenged each other to try. Loss is never easy, but there is comfort in being grateful.

We talked about this earlier in our study regarding King David and the death of his infant son. King David loved God and he prayed for healing that did not come; however, David went on to live for the Lord and understood that God still loved him. David did not blame God, and neither do I blame God for Ron's death or any other pain that comes as a result of living here on earth.

Someone else might argue that their illness is not the result of a poor choice, but rather a shock that happened to them without warning. A perfect example of this is Job from the Bible. Job had no idea all the calamity that was coming to him, but he continued to trust God through death, financial ruin, sickness and more. Job trusted God and relied on Him to restore all that was lost, even though he had no idea that God was working miracles on his behalf. God does not bring bad things into our lives. Rather, we have to realize that we live in a fallen world where death, destruction, calamity and strife are ever present. We will not see these misfortunes cease until we are residents of heaven.

When we notice ourselves looking for others to blame, we need to stop for a moment. This allows us to see that sometimes things are happening to us because of the words we spoke, actions we performed, or people we associated with. Always blaming others will never lead to a peaceful life that grows in God. We need to be brutally honest with ourselves and take a hard look at the life we are leading.

How many times have we blamed the judge when we lost a match or didn't place in our forms competition? Maybe the judge missed a point, but if we were truly the better prepared athlete, we still would have won. It's time we stop and judge our own training, effort and determination to succeed rather than blaming the coach, judge, or the other competitor. We will never become better martial artists if we look for others to blame in our training instead of looking inward at ourselves first.

Seek Knowledge

One of the reasons people start martial arts is to learn something new. They want to learn about the traditions, discipline, and the art itself. They come seeking knowledge about a new activity they can add to their life and, for some, to their family. No matter the reason, gaining knowledge is what helps us grow mentally, spiritually, and even professionally.

The Bible says a lot about learning:

- Deuteronomy 31:12 tells us to *"learn to fear the Lord your God"*
- Proverbs 1:5 instructs the *"wise to listen and add to their learning"*
- Isaiah 1:16-17 says, *"Stop doing wrong and learn to do right!"*
- Christ instructs us in Matthew 11:29 to *"Take my yoke upon you and learn from me..."*

These verses only highlight a few places where we are admonished to learn, but it's clear that learning is important. When you first accept the Lord as your Savior, you are not expected to know everything. The Bible even compares new believers to a newborn who requires milk as their diet to grow. But as we grow in our understanding and knowledge of God, we move from drinking milk to eating solid food, just as an infant does as he or she grows.

This same principle can be applied to our martial arts training. Often when we start a new activity, we are so excited that we want to jump right into the deep end without first learning how to navigate the shallow waters. However, we need to take baby steps first. This progression of knowledge is demonstrated by the advancement in belts. The white belt signifies innocence and purity regarding the system you are enrolled in. The white belt says that you have an open mind and are ready to learn anything new. As you progress in your learning, the color of your belt changes to represent that new knowledge. Each belt has its own meaning – my personal favorite is green because it means growth! Any onlooker can see that a student has trained and worked to master their art by simply looking at the color of their belt.

When you finally obtain your black belt, it does not mean that your learning has stopped. In fact, just the opposite is true, as the rank of black belt is viewed as a new beginning where you apply all the knowledge you have obtained and use the tools you have been given. The black belt represents the commitment of the student to overcome difficult tasks using both physical achievement and mental determination.

Moving up in belt rank is a great analogy to our walk as Christians. We start as a new Christian eager to learn about the things of God. We grow daily by reading His word, spending time in prayer, and gathering with others who also love Him. As we continue to build our relationship with God and learn about His teaching, we are moving from white belt to black belt in our Christian lives. This movement comes from seeking knowledge – which is what Proverbs 19:2 and 8 are telling us to do. Getting your black belt does not happen in a week. It's not a fast climb because there is so much to learn, to evaluate, and to understand. You must approach this journey with the understanding that you will embrace knowledge and develop as a martial artist over time, just as you move through your life as a Christian – growing daily in the knowledge of God.

Grow from the Knowledge

I am a true believer in life-long learning. At age 49 I decided to start my sixth college degree – a doctorate in Educational Leadership. However, back when I was in first grade, you would probably not have convinced my mom that I loved school. As a first grader I had to transition to all-day school from my half-day kindergarten experience. Around noon every day I developed a mysterious stomachache, and my teacher would send me to the sick bed while she called my mom. The truth was I just wanted to go to my grandma's house, and I told my mom, "A half day of school was enough for anybody." That was a favorite story that my grandmother loved to tell and one I continued to be reminded of by my parents.

While I might not have appreciated school at an early age, I have grown to love school and continually look for opportunities to learn. During this doctoral program, I have been especially challenged in my writing and thinking. Writing as a researcher has been a new experience and I have had to process a lot of corrections from my professors.

This same correction is applied regularly in the dojo. Students of every belt color face correction during their training. Without this correction, we would never master the art, learn proper techniques, develop discipline, or understand the traditions of martial arts. Verse 25 is an excellent guide to help us through this process of correction and continuing down our path of learning. The Living Bible says: *"Punish a mocker and others will learn from his example. Reprove a wise man and he will be the wiser."* There is a great difference between those who learn from correction and those who reject it. The saying, "You can either get bitter or get better" applies here. How we respond to correction will determine how we grow in wisdom as well as in our learning and training. The next time you are corrected or even criticized, listen carefully to all that is said before you make a judgement. You might find that the correction is much needed, and you will add to your base of knowledge.

If you are like the mocker in verse 25 you will surely stunt your growth. *Mockers* say they can do things their way and they don't need to listen to anyone. They are close-minded and lack the capacity to look outside their own box. Like a plant that needs water to grow, the correction applied to a wise person's life helps them grow. Without water the plant, like the mocker, will stay the same and eventually die. Verse 27 tells us the same thing: *"Stop listening to instruction, my son, and you will stray from the words of knowledge."* God's Word implores us to strive to be life-long learners, continually looking for opportunities to grow in our relationship with Him by feeding our lives with the knowledge of Christ and His plan for us.

Points to Remember

- *Own your own behavior and don't blame God or others for your decisions or the consequences of those decisions.*

- *Learn something new so you continually grow in all areas of your life - especially in your knowledge of the Lord.*
- *Love learning. Embrace it all your life.*

| 20 |

God's Candle

Wine is a mocker and beer a brawler; whoever is led astray by them is not wise.

²A king's wrath strikes terror like the roar of a lion; those who anger him forfeit their lives.

³It is to one's honor to avoid strife, but every fool is quick to quarrel.

⁴Sluggards do not plow in season; so at harvest time they look but find nothing.

⁵The purposes of a person's heart are deep waters, but one who has insight draws them out.

⁶Many claim to have unfailing love, but a faithful person who can find?

⁷The righteous lead blameless lives; blessed are their children after them.

⁸When a king sits on his throne to judge, he winnows out all evil with his eyes.

⁹Who can say, "I have kept my heart pure; I am clean and without sin"?

¹⁰Differing weights and differing measures the Lord detests them both.

¹¹Even small children are known by their actions, so is their conduct really pure and upright?

¹²Ears that hear and eyes that see the Lord has made them both.

¹³Do not love sleep or you will grow poor; stay awake and you will have food to spare.

¹⁴It's no good, it's no good!" says the buyer then goes off and boasts about the purchase.

¹⁵Gold there is, and rubies in abundance, but lips that speak knowledge are a rare jewel.

¹⁶Take the garment of one who puts up security for a stranger; hold it in pledge if it is done for an outsider.

¹⁷Food gained by fraud tastes sweet, but one ends up with a mouth full of gravel.

¹⁸Plans are established by seeking advice; so if you wage war, obtain guidance.

¹⁹A gossip betrays a confidence; so avoid anyone who talks too much.

²⁰If someone curses their father or mother, their lamp will be snuffed out in pitch darkness.

²¹An inheritance claimed too soon will not be blessed at the end.

²²Do not say, "I'll pay you back for this wrong!" Wait for the Lord, and he will avenge you.

²³The Lord detests differing weights, and dishonest scales do not please him.

²⁴A person's steps are directed by the Lord. How then can anyone understand their own way?

²⁵It is a trap to dedicate something rashly and only later to consider one's vows.

²⁶A wise king winnows out the wicked; he drives the threshing wheel over them.

²⁷The human spirit is the lamp of the Lord that sheds light on one's inmost being.

²⁸Love and faithfulness keep a king safe; through love his throne is made secure.

²⁹The glory of young men is their strength, gray hair the splendor of the old.

[30]Blows and wounds scrub away evil, and beatings purge the inmost being.

Chapter 20: Daily Devotional

You know that feeling you get and you're just not sure why you feel that way? We call that our conscience. Conscience is a mysterious concept, but it's best defined as a sense of awareness or recognition of something within or outside of yourself. As Christians, our conscience is described as God's candle inside of us. This candle illuminates the right thinking and righteous living that God instructs us to follow. As we adhere to this way of living, our conscience might say things to us like, "I shouldn't say that" or "I should act differently." The principles of Chapter 20 teach some of those things God's candle might expose in us.

Cheaters Never Win

You might read that heading and think, "Yes, they do!" Admittedly, I would agree with you to some extent. Over my 28 years of teaching I have dealt with many students who cheated by making copies of each other's work, copying text directly from the internet and calling it their own, and taking pictures of online tests and sharing them with others. As an instructor, cheating is so defeating to me because you work hard to provide good instruction and deliver content in a meaningful way, and some students just don't seem to care. They simply want to get the grade and pass the class regardless of how it's done.

Do cheaters get the grade? Pass the class? Most of the time. I do not know of every cheating incident in my classes; however, I do talk with students who I felt have been academically dishonest. The range of responses during this conversation can be disheartening. Many students argue that they are not cheating. They see their work as their best effort because it's their way of survival. In other words, they don't know how to do the work so getting help (i.e. cheating) is resourceful. One student even found the answer key to an assignment by Googling it and submitted that very answer key as his work. When questioned, he could not understand why I was upset with him. In his mind, he did what it took to get the answers.

We see cheating in martial arts. People who claim to be experts in their art, but don't actually have any credentials, cheat students out of quality instruction and money. At tournaments, judges may score a student from their school higher than another when it's not deserved, and thus cheat another student out of an award. In the dojo, instructors cheat students when they are unprepared to teach the class.

Cheating is pervasive in our society and many seem to think it's okay. However, God is very clear about how He feels about being honest. In our discussion of Chapter 11 we read in verse 1, *"The Lord hates cheating and delights in honesty"* (Living Bible). That seems very easy to understand, but to give it even more emphasis, Proverbs 20 says it again. Let's look at verses 10, 17 and 23. We learned about using dishonest weights during Jesus's time in Chapter 11 and God continues to use the analogy of weights and measures to help us understand how serious He is about this issue. Proverbs is very clear in telling us that God hates any form of dishonesty. He despises it so badly that he compares liars to murderers in Revelation 21:8: *"But the cowardly, the unbelieving, the vile, the murderers, the sexually immoral, those who practice magic arts, the idolaters and all liars—they will be consigned to the fiery lake of burning sulfur. This is the second death."*

When you obtain anything because you did it dishonestly, verse 17 says it will be like *"gravel in your mouth."* Just imagine how that would feel! Knowing this, you have to wonder if getting whatever you wanted by using dishonest measures is really worth it. Do you feel the same satisfaction as you would have by working hard and doing the right thing? What more would you have learned by not cheating and simply doing the work yourself? There are short and long-term results of being dishonest. In short, fraudulent gain is sweet for only a short while (verse 17) and in the long, riches gained quickly don't last (verse 21).

Don't get confused and let the world convince you that being dishonest is okay or simply a way of survival. This is often an excuse for being lazy. Isaiah 5:20 writes, *"Woe to those who call evil good and good evil, who put darkness for light and light for darkness, who put bitter for sweet and sweet for bitter."* The Living Bible uses the words *"what is right is wrong and what is wrong is right."* Sin is sin and for God there is no gray area.

Age Does Not Matter

One of my favorite verses is Proverbs 20:11: *"Even small children are known by their actions, so is their conduct really pure and upright?"* One of the reasons I love this verse is because it was the *E* verse my children learned in their elementary school education. As kindergartners, they both learned a Bible verse for every letter of the alphabet, and I am reminded of that when I read this verse. The other reason it's one of my favorites is because it applies so much to our martial arts instruction. Over the years of owning our school we have taught students of all ages, but by far the greatest number of students are children. Children can be terrific students and watching them learn is one of the greatest benefits of teaching.

Children come with all kinds of personalities, but regardless if they are shy or outgoing, most of them love to play. Using "play" is one way to effectively teach martial arts. Games are used to disguise what seems like hard work. Exercise is fun when it's done in such a way that it doesn't seem like exercise. Games have rules and structure, just as martial arts does, and this discipline of playing the game correctly carries over into the martial arts instruction. Students are given incentives in games to encourage them to work hard and they are given incentives in their martial arts training such as being the class leader, demonstrating their form to the class, and earning promotions. Adults appreciate incentives as well. While they might not care about being the first one through the obstacle course, they do appreciate praise for their demonstration of what they learned in class.

During class, the instructor can watch the students' conduct and attitude in how they play, how they process instruction, and how they receive praise. We expect adults to be respectful in all these situations, and we should also expect the same from our children. As instructors and parents, we must set an example that helps children know what actions are acceptable in the dojo and how to carry those into their daily lives. Age is no respecter of bad conduct. It's likely we have all seen unruly, disobedient, and misbehaved children and we quickly form an opinion of that child (and often the parenting of that child.)

When you are an instructor and teacher you work with many students, and often you think of them by their conduct. For example, when we were picking out names for our own children, Chris or I would suggest a name but then the other one would say, "No! I had a student with that name and he/she was awful/mean/disrespectful." We didn't want to give our child a name that we associated with bad behavior. That may seem silly, but I'm sure I'm not the only teacher who has thought that way!

Age is no excuse for bad behavior. Children are known by their behavior just as adults are. It's important that children are taught at an early age to follow the instructions for good behavior found in Proverbs 20, including:

- Don't gossip (verse 19)
- Don't cheat (verse 10)
- Avoid fighting (verse 3)
- Be a hard worker (verses 4 and 13)

When we are diligent to teach and model this behavior to our children, verse 7 tells us we will be blessed and so will our children after us.

Stay Out of a Fight

We've talked about avoiding strife in previous chapters and how some people start martial arts training just to learn how to fight. Physically defeating opponents and defending against threats is part of the sport, but it's not the heart of the art. Taekwondo is really about enlightenment and growth, learning to forgive, and refraining from violent behaviors. Some might say that walking away from a fight shows weakness; however, if you have a real understanding of martial arts, you know that the opposite is true. Showing wise restraint can be more difficult than letting go of your emotions, words, and actions when you are confronted with a challenging situation.

Verse 3 admonishes us to follow the same teaching as the tenets of taekwondo. The Living Bible reads, *"It is an honor for a man to stay out of a fight. Only fools insist on quarreling."* Taekwondo tenets include courtesy, integrity, perseverance, self-control, and indomitable spirit. It often takes a great deal of self-control to stay out of a fight, but if we are exercising our martial arts training and following the wisdom of the Bible, we will choose to not fight and avoid the conflict if possible.

There is a great example in the Bible of how two men could have easily gotten into a dispute because they wanted their own way. In Genesis 13:5-12 we read how Abraham and Lot were having problems because their servants were quarreling over grazing rights for their herds. Abraham shows us exactly how to apply verse 3. The Bible says in Genesis 13:8, *"So Abram said to Lot, "Let's not have any quarreling between you and me, or between your herdsmen and mine, for we are brothers."* Abraham proposed that Lot look at the land and pick the side he wanted. Abraham would then take the other side. Some may say that Abraham backed down and showed weakness. According to scripture, we see it was an honor for Abraham to avoid fighting with Lot and it showed great character. In turn, God blessed Abraham and made him the father of many nations.

When we avoid strife with others, we are demonstrating the love of Christ. This demonstration of love is done when we are walking in the wisdom of God. Let God order your steps (verse 24) so you can live a life full of blessing just as Abraham did.

Consider Your Promise

Dedication means to set apart or to devote to something. When you are dedicated to martial arts you will set apart time to go to class, money for equipment and a uniform, and energy to put into your training. You might think of dedication as it relates to marriage – you said vows at your wedding and dedicated yourself to your spouse. You might have dedicated your children to the Lord and vowed to raise them in a godly home. You might think of being dedicated to your job and working there for thirty-plus years. Being dedicated is an admirable quality that speaks highly about your character and commitment.

For some, being dedicated is an unfulfilled promise – merely a fleeting commitment that is said in the moment. You are very passionate about an opportunity and quickly claim that you are dedicated to it – fully, completely, and at all cost. When dedication is done out of haste or excitement of the moment, it loses its luster quickly if it hasn't been seriously considered. Verse 25 warns us about making such decisions. It reads, *"It is a trap to dedicate something rashly and only later to consider one's vows."*

We have seen this in our martial arts schools more than once. A family will come and try out a class. They are so excited that they buy all the equipment, order uniforms, and sign up for a year contract on the first visit. This is great if they have considered it completely and know how this commitment will fit into their family schedule. I don't ever want to discourage a family from becoming part of our martial arts school, but we also invite them to try it once and decide if it's a good fit before making a heavy investment. Unfortunately, some families who made this decision rashly stop coming because there is not enough time in the day to be involved in everything.

When people make promises they typically have good intentions, but if they fail to live up to their promise it casts doubt on their character. You know the type of person who makes promises and never delivers – they promise to be there, but never show up. They promise to pay their tuition, but always forget the checkbook. They promise to help you with a project but leave you to do it yourself. We all know someone like this and while you want to believe them, it gets harder and harder as their promises continue to fail.

There are examples in the Bible of both good and bad vows of devotion. For example, Jephthah promised the Lord he would offer to the Lord whoever came out to meet him after battle. The result was he lost his daughter. Jephthah did not think this promise through! On the flip side, there is Hannah who offered to give her son back to God if she could conceive a son. She did and her son, Samuel, became a great prophet of the day.

The Bible tells us to be careful what we promise. Even the best of intentions should not be your determining factor for saying yes to everything. "Yes" might be nice, but often "No" is necessary when you have too much on your plate. Think first about what you are promising to and determine if it's reasonable. You will only disappoint others and hurt yourself if you continually fail to finish what you said you were devoted to.

Points to Remember

- *Don't be a cheater. Prepare and work hard so you will appreciate the effort of your labor.*
- *When people think of you, they should have a picture of a good, righteous person - regardless of how old you are.*
- *Self-control can be a hard thing, but it brings blessings on you in the long run.*
- *Consider the vow you are making. Can you really keep it? If not, don't make the promise to do it.*

| 21 |

Get Prepared

In the Lord's hand the king's heart is a stream of water that he channels toward all who please him.

²A person may think their own ways are right, but the Lord weighs the heart.

³To do what is right and just is more acceptable to the Lord than sacrifice.

⁴Haughty eyes and a proud heart the unplowed field of the wicked produce sin.

⁵The plans of the diligent lead to profit as surely as haste leads to poverty.

⁶A fortune made by a lying tongue is a fleeting vapor and a deadly snare.

⁷The violence of the wicked will drag them away, for they refuse to do what is right.

⁸The way of the guilty is devious, but the conduct of the innocent is upright.

⁹Better to live on a corner of the roof than share a house with a quarrelsome wife.

¹⁰The wicked crave evil; their neighbors get no mercy from them.

¹¹When a mocker is punished, the simple gain wisdom; by paying attention to the wise they get knowledge.

¹²The Righteous One takes note of the house of the wicked and brings the wicked to ruin.

¹³Whoever shuts their ears to the cry of the poor will also cry out and not be answered.

¹⁴A gift given in secret soothes anger, and a bribe concealed in the cloak pacifies great wrath.

¹⁵When justice is done, it brings joy to the righteous but terror to evildoers.

¹⁶Whoever strays from the path of prudence comes to rest in the company of the dead.

¹⁷Whoever loves pleasure will become poor; whoever loves wine and olive oil will never be rich.

¹⁸The wicked become a ransom for the righteous, and the unfaithful for the upright.

¹⁹Better to live in a desert than with a quarrelsome and nagging wife.

²⁰The wise store up choice food and olive oil, but fools gulp theirs down.

²¹Whoever pursues righteousness and love finds life, prosperity and honor.

²²One who is wise can go up against the city of the mighty and pull down the stronghold in which they trust.

²³Those who guard their mouths and their tongues keep themselves from calamity.

²⁴The proud and arrogant person—"Mocker" is his name— behaves with insolent fury.

²⁵The craving of a sluggard will be the death of him, because his hands refuse to work.

²⁶All day long he craves for more, but the righteous give without sparing.

²⁷The sacrifice of the wicked is detestable— how much more so when brought with evil intent!

²⁸A false witness will perish but a careful listener will testify successfully.

²⁹The wicked put up a bold front, but the upright give thought to their ways.

³⁰There is no wisdom, no insight, no plan that can succeed against the Lord.

³¹The horse is made ready for the day of battle, but victory rests with the Lord.

Chapter 21: Daily Devotional

I love To-Do lists. They help me control the day, so the day does not control me. Crossing things off my list is completely rewarding and sometimes I write things on the list that I've already finished just so I can cross them off! Before the end of each day I prep for the next day – my work and exercise bags are packed, my lessons are ready for class, and my to-do list is written for tomorrow. This preparation makes me more self-disciplined and thus more productive. Being prepared for today, tomorrow, and the future is a good thing. While God ultimately knows all that will happen to us in our lives, He still expects us to prepare for rainy days and life events. Proverbs 21 instructs us to prepare our plans in life, prepare our minds to learn, and prepare our savings account for the future.

What's Your Motive?

A motive is the reason behind why you are doing something. Think about it: what is your reason or motive behind your martial arts training? Each of us have a motive for joining a school such as losing weight, getting in shape, or learning self-defense.

Another type of motive is an *ulterior* motive which is the same thing – except it's hidden. You are doing something for a reason that you are not telling others. An example of an ulterior motive might be when your child cleans their room and tells you they are just wanting to help out. While you really hope that is the case, you later find out that they want to spend the night with a friend and cleaning their room was their ulterior motive in hopes that you would say yes.

People have ulterior motives for many things. In the book of Matthew, Jesus calls out the people who do good acts for appearances only – not for a true sense of compassion for others. Their actions are good, but their motives are not. They want people to acknowledge how great they are for generosity; however, this acknowledgement will be their only reward. God knows their heart and He rewards those with a pure motive.

Jesus also calls out the religious leaders in Matthew 6:5-6 for standing on the street corners and praying out loud. He's not calling them out for praying; he's saying that their motive is not to commune with God, but to show-off how spiritual they think they are and get praise from men. Again, this praise will be their only reward. Jesus says that whatever you do – giving, helping, praying – do it in private so that it's not about you, but rather about Him. Getting praise from others is not a bad thing and to be honest, it makes us feel good as a person. This praise is even better when you have glorified God with your work and people see your heart for Christ.

How do you "prepare" your motives? Verse 2 reads, *"A person may think their own ways are right, but the Lord weighs the heart."* It's easy to justify anything we do with an excuse or an explanation that sounds legit. So, to check your motives, simply ask God if He would be happy with the real reason behind the actions. He already knows your heart so this should be an easy question and answer.

For example, if you truly came early to class to help others prepare and not with the idea of getting "brownie" points from the instructor, then you're good. Be a helper. If you truly came to class early to help clean the locker room areas and not ask for a break on this month's tuition, then you're good. Be a cleaner. If you truly stayed late to stock the inventory shelves and not just want a free shirt, then you're good. Be a stocker.

God knows your heart from the start, but you know what? Eventually, others will start to figure you out too. What do you want people to know about your motives? The Bible tells us what our motives should be in Colossians 3:23, *"Whatever you do, work at it with all your heart, as working for the Lord, not for human masters."* Your motives should be to glorify God in all you do.

Prepare to Learn

There are upper belts in class who assist the master instructor with teaching. These students have been training longer and, therefore, know the routines of the school and have a better understanding of the techniques being taught. They have knowledge to give and can be a good resource to help during class when the master instructor is working with others. Not only can these students help you to do a form correctly, they can also share what *NOT* to do so that you act, perform, and present in the way your master instructor expects. The tips you get from classmates will help you earn a promotion and perform well at belt tests... *IF* you listen and take their advice to heart.

If you think you will only listen to the master instructor, you may be missing out on how to avoid typical student pitfalls. Just like we have pastors who help us along our spiritual journey, our classmates can help us in our martial arts journey. It is better to learn from those who have already walked down the path we are embarking upon. That way, we can learn from their mistakes. We can do this by listening, observing, and taking counsel instead of learning the hard way. Verse 11 calls this kind of student "wise." There is no reason to attend the "school of hard knocks" when you can have the wisdom of learning from others.

To be prepared for learning, you need to be open-minded to receiving instruction and correction. Proverbs 19:25 says, *"Flog a mocker, and the simple will learn prudence rebuke the discerning, and they will gain knowledge."* When you are prepared to learn, your learning potential is unlimited!

Prepare for Battle

During my educational career, I served as a high school building administrator and one thing I disliked were the confrontational or correcting conversations I needed to have with teachers. Most people have a difficult time accepting reprimand and correction, and I struggled giving it. As a harmonizer, I wanted to make people happy, not be the bad guy. Many times I practiced those conversations with my supervisor, wrote them out on paper, and watched myself in the mirror as I tried to do my job, but also show the love of Christ. I did these things to prepare so the conversation would communicate what I needed to get across and so I would say it in a professional, thoughtful manner. To me, these conversations were like a battle – mostly a battle for me to control my emotions, communicate effectively, and listen intently.

Think about the things that you prepare for and why you are preparing. How many times have you practiced a form in your living room to be prepared for a belt test? Why did you do that? Simple – so you would be promoted to the next rank. The word "battle" may sound like a harsh word, but it really means anything that you are trying to learn, any achievement you are trying to accomplish, any conversation you'll have, or skill you are learning – it can really be anything you are facing. Changing the word from "battle" to "opportunity" might be another way to look at it. "Battle" does not need to be negative but can rather be seen as a welcome challenge. After all, challenges are what keep us learning and growing.

As we read in verse 31, God expects us to do our part to be prepared for this battle or challenge. While all our planning can be futile without God's help, He still expects us to come prepared. For example, if you are scheduled to test for your next belt, you would come to class on a regular basis and practice the belt requirements. If you are going to a tournament, you would train and prepare for the competition. If I were running a marathon, I would print a running schedule and follow it daily to be ready on race day. I wouldn't show up to race day with my longest run being only 7 miles! Doing these things is our part of preparation. God will accomplish His purposes and He will be able to use you if you have done your prep work and come prepared to the battle.

Living a life for Christ might feel like a battle some days. The Bible tells us how to prepare for that battle in Ephesians 6:10-18. The scripture uses the analogy of putting on armor like a soldier to fight off the enemy. In our daily life you might not actually put on a helmet – unless you are in sparring class – but instead you "gear up" by reading the Bible, spending time in prayer and relying on God's power for your daily living. When you go to sparring class, think of all the things you put on before the fight. Now, translate that picture into your spiritual life. You wouldn't approach the fighting ring without your protective gear, and you should not approach life without God's protective armor.

Prepare for the Future

Did you know the Bible offers a plan for saving money? I Corinthians 16:2 suggests a way for sticking to a savings plan: "*On the first day of every week, each one of you should set aside a sum of money in keeping with your income, saving it up, so that when I come no collections will have to be made.*" In this verse, Paul is speaking to the churches of his time and instructing them on how to save to advance the kingdom of God by supporting missionaries. Many Christians have different theories on saving. Some say there is no need to save because God will take care of them, and they quote Matthew 6:19-20 as their source for this opinion. However, savings is indeed a Biblical principle.

A key ingredient in this savings plan is diligence. Verse 5 says *"The plans of the diligent lead to profit as surely as haste leads to poverty."* Consider the ant in Proverbs 6:6-11. The ant has no leader but works diligently to store up for the winter. Following the ant, scripture references the lazy person who does not work and falls into poverty, which is just the opposite of the diligent ant. While saving might seem like a mundane task and with a low interest rate may seem to never accumulate, God instructs us to remain diligent. If you have ever studied compounding interest you will know that interest on interest can add up quickly if you remain faithful to put money into savings. Maybe not in the short run, but in the long run you will see your investment climb.

Another financial area that Proverbs 21 addresses is *how* to spend your money. Read verse 17, *"Whoever loves pleasure will become poor; whoever loves wine and olive oil will never be rich."* Let's be clear that God is not telling us to never buy things that bring us pleasure. If that were the case, we would never go on family vacations – something we love to do! He's simply telling us to be smart with our money. If you make purchases that your budget cannot support or habitually spend more money than you make, you will become poor. Learning how to create a budget is wise in helping prepare for future expenses and unplanned emergencies. Ants understand this, so it should be pretty simple for us humans to understand!

Some business students from a local college visited our school because they wanted to interview Chris about running their own gym. One student made the comment, "I could never have enough money to own all this." Chris explained that what we have today did not happen overnight. It took years of sacrifice and spending money on the important things, not just the frivolous. We had a vision for our school and continually made financial decisions that supported that goal. Little by little we made purchases within our school budget that helped us grow and obtain the equipment and necessities we need to operate the school. Some months we didn't move forward, some months we took one step forward and two steps back, and other months we made great gains. Financial planning and preparation is a marathon, not a 100-meter dash and you just have to put in the miles.

Points to Remember

- *Preparation is the key to success. Living a life for Christ requires us to prepare our motives, thoughts and actions to achieve what He has called us to be.*

- *Stay diligent in doing the mundane tasks of preparation. You will be thankful that you are ready when the battle comes.*
- *Like the ant prepares for the winter, so we should prepare for financial situations before they surprise us.*

| 22 |

A Humble Attitude

A good name is more desirable than great riches, to be esteemed is better than silver or gold.

²Rich and poor have this in common, The Lord is the Maker of them all.

³The prudent see danger and take refuge, but the simple keep going and pay the penalty.

⁴Humility is the fear of the Lord; its wages are riches and honorand life.

⁵In the paths of the wicked are snares and pitfalls, but those who would preserve their life stay far from them.

⁶Start children off on the way they should go, and even when they are old they will not turn from it.

⁷The rich rule over the poor, and the borrower is slave to the lender.

⁸Whoever sows injustice reaps calamity, and the rod they wield in fury will be broken.

⁹The generous will themselves be blessed, for they share their food with the poor.

¹⁰Drive out the mocker, and out goes strife; quarrels and insults are ended.

¹¹One who loves a pure heart and who speaks with grace will have the king for a friend.

[12]The eyes of the Lord keep watch over knowledge, but he frustrates the words of the unfaithful.

[13]The sluggard says, "There's a lion outside! I'll be killed in the public square!"

[14]The mouth of an adulterous woman is a deep pit; a man who is under the Lord's wrath falls into it.

[15]Folly is bound up in the heart of a child, but the rod of discipline will drive it far away.

[16]One who oppresses the poor to increase his wealth and one who gives gifts to the rich—both come to poverty.

[17]Pay attention and turn your ear to the sayings of the wise; apply your heart to what I teach,

[18]for it is pleasing when you keep them in your heart and have all of them ready on your lips.

[19]So that your trust may be in the Lord, I teach you today, even you.

[20]Have I not written thirty sayings for you, sayings of counsel and knowledge,

[21]teaching you to be honest and to speak the truth, so that you bring back truthful reports to those you serve?

[22]Do not exploit the poor because they are poor and do not crush the needy in court,

[23]for the Lord will take up their case and will exact life for life.

[24]Do not make friends with a hot-tempered person, do not associate with one easily angered,

[25]or you may learn their ways and get yourself ensnared.

[26]Do not be one who shakes hands in pledge or puts up security for debts;

[27]if you lack the means to pay, your very bed will be snatched from under you.

[28]Do not move an ancient boundary stone set up by your ancestors.

[29]Do you see someone skilled in their work? They will serve before kings; they will not serve before officials of low rank.

Chapter 22: Daily Devotional

In order to learn anything, we must approach the learning with a sense of humility. A humble attitude sets the stage for foundational learning that all other learning can be built upon. When we are humble to learn, eager to listen and willing to work hard, God has promised that success will come our way. We will advance to new levels and doors will be opened for us.

Without this sense of humility, an attitude of arrogance rises that closes the door to new ideas, different perspectives, and creative suggestions. Over the years, martial artists have come to our school and, because they previously trained somewhere else, feel they know more than our instructors. They challenge the techniques being taught and argue that their training is superior. While some have had great skill and potential, their mindset closed the door to learning new, and possibly better, skills and instruction. Learning is an act that never stops and should be embraced in all areas of life.

Training for a Lifetime

There is a lot to be said about a good education. Many educational institutions show salary figures a person would earn with a bachelor's degree, compared to a person without a bachelor's degree. Statistics show any type of credentials or skills-based training will greatly impact your financial situation and provide you with substantial benefits over time. Not only does a good education provide you with monetary gains, it also allows you to network with others, build relationships, become a better communicator and critical thinker, and instill a sense of accomplishment and greater discipline. There are many other benefits to add to this list, but one of the greatest is that no one can take this training from you. Once you earn an education, it's yours for a lifetime.

The same is true of your martial arts training. The knowledge you gain from learning and the discipline your training instills in you is yours – for a lifetime. The foundation of this learning must be solid to allow you to build upon it. Just as a house is built on a solid foundation, we can build our solid martial arts foundation through class attendance, diligent practice, and consistently applying the teachings of our master instructors. We can compare this solid foundational training to the words of Jesus in Matthew: *"Therefore everyone who hears these words of mine and puts them into practice is like a wise man who built his house on the rock. The rain came down, the streams rose, and the winds blew and beat against that house; yet it did not fall, because it had its foundation on the rock"* (Matthew 7:24-25).

Proverbs 22 tells us a lot about training and discipline. In our discussion in Chapter 4, I used the phrase "guard your grill" as it relates your training. This also applies to what the writer is teaching in verse 5: *"...those who would preserve their life stay far from them."* "Them" can be applied to a lot of areas in our life:

- people who negatively influence us
- places that dishonor God
- thoughts that steal our joy
- activities that lead us down the wrong path

Learning how to guard ourselves is part of the training we receive as children, and the instruction we get as martial artists new to the sport. This instruction is ours for life. Verse 6 reads, *"Start children off on the way they should go, and even when they are old they will not turn from it."* The training becomes embedded in us and is part of who we are as we grow older. We continue to draw on it throughout our lives and our martial arts development.

Today, my grown children remind me of times when I disciplined them. We laugh about it now, but it was not fun at the time. Both of my children had a strong will which they tried to use to get what they wanted. My daughter would scream when we put her in the car seat, simply because she wanted out. My son would not go to bed at night and fought to get his way. These might sound like normal child behaviors, but they were not tolerated in our house. My husband and I lovingly disciplined our kids to understand that we were the authority in the home and to respect authority. This does not mean they never fought us again, but it does mean that both of my children have a respect for authority and for those that serve above them. We trained them at an early age, and it is very present in their lives as adults.

Understanding the importance of authority will serve as a guard to protect you from a bruised reputation, loss of a job, or ruined relationships. How can your training be embedded for a lifetime? We can find the answers in verses 17-19.

1. Pay attention: maintain your focus on what is being taught
2. Listen: be intentional in your focus. Don't just hear the words, listen to them.
3. Apply the teaching: once you have heard the instruction, do it. Demonstrate your understanding.
4. Be prepared: the verse reads *"ready on your lips."* Know how to act, what to say and when to respond because you have trained for the task.
5. Trust in the Lord: know He will help you recall your training at the right time

Follow these five steps to continue in your educational journey and build on the foundations of your early teaching.

What's in You?

Both of our children ran in a track club when they were young. At one meet, Jenna was waiting in her check-in station when another girl in her 200-meter heat asked her, "So, what are you mixed with?" The confused look on Jenna's face caused the girl to explain that she herself was biracial and she wanted to know Jenna's biracial make-up too. (Our kids are a "mix" that comes from a white mother and Mexican father.) Once the confusion passed, the young girls shared their racial make-up with each other. There was no disrespect intended – just two girls sharing about who they were.

As a martial artist, you may have received training in various styles and disciplines from arnis to taekwondo. You may attend a school that offers multiple opportunities for learning to give you a well-rounded training. At our gym alone, Chris's base is taekwondo, but he also wrestled in high school and college, so he incorporates grappling into his teaching. His father trains in arnis and offers classes for those interested in this art. Another student competes professionally in the mixed martial arts circuit and gives special training for those interested in MMA. All of these opportunities become pieces of what your martial arts training is mixed with and encompasses a broader base of knowledge.

Your training is what is "in you." Our pastor used to give an analogy about the importance of what is in you. He said that if you have a glass of water and you shake that glass of water, water will come out. What you store inside of you will come out when you are faced with adversity. It's just like if you were attacked on the street. Your martial arts training would likely come out of you to defend yourself. Whatever we put in our minds is what will be manifested when we encounter events in life. The question is, "What's in you that will come out?"

As a martial artist, the tenets of taekwondo along with the physical training should be embedded in you. As a Christian, the qualities of Christ should be embedded in us. To guarantee that what comes out of you is beneficial to others and pleasing to God, you can follow the basic instructions in the Bible. Verses 20-21 tell us that the Bible has words of counsel and knowledge that teach us to use true and reliable words. When you put these types of words in you, this will be the language that comes out when you are shaken. The way to ensure what's in you is wise requires spending time with God daily and getting to know the words and actions He wants to come out of you, so you then can show His love to others.

Humility and Hard Work

For many years I served as the Christian Education director at our church and, while we had no official credentials, Chris and I were considered the children's pastors. The time came when we felt like God was directing us to leave our church and serve in a church in another community. Our new pastor recognized that we were workers and immediately plugged us into working the children's program. Our first summer, we took kids to church camp and Chris served as a group leader while I was put in the kitchen. In all honesty, I felt completely defeated, as if I no longer had value. I remember walking the campus at night telling God I had no ministry and I felt like He had nothing for me any longer. I was reduced to cutting onions in the kitchen. You talk about pride – that's it! The Bible is very clear that not everyone will be the pastor, but that every individual has a valuable part in His Kingdom. I Corinthians 12:14 tells us of the diversity needed in the church, *"Even so the body is not made up of one part but of many."* What I needed was a dose of humility.

There are two things in Proverbs 22 that bring honor to God – humility and hard work. While some people might not be able to see the connection between these two, the Bible tells us that God connects them by requiring them of us and blessing us for doing them. Verse 4 reads, *"Humility is the fear of the Lord; its wages are riches and honor and life."* Fearing the Lord means to reverence Him, and when we reverence Him, we will work at any job as if we are working for Him, not just the boss. As a kitchen worker I created my own pity party and failed to see that my job of feeding all these kids was just as important as my husband's job of taking them to daily activities and nightly services. I might have done the work, but my attitude did not bring honor to God or myself.

Humility opens the door for learning and hard work helps you walk through it. Working hard means not making excuses as the sluggard does who is described in verse 13. Hard work will cause you to be described as the man in verse 29, *"Do you know a hard-working man? He shall be successful and stand before kings"* (Living Bible). A hard-working person is humble enough to take any assignment given to him or her and tackle it with all their might. Humility says, "I don't know it all; I'm not better than anyone; I'm here to serve." God's promise for a person with that attitude is wealth, honor, life, and success.

Look at the martial arts belt you wear around your waist. Regardless of what color it is, you have a place in your dojo. If you do not like that place, you simply need to be humble to learn and work hard to advance.

Points to Remember

- *Embrace instruction and training. Make learning a part of who you are, so it guides your words and actions.*
- *Put the Word of God in you. What's in you will come out when the world shakes you.*
- *There's no substitute for hard work. Take the job given to you and give it all you have.*

| 23 |

The Big Picture

When you sit to dine with a ruler, note well what is before you, ²and put a knife to your throat if you are given to gluttony.

³Do not crave his delicacies, for that food is deceptive.

⁴Do not wear yourself out to get rich; do not trust your own cleverness.

⁵Cast but a glance at riches, and they are gone, for they will surely sprout wings and fly off to the sky like an eagle.

⁶Do not eat the food of a begrudging host, do not crave his delicacies

⁷for he is the kind of person who is always thinking about the cost. "Eat and drink," he says to you, but his heart is not with you.

⁸You will vomit up the little you have eaten and will have wasted your compliments.

⁹Do not speak to fools, for they will scorn your prudent words.

¹⁰Do not move an ancient boundary stone or encroach on the fields of the fatherless,

¹¹for their Defender is strong; he will take up their case against you.

¹²Apply your heart to instruction and your ears to words of knowledge.

¹³Do not withhold discipline from a child; if you punish them with the rod, they will not die.

¹⁴Punish them with the rod and save them from death.

[15]My son, if your heart is wise, then my heart will be glad indeed

[16]my inmost being will rejoice when your lips speak what is right.

[17]Do not let your heart envy sinners, but always be zealous for the fear of the Lord.

[18]There is surely a future hope for you, and your hope will not be cut off.

[19]Listen, my son, and be wise, and set your heart on the right path:

[20]Do not join those who drink too much wine or gorge themselves on meat,

[21]for drunkards and gluttons become poor, and drowsiness clothes them in rags.

[22]Listen to your father, who gave you life, and do not despise your mother when she is old.

[23]Buy the truth and do not sell it—wisdom, instruction and insight as well.

[24]The father of a righteous child has great joy; a man who fathers a wise son rejoices in him.

[25]May your father and mother rejoice; may she who gave you birth be joyful!

[26]My son, give me your heart and let your eyes delight in my ways,

[27]for an adulterous woman is a deep pit, and a wayward wife is a narrow well.

[28]Like a bandit she lies in wait and multiplies the unfaithful among men.

[29]Who has woe? Who has sorrow? Who has strife? Who has complaints? Who has needless bruises? Who has bloodshot eyes?

[30]Those who linger over wine, who go to sample bowls of mixed wine.

[31]Do not gaze at wine when it is red, when it sparkles in the cup, when it goes down smoothly!

[32]In the end it bites like a snake and poisons like a viper.

[33]Your eyes will see strange sights, and your mind will imagine confusing things.

[34]You will be like one sleeping on the high seas, lying on top of the rigging.

[35]"They hit me," you will say, "but I'm not hurt! They beat me, but I don't feel it! When will I wake up so I can find another drink?"

Chapter 23: Daily Devotional

"He can't see the forest for the trees." This is an expression that is said when someone is so wrapped up in the details that they cannot see the big picture. Often the details of a situation can deter you from focusing on the greater problem or answering the bigger need. In an interview, a Vietnam Air Force pilot described how his training taught him that he must be thinking about the flight six miles ahead, not just the present space they were in. This pilot's training taught him to always be looking forward.

This chapter of Proverbs encourages us to not get lost in the details of the trees. It's easy to get distracted by the world and take our eyes, thoughts, and focus off of Christ. As we'll see in this chapter, it's important to tend to details, but not at the expense of losing sight of the big picture. Ultimately, by keeping your focus on Christ, you will be a blessing to others, become a better version of yourself, and avoid many pitfalls of life.

Focus on the Important

Having financial means is an important concern in our world today and while we need to plan for our financial future by budgeting and creating retirement eggs, it should not be the priority that consumes our minds. Money can be a scary and stressful thing if you allow it to overtake you. There was a recent news report of a man who got so caught up in day trading on the stock market that he committed suicide when he saw how much money he lost in one day. God has a plan to keep us financially blessed by following the directions he provides in His Word. God does not intend for us to miss the blessings of wealth. In fact in Proverbs 22, we just read that God will provide riches, honor and life to those that fear (reverence) Him. It's our job to plan, as we learned in Proverbs 21, and trust God to do His part as He has promised.

Instead of money, our most important concern should be doing what Christ has called us to do and who He has called us to be. Riches are here today, gone tomorrow, as we read in verse 5. Just look at the many people who have won the lottery or made millions in their jobs, only to lose it all. The Bible states in 1 John 2:17 that *The world and its desires pass away, but whoever does the will of God lives forever."*

What does it mean for us to do God's will? The poet C.T. Studd said it best: "Only one life, 'twill soon be past, only what's done for Christ will last." I told you in a previous chapter that we have never made a living off of operating our martial arts school and Chris and I have always worked full-time jobs. God has blessed us to pay the bills, keep the doors open, and have all we need. In doing this, we have made wonderful friendships, prayed with hundreds of individuals and families, and ministered to countless families in need. We always saw the martial arts school as our mission field. Some have raised an eyebrow when we equate martial arts to mission work, but God can truly use anything and anyone to do His will. Chris and I are content with what we have at Ultimate Martial Arts and look back over the years to see how God graciously provided. We have been in business since 1994, growing from our basement to a beautiful space at our local mall. "Riches" does not always mean money – I believe riches also include the peace, joy, and blessings we receive.

Some of the blessings we have received have come in unusual ways. People have blessed us over the years by cleaning the school, mowing our yard, buying us supper, giving unexpected gifts, taking care of our dogs, fixing our cars, and, most importantly, being our friends. God has been good because we have focused on the most important – allowing Him to use us to interact with others and be the hands and feet of

Christ. Verse 4 tells us to not *"weary yourself trying to get rich"* (Living Bible). This is a lesson I had to learn and really work on to trust God with – especially when I could not see how we were going to pay the rent at the school. We weren't trying to get rich, rather, we were just trying to get by.

During those times and during the entire lifespan of our school, Chris has always given away lessons by allowing people to work off their tuition. I learned to not be surprised when I saw someone mowing my lawn or pulling weeds in the front yard. We didn't worry about getting rich, and I even learned that if we were faithful in a little, God was always faithful in the big. Chris's goal was to get people in the school where he could demonstrate Christ to others. It is fun to see what God will do when we let go of the things that seem so important and let Him use us.

Don't Envy Those Who Have "It"

You define "it." "It" can be anything someone else has that you want and are envious of.

Have you ever had a student in your dojo who it seems everything just comes easily to? Their forms are flawless, their techniques are sharp, and their fighting skills are solid. This student can speak commands in Japanese as if he or she were a native, can endure the physical demands of class, and can learn a new weapons form in a day. You, on the other hand, can't seem to get your belt tied right, forget your sparring gear at home, and get the moves in Won-Hyo and Yul-Gok mixed up on a regular basis. You want to be like that student, but it just does not come naturally to you.

At this point you have a choice – you can either become bitter or better. Bitter would say, "That guy gets all the breaks. Master Rangel just likes him more. I can't get better because no one will help me." Better says, "If I work hard, good things will happen. I just need to use focus and concentration to develop myself and improve my skills."

Envy is a cancer that robs us from achieving our best. If we focus on what we don't have, we will never uncover what we do have. Christ has given us unique talents and abilities that we can't compare to others. For example, one talent I absolutely do not have is musical abilities. I cannot sing to save my life and my piano teacher in 3rd grade told me I should just quit. I used to want to be the person who led worship on stage at church and envied those who could. However, since I can't sing, I found what I can do and that is teach. Envy and self-pity can rob you and others of your unique talents. What if I had never started teaching and just got mad because I couldn't lead worship? Well, there would have been a lot of children who would have never learned about Jesus and given their hearts to Him.

If you can never do your form to the level of the other student in your dojo, that's okay. You can do your form with all you have, using your best abilities, and infusing all the energy you can possibly muster. In high school I tried out for the drill team (today it's called the dance team) even though I could not dance. Doing choreography and executing dance moves were another of those abilities God did not give me, but I tried out anyway and made the team. I couldn't dance, but I could smile. I smiled so hard through that try-out my face nearly fell off. All the judges scored me low on dance ability, but I won them over with my smile!

Don't focus on what you can't do; focus on what you *can* do. Do you have a loud voice? Then kihap with all your might. Do you have great posture? Then stand tall and proud when you present your form. Do you have a good vertical? Then get as high as you can when you demonstrate your roundhouse.

If you follow God's instruction of working hard, planning ahead, and putting Him first, you will experience blessings that are as unique to you as your talents are. Regardless if we always follow God's ways, there will be people in our lives who seem to get ahead without following the rules and are unhampered by Christian responsibilities. When we encounter those types of people, verses 17-18 provide great advice and hope for us to follow: *"Do not let your heart envy sinners, but always be zealous for the fear of the Lord. There is surely a future hope for you and your hope will not be cut off."* Keep doing you. God promises a hope and future even if we don't experience it in this life.

Your Mom was Right

Does your mom ever remind you that she was right? I know I like to do this to my own children. If we are honest, there are likely times when all of us have thought we knew more than our parents, or anyone else for that matter. Most of the time that is faulty thinking, and we would be smart to rely on the experience of our parents. The writer of Proverbs tells us in verse 22, *"Listen to your father's advice and don't despise an old mother's experience"* (Living Bible). Our parents have good insight that can help us navigate the challenges and decisions of our life. Children often have the same tendencies of their parents and it's probable that children will face similar situations in their lives as their parents did. If the child will listen to their parental advice, they can avoid the pitfalls that their parents experienced and react in a different – and better – way.

As parents, we know our kids. Jenna is a mini-me and Jared is a mini-Chris. In most situations Jenna will react just like I would, while Jared will behave just like Chris. For example, Chris is a dreamer and is always coming up with new ideas for a business we should start. Jared is a dreamer too. When he was trying to decide what vocation to pursue, he thought he would become a specialist in the Coast Guard, then a snowboard instructor in Colorado, and then a police officer in Texas. He finally settled on being a firefighter and finished his degree and training, but not without lots of changes in the direction he wanted to go. Because we know that Jared is a dreamer like Chris, it helped us as parents approach his ever-changing directions and guide him in the way that best suited his personality.

If we want our children to heed our advice, it comes down to our delivery. Verse 23 reads, *"...hold on tightly to all the good sense you can get"*

(Living Bible). To help our children listen, embrace and apply the advice we offer, we have to consider how we say it. Being bossy, demanding, preachy, negative or condescending will get you nowhere. Like that saying, "You can catch more flies with honey than with vinegar" so it is with how you catch the respect of your child to listen. We know from verse 23 that getting good advice is smart, so learn to deliver your message in such a way that it's a *conversation* with your child instead of correction. How would you like to be talked to? After you answer that question, talk to your children the same way. Statements like "because I said so" or "I'm right because I'm the mom" do not provide children with the "why" they need to hear. Helping them understand your instructions will help them learn from your teaching.

The next two verses (24 and 25) are the blessings of creating a relationship with your children in which they listen, embrace, and apply your advice and experience. As a parent you will experience great joy, you will delight in your children, you will be glad, and you will rejoice! Those are the blessings that every parent longs for and cherishes. Having "advice-giving" conversations with your teenage children can be difficult, but if you start when they are toddlers it makes the teenage years much easier and you will really see the blessings when they are adults.

There is no area of life immune to our thinking that we are better than or know more than someone else. Think about this type of advice-giving, experience-sharing conversation in other areas of your life – particularly at the dojo. Replace "parent" with the name of your master instructor and children ("son") with your name. You might be a black belt and truly know your art; however, the experience of the instructor who taught you is still greater simply because of time. This time has afforded him or her more opportunities to learn, to compete, to instruct, and to discipline. There is always more to learn, and if you embrace being a life-long learner (verse 23) you will be the pride and joy of your instructor. You will be the student he or she will brag about, endorse, and promote both in and out of the dojo.

Points to Remember

- *Ask the Lord where you can be a blessing to others. You might be surprised to learn that your martial arts training is just the avenue to speak into someone's life.*
- *Whatever you attempt to do, give it all you've got. You have different talents that will come to light when you just do you.*
- *Don't be a know-it-all. Heed the lessons you can learn when you listen.*

| 24 |

Show Respect

Do not envy the wicked, do not desire their company;
²for their hearts plot violence, and their lips talk about making trouble.

³By wisdom a house is built, and through understanding it is established;

⁴Through knowledge its rooms are filled with rare and beautiful treasures.

⁵The wise prevail through great power, and those who have knowledge muster their strength.

⁶Surely you need guidance to wage war, and victory is won through many advisers.

⁷Wisdom is too high for fools; in the assembly at the gate they must not open their mouths.

⁸Whoever plots evil will be known as a schemer. The schemes of folly are sin, and people detest a mocker.

¹⁰If you falter in a time of trouble, how small is your strength!

¹¹ Rescue those being led away to death; hold back those staggering toward slaughter.

¹²If you say, "But we knew nothing about this," does not he who weighs the heart perceive it? Does not he who guards your life know it? Will he not repay everyone according to what they have done?

¹³Eat honey, my son, for it is good; honey from the comb is sweet to your taste.

¹⁴ Know also that wisdom is like honey for you: If you find it, there is a future hope for you, and your hope will not be cut off.

¹⁵Do not lurk like a thief near the house of the righteous, do not plunder their dwelling place;

¹⁶ for though the righteous fall seven times, they rise again, but the wicked stumble when calamity strikes.

¹⁷Do not gloat when your enemy falls; when they stumble, do not let your heart rejoice,

¹⁸ or the Lord will see and disapprove and turn his wrath away from them.

¹⁹Do not fret because of evildoers or be envious of the wicked,

²⁰ for the evildoer has no future hope, and the lamp of the wicked will be snuffed out.

²¹ Fear the Lord and the king, my son, and do not join with rebellious officials,

²² for those two will send sudden destruction on them, and who knows what calamities they can bring?

²³These also are sayings of the wise: To show partiality in judging is not good:

²⁴ Whoever says to the guilty, "You are innocent," will be cursed by peoples and denounced by nations.

²⁵ But it will go well with those who convict the guilty, and rich blessing will come on them.

²⁶An honest answer is like a kiss on the lips.

²⁷Put your outdoor work in order and get your fields ready; after that, build your house.

²⁸Do not testify against your neighbor without cause— would you use your lips to mislead?

²⁹ Do not say, "I'll do to them as they have done to me; I'll pay them back for what they did."

³⁰I went past the field of a sluggard, past the vineyard of someone who has no sense;

[31] thorns had come up everywhere, the ground was covered with weeds, and the stone wall was in ruins.

[32] I applied my heart to what I observed and learned a lesson from what I saw:

[33] A little sleep, a little slumber, a little folding of the hands to rest—

[34] and poverty will come on you like a thief and scarcity like an armed man.

Chapter 24: Daily Devotional

The principles of Proverbs 24 have played out many times in Chris's training. Wisdom, as we have learned, includes being humble. As I mentioned at the beginning of this book and again in Chapter 4, Chris showed no humility when he won a fight and got his nose broken because of his boastful attitude. He did not have the correct mental game, as this Proverb teaches us we should have. He also did not have "true iron" in his life; no one would give him an honest answer about his conduct in the ring. His opponent adhered to verse 29 and got his revenge against Chris's arrogance. Fast-forward over the years of owning a school and having a relationship with Christ, Chris has grown to value respect and he works hard to instill it in his students in the way they compete in the ring, how they kneel at attention at ringside, and how they interact with judges.

The way we act and train shows a lot about our character. To improve ourselves physically, mentally, and spiritually takes a daily focus on the things of God and the wisdom He expects us to seek. Focus on the truths in this Proverb to grow in each of the tenets of taekwondo.

A Smart Athlete

When I run marathons, I have learned to not look at any runner and think, "I can beat her!" Shape, size, height, and weight are no determinants for a runner who can finish the race before you. Even a runner with a tracheotomy in his throat beat me once! The same goes for martial arts. I have witnessed our best students lose to a student who I thought had no chance against us. The old saying, "Don't judge a book by its cover" applies here. As a competitor, we should not underestimate anyone or take anyone for granted. I'm sure you have witnessed an athletic competition when the better team lost because they did not respect their opponent enough to play their best.

As a martial artist, you work hard to prepare physically, but how much emphasis do you put on the mental part of the game? The creed at our martial arts school is "to prepare ourselves physically, mentally and spiritually with great character." It's important that all three tenets of this creed get equal commitment. Verse 5 helps us understand this thinking: *"A wise man is mightier than a strong man. Wisdom is mightier than strength"* (Living Bible). This seems a little contradictory to traditional thinking where we predict the best physically shaped athlete will win the competition, but Proverbs tells us that wisdom is equally as important.

As an example, let's look at my husband, Chris. Chris is a man of small stature, coming in at 5'4" and 150 pounds, but he rarely loses a fight. He watches his opponents and learns from them and uses the wisdom he has gained from that observation to give him an advantage in the ring. This is true of many athletes and teams – they watch film, study the tendencies of their opponent, and identify their weaknesses before they even step on the mat. This is not to say that you should not train or physically prepare for the competition. But do not be fooled by someone you think you can "take." Wisdom is a vital part of strength.

Take this same thinking and apply it to our lives outside of the dojo. There are many things we think we can handle or easily overcome without much effort, but rather these things may take time, consideration, and commitment. Look at obesity for example. Today's world promotes unhealthy eating in many arenas. It's much less expensive to go to the store and purchase unhealthy food than to buy produce or healthy alternatives. Fast food is quick and convenient, but it often lacks the nutritional value we need to maintain a healthy lifestyle.

We met a friend a short time ago who was an amazing BMX biker and won many accolades for his biking talents. Not long into his career, he learned he had a brain tumor that sidelined his physical game and forced him to focus on his mental game, which was how to eat in such a way that helped his brain and overall health. It's easy to go through life and just eat whatever, whenever you want. We are blessed in America that food can be easily obtained for the majority of our citizens and we blindly eat without thinking of the consequences. Our friend's brain tumor was not caused because he did not take care of his body, but it focused him to become wise about another area that impacted him: his nutrition. Striving for wisdom is a daily battle, just as is our physical condition. Wisdom should be applied to all areas of our lives – both in and out of the dojo.

Times of Trouble

We will all have trouble – it's no respecter of persons, and while we certainly don't like going through trouble, the lessons and growth we experience on the other side can be life-changing. While you are wading through the sea of trouble, verse 10 can provide you with a pep talk. You know, the talk your coach gives you when the training is tough. Verse 10 reads, *"If you falter in times of trouble, how small is your strength!"* I've heard many of Chris's pep talks to his students – some are not very uplifting like, "You better not lose to this kid," but others are pretty motivating. Some students, however, do respond better to the more direct approach! His goal in this moment is to remind the student to compete like a smart athlete who does not take the opponent for granted.

Training for a competition is always tough. We have an athlete who grew up in our community and now fights on the MMA circuit. When he comes home to visit family, he always works out at our gym. Watching him train and prepare for a fight is nothing less than incredible. Just hearing his stories of the amount of time he puts in the gym and the amount of weight he cuts is mind-blowing. He puts his body through a rigorous training camp, but he has a goal in mind and the daily challenges do not distract him from the bigger goal.

There is a story in the Bible where a man just couldn't overcome the daily troubles of life. If you turn in your Bible to Jeremiah chapter 12, you will read of Jeremiah's complaint to God. Jeremiah was complaining about the fairness of life – a complaint that we have all probably uttered at one point or another. Starting in verse 5 of this chapter, God answered Jeremiah and said, "If you can't handle the small stuff, how will you handle anything bigger?" (my paraphrase). Verse 5 hits the nail on the head: *"If you have raced with men on foot and they have worn you out, how can you compete with horses? If you stumble in the safe country, how will you manage in the thickets by the Jordan?"*

Sorry to break it to you, but life is going to throw you trouble. Many of these troubles are small potatoes that just happen in everyday life. You're tired from training? Well, suck it up! You're losing the match and you're frustrated? Well, refocus and use your training to gain an advantage. You stubbed your toe? There's an ice pack after the fight is over. Pushing through the small things builds our character, faith, and confidence to tackle the bigger challenges of life... and there will always be bigger ones to come. Don't throw up your hands in defeat, *"because the one who is in you is greater than the one who is in the world"* (I John 4:4). The trouble you face today is training you to overcome the more difficult situations you will face in the future.

An Honest Answer

It's hard to hear the truth sometimes. I remember when we took our daughter to her first pitching lessons. Her pitching coach was a good friend of ours and had taught many young girls to pitch. I told my friend to be honest with us about Jenna's abilities. "If she isn't cut out for this, please just tell me the truth." Chris and I have been coaches for many years and know that parents often look at their kids with blinders on. We didn't want to be those parents and truly wanted an honest answer. I knew my friend trusted me enough to not be offended by her honest answer.

In verse 26 the writer says, *"An honest answer is like a kiss on the lips."* In Proverbs a kiss was a sign of true friendship. It's the honest answer you give someone and you don't worry about hurting their feelings. You tell them just like you see it because you know that it will help them improve or avoid hurt. This type of answer really shows true friendship – if you love someone enough you will tell them the truth and if the friend trusts that friendship, they will appreciate you for it. But, let's face it, this is not easy. Giving "happy" answers is much easier than giving honest answers that run the risk of causing an offense.

Consider your martial arts instructor. If you signed up for class, paid your tuition and truly want to learn this art, you would expect correction. At any belt level there is always room for improvement, and it is your instructor's job to provide that corrective instruction to help you learn and improve. But what if your instructor is afraid of hurting your feelings and always tells you what a great job you are doing, without giving any constructive criticism? Filled with confidence, you sign up for a tournament and pay your entry fee to compete, expecting to be a viable contender. Then you finish dead last. Not only do you finish dead last, you are embarrassed because after seeing the others in your division you realize that you know absolutely nothing! Your embarrassment grows into anger and you quit martial arts because of it. If you had just been told the truth and given honest correction, all of this would have been avoided.

There are people who give truthful answers in a harsh way – you might call it "brutally honest" – and go overboard in their version of honesty. But what we are talking about here is that friend or instructor who has your best interests at heart and no other motive. You will know that person – just like I knew my friend when I asked her about my daughter's pitching abilities. That person cares about you and with that knowledge, it's easier to swallow the pill of truth.

Rule Reversal

The Golden Rule: *"Do to others as you would have them do to you"* (Luke 6:31). It's very likely that you have heard of this rule. Most people, Christ-followers or not, have used this rule to measure their kindness to others. If used, it is a good measuring stick to help us pause before we speak or act and consider the impact of our actions. Did you know there is a reverse version of the Golden Rule in Proverbs 24:29? *"Do not say, "I'll do to them as they have done to me; I'll pay them back for what they did."* This version says, "I'll get revenge" which is a very worldly reaction to most injustices. Revenge, however, is not God's way of dealing with injustice. If we apply this to our own lives, we should probably be thankful that revenge is NOT God's way.

Proverbs 24 gives us ways to reverse the way the rule is written in verse 29. Look at verses 17 and 28. In verse 17 we are told not to gloat over your enemies. If we are applying the Golden Rule, gloating is not something we would want done to us when we fail. Verse 28 tells us to not lie about others. Having lies told about you is very hurtful.

As martial artists, our challenge is to daily be respectful in all areas of our lives. Respect is not reserved for the upper belts in the dojo, but it is a characteristic that others would use to describe us in our everyday lives. Consider your actions today or even the past week. Would they pass the Golden Rule test or would they have the reverse of verse 29? Our challenge is to demonstrate the Christian martial artist character God has called us to show.

Points to Remember

- *Don't approach life with only having focused on the physical elements of training. Train in all three areas -- physical, mental, and spiritual -- to truly be prepared for the troubles ahead.*
- *Don't sweat the small stuff. And most stuff is small. There are bigger things on the horizon for you if you can overcome the daily obstacles in your path.*
- *Good friends tell each other the truth even if it hurts. This truthfulness can prevent long-lasting pain and preserve a solid friendship.*

| 25 |

Boundaries Protect Us

These are more proverbs of Solomon, compiled by the men of Hezekiah king of Judah:

²It is the glory of God to conceal a matter; to search out a matter is the glory of kings.

³As the heavens are high and the earth is deep, so the hearts of kings are unsearchable.

⁴Remove the dross from the silver, and a silversmith can produce a vessel;

⁵remove wicked officials from the king's presence, and his throne will be established through righteousness.

⁶Do not exalt yourself in the king's presence, and do not claim a place among his great men;

⁷it is better for him to say to you, "Come up here," than for him to humiliate you before his nobles.

⁸What you have seen with your eyes do not bring hastily to court, for what will you do in the end if your neighbor puts you to shame?

⁹If you take your neighbor to court, do not betray another's confidence,

¹⁰or the one who hears it may shame you and the charge against you will stand.

¹¹Like apples of gold in settings of silver is a ruling rightly given.

[12]Like an earring of gold or an ornament of fine gold is the rebuke of a wise judge to a listening ear.

[13]Like a snow-cooled drink at harvest time is a trustworthy messenger to the one who sends him; he refreshes the spirit of his master.

[14]Like clouds and wind without rain is one who boasts of gifts never given.

[15]Through patience a ruler can be persuaded, and a gentle tongue can break a bone.

[16]If you find honey, eat just enough— too much of it, and you will vomit.

[17]Seldom set foot in your neighbor's house— too much of you, and they will hate you.

[18]Like a club or a sword or a sharp arrow is one who gives false testimony against a neighbor.

[19]Like a broken tooth or a lame foot is reliance on the unfaithful in a time of trouble.

[20]Like one who takes away a garment on a cold day, or like vinegar poured on a wound, is one who sings songs to a heavy heart.

[21]If your enemy is hungry, give him food to eat; if he is thirsty, give him water to drink.

[22]In doing this, you will heap burning coals on his head, and the Lord will reward you.

[23]Like a north wind that brings unexpected rain is a sly tongue—which provokes a horrified look.

[24]Better to live on a corner of the roof than share a house with a quarrelsome wife.

[25]Like cold water to a weary soul is good news from a distant land.

[26]Like a muddied spring or a polluted well are the righteous who give way to the wicked.

[27]It is not good to eat too much honey, nor is it honorable to search out matters that are too deep.

[28]Like a city whose walls are broken through is a person who lacks self-control.

Chapter 25: Daily Devotional

Boundaries don't sound like a fun topic, but they truly are designed to help us lead a more fulfilling life. What comes to mind when you think of "boundaries?" Does this word produce a positive or negative connotation? Boundaries make me think of fences that keep animals in, lines on the road that keep cars in their lane, and ropes in a theatre that guide you to the ticket booth. If you see them as a positive, you probably find them as freeing because they define the limits without you having to think about them. I don't need to think about how fast I can drive – the speed limit tells me that. I don't have to create my open lanes in the pool – the ropes do that for me. If you see boundaries as negative, you likely feel they confine you from fun, restrict your freedom, and limit your opportunities.

Regardless of the lens you use to view boundaries, God puts them in our lives to protect us from the attacks of the enemy and to lead a safe and happy life. There are boundaries for how we talk, act, eat, spend money, and interact with others – all of which are designed by a God that loves us.

A Life with Boundaries

People might say that they want to do whatever they want. They don't want to be limited or restrained. An out-of-control lifestyle might sound fun for a while, but the end result is usually negative. The truth is we all want and need boundaries. They keep and make us feel safe; they ward off dangers and pitfalls; they help us maintain a focused life. Think of the boundaries of a martial arts ring – you must stay in those boundaries when you demonstrate your form and when you fight an opponent. The boundaries of the ring help us know where we are during our form presentation. They keep us from overstriding and ending up in the next ring, or from hitting your judges with your sticks. I have witnessed beginner students who have not quite mastered the art of their form and end up in the judge's lap at some point in their demonstration. They haven't learned how to stay within the boundaries of their ring, but that mastery will come as they continue to learn and practice.

The same is true of our Christian walk. As new Christians, we seem to walk outside the boundaries God has set for us quite a lot. This is often because we just don't know any better or haven't developed the spiritual toughness to say no to temptations. God has promised that He will teach us if we will listen to His voice. Isaiah 41:10 reminds us of God's promise of what we need to do when we just don't understand. *"So do not fear, for I am with you; do not be dismayed, for I am your God. I will strengthen you and help you; I will uphold you with my righteous right hand."*

We might step out of the ring, but God promises to help us get back in. John 14:16 reads, *"And I will ask the Father, and he will give you another advocate to help you and be with you forever."* The job of the Holy Spirit is to teach us and remind us when we are out of bounds. Our job is to listen and obey. The longer we walk with the Lord, the less these boundaries feel like boundaries. They just become who you are and how you live. You don't think about taking someone's gear from their unlocked, open locker – you just don't think that way anymore. It might have been a temptation at one point in your life, but it no longer is because you have transformed who you are in Christ.

If you continually step out of bounds and refuse to learn, your life will quickly spin out of control. Verse 28 reads, *"Like a city whose walls are broken through is a person who lacks self-control."* City walls in biblical times provided protection and defense for the citizens. While they restricted the coming and goings of the people, you did not want a city without walls because it would have left the inhabitants vulnerable to attacks by other nations or bandits. Self-control is the walls of our lives. By submitting to God and practicing self-control, we will learn to respond to the pressures of life in a way that shows Christ to others. Consider the things that are spinning out of control in your life and work on rebuilding that wall.

Don't Overdo It

A way to build boundaries is to not overindulge. It's like eating a Thanksgiving meal – it smells so good and your eyes become bigger than your stomach. You eat without thought because the food is wonderful, and seconds turn into thirds. Then it hits – the feeling of overeating. Now you are miserable, and your pants are too tight. It's easy to overindulge and not think about the consequences because it sure tastes good at the time. Proverbs 25:16 gives us great wisdom about this very thing: *"If you find honey, eat just enough -- too much of it, and you will vomit."*

It's okay to have fun, but we shouldn't live only for pleasure, ignoring all the other things in life. Jesus talks about it in Mark 4:19: *"but the worries of this life, the deceitfulness of wealth, and the desires for other things come in and choke the word, making it unfruitful."* Packing your life with material or worldly pursuits chokes out your time with God and His will for you. There is a balance and one cannot overtake the other. This is even true of our martial arts training. Martial arts is an amazing sport with endless benefits, but like anything else it has its boundaries. Your training should not take over your life – that's a surefire way to break down your walls, as we learned in verse 28. Martial arts has a physical training element that could take over your daily time and calendar, but it also has a mental element that focuses on meditation and controlling your mind. Meditation in your martial arts training can increase your awareness, calm, and focus, but, like anything else, it has its place and requires a balance. It too can be a foothold for the devil to gain access to your life and tear down your walls of self-control.

Stop for a moment and think about the places you overindulge. If you wrote out your day, hour by hour, where did you spend your time, thoughts, money, and energy? Look for anything that has taken too much indulgence and tipped the scales out of balance. Is your martial arts in balance with everything else in life? Anything that separates us from God can be a negative indulgence in our lives no matter how innocent it seems. God might be calling you to a new place in life and calling you out of something that could be hindering your walk with Him even if that something is "good" for you. Maybe it's exercise. Let's say you stay at the gym three hours every night and you come home too tired to spend time with God. If you are feeling a tug on your heart, that's God's way of saying this "good" thing has become a hindrance and to maintain your spiritual walls you might need to cut back to one hour at the gym for now. God knows what you need and just like sleep and exercise, you need a daily renewing of your mind and spirit by spending time with Him.

Put Boundaries in your Actions

Boundaries in your actions are another way to maintain strong spiritual walls. One way to have action boundaries is to act humble. Verses 6-7 tell us, *"Don't demand an audience with the king as though you were some powerful prince. It is better to wait for an invitation rather than be sent back to the end of the line, publicly disgraced"* (Living Bible). These verses tell us to not to think more of ourselves than we should. Taking a big bullhorn and shouting, "Hey, look at me! Look at how great I am!" does not get people to think highly of you. Instead, the Bible teaches us to do things the right way with integrity, that is not honor seeking, but rather quietly and faithfully as if we are doing it for the Lord. People will notice this type of attitude because actions speak louder than words. Jesus was so adamant about acting humbly that he teaches on humility in Luke 14:7-11. He teaches that true humility is not putting yourself down, but rather knowing who you are in Christ and comparing yourself only to Him and his standards.

Another action boundary is found in verses 8-9. In these verses, the writer of Proverbs is telling us to not be hot-tempered and spread gossip in anger. Have you ever heard the advice that if you are mad about something, you should count to 10 before you speak? That might really serve you well if you are prone to talking before you think. In that adrenaline-fueled moment of anger, you might say something you regret. Then, guess what? You can't get that toothpaste back in the tube. Those words are out there and nothing you can do can take them away. You might lose your friendships and ruin your reputation if you cannot set this action boundary in your life.

This can be a hard boundary to establish for many. In James 3:5, the Bible talks about how powerful the tongue is. *"So also the tongue is a small thing, but what enormous damage it can do"* (Living Bible). It takes work to control our tongue and even if we cannot achieve perfect control of it, we are still called to try. Remember, the Holy Spirit will help us and teach us as we daily learn and listen to the voice of God.

Points to Remember

- *Self-control is the wall of protection for our lives. Building and maintaining the wall requires our daily commitment to living within God's boundaries.*
- *Even the "good" things in life should have balance. If anything is taking the place of your time with God, you should reevaluate the priority and time you give it.*
- *Your life needs action boundaries. How you act will help you build strong spiritual walls in your life.*

| 26 |

Don't Be a Fool

Like snow in summer or rain in harvest, honor is not fitting for a fool.

²Like a fluttering sparrow or a darting swallow, an undeserved curse does not come to rest.

³A whip for the horse, a bridle for the donkey, and a rod for the backs of fools!

⁴Do not answer a fool according to his folly, or you yourself will be just like him.

⁵Answer a fool according to his folly, or he will be wise in his own eyes.

⁶Sending a message by the hands of a fool is like cutting off one's feet or drinking poison.

⁷Like the useless legs of one who is lame is a proverb in the mouth of a fool.

⁸Like tying a stone in a sling is the giving of honor to a fool.

⁹Like a thorn bush in a drunkard's hand is a proverb in the mouth of a fool.

¹⁰Like an archer who wounds at random is one who hires a fool or any passer-by.

¹¹As a dog returns to its vomit, so fools repeat their folly.

¹²Do you see a person wise in their own eyes? There is more hope for a fool than for them.

¹³A sluggard says, "There's a lion in the road, a fierce lion roaming the streets!"

¹⁴As a door turns on its hinges, so a sluggard turns on his bed.

¹⁵A sluggard buries his hand in the dish; he is too lazy to bring it back to his mouth.

¹⁶A sluggard is wiser in his own eyes than seven people who answer discreetly.

¹⁷Like one who grabs a stray dog by the ears is someone who rushes into a quarrel not their own.

¹⁸Like a maniac shooting flaming arrows of death

¹⁹is one who deceives their neighbor and says, "I was only joking!"

²⁰Without wood a fire goes out; without a gossip a quarrel dies down.

²¹As charcoal to embers and as wood to fire, so is a quarrelsome person for kindling strife.

²²The words of a gossip are like choice morsels; they go down to the inmost parts.

²³Like a coating of silver dross on earthenware are fervent lips with an evil heart.

²⁴Enemies disguise themselves with their lips, but in their hearts they harbor deceit.

²⁵Though their speech is charming, do not believe them, for seven abominations fill their hearts. ²⁶Their malice may be concealed by deception, but their wickedness will be exposed in the assembly.

²⁷Whoever digs a pit will fall into it; if someone rolls a stone, it will roll back on them.

²⁸A lying tongue hates those it hurts, and a flattering mouth works ruin.

Chapter 26: Daily Devotional

Let me be completely honest: I love school! I have been in school for my entire life, from being a student, to a teacher, to a high school administrator, to now a college professor – it's all I've known for my entire career. Someone like me who has been in school or works toward a degree could be characterized as "educated." Being educated can mean learning more "head knowledge," but it is truly powerful when knowledge becomes "heart knowledge" as well. Just because someone says they are educated, does not mean they are not what Proverbs 26 calls a fool. A fool can be educated, but they refuse to allow their head knowledge to impact their life and alter who they are. A change of heart is what God is saying that a fool needs in order to become wise.

Look how many times Proverbs 26 uses the word "fool" or the word "rebel" in the Living Bible. It's clear in this chapter that being a fool is not a desirable characteristic for anyone. A fool's ways are hopeless because they are so contradictory to the life God has called us to live, but God can help guide the fool to a place of wisdom if they have a change of heart.

A Hopeless Path

The first 11 verses in this chapter show us how to interact with fools. What is a fool exactly? It's a person who lacks judgment or sense. To me, being called a "fool" would be one of the greatest insults because a fool lacks the capacity to show any common sense. Let's look at the top 10 ways to work with a fool from this chapter.

1. A fool should not be given any honor. The Bible compares giving honor to a fool as getting snow in the summer -- it just doesn't happen (verse 1).
2. Fools must be taught using strict measures. They don't listen, so the Bible says that you must *put a rod to his back* like you would train a *horse with a whip* (verse 3). Fools are so resistant to teach-

ing that you must be direct with your words and firm in your actions.

3. It's a waste of time to argue with a fool. Regardless of your efforts, they will remain a fool. You will simply be stooping to their level and will gain nothing in the end (verse 4).

4. Verse 5 seems like a contradiction to verse 4, but they are really saying the same thing by showing the contradiction between reason and stupidity. You might realize that answering a fool is a waste of time, but on the other hand, giving an answer might show how stupid the fool is and expose their ignorance. So, you must decide – is it worth exposing the fool's idiocy or are you better to just walk away?

5. Fools twist your words. You cannot entrust anything of importance to a fool. Telling a fool to deliver a message or perform a job can backfire because they will not follow instructions and change the delivery to meet their thinking. Verse 6 says that trusting a fool is as dumb as drinking poison!

6. Trying to give a fool advice is pointless. Fools are so oblivious to wisdom that no matter if they memorize a proverb word for word and can recite it at the drop of a hat, it will not impact them. It's as useless as a paralyzed body part (verse 7). Fools do not have a receptive attitude and words, no matter how good they are, are just words to them.

7. What does a slingshot do? It catapults an object at a distance further than you can throw with your arm. By tying a rock into the sling, it makes the sling unusable. In fact, the rock that you tied in the sling could easily come back and hit you! Verse 8 is comparing this useless sling to giving honor to a fool. Imagine a situation where your co-worker is causing constant issues and ruining morale at work. Your boss decides that by promoting this person the discord will stop, causing the person to improve his or her attitude and become a loyal, happy employee. This typically never works. This person needs a heart change, not a job change. This employee now has the power to inflict real discord

at work and things just got worse. Giving honor to a fool is never a good idea.

8. Fools cannot process advice. In verse 9 the fool is compared to a drunk person with a thornbush. A drunkard can be so intoxicated that they cannot even feel the prick of the thorns. Alcohol can dull your senses and cause you to make irrational decisions. The prick of a thorn on a sober person would caution them to stay away and to remove the thorn before it causes further damage. The fool is like the drunkard who cannot feel the thorn because they cannot process corrective advice that hurts – it's the type of advice that needs to be told, but can hurt when you get it. The fool will take that advice and think you are talking about someone else. It surely cannot apply to them! The fool will only apply that advice to whomever they are rebelling against at the time.

9. Fools will ruin your business. If you are a business owner, do your research before hiring anyone. Your new hire should be qualified and have references speaking of characteristics that promote teamwork and collaboration. Hiring a fool will bring trouble and toxic behavior that will negatively impact your work culture. You will likely get more work out of an untrained, unskilled worker than a professional fool.

    1. If you make the mistake and hire a fool, you will likely have to work through four steps to get rid of them.
        1. Reassignment – give them another job and see if they can do it.
        2. Remove responsibilities and any future opportunities for advancement.
        3. Demote the person to a lower status or pay grade.
        4. Terminate – they have to go.

10. Fools never learn. This is the definition of insanity: doing the same thing over and over and expecting different results. The fool repeats the same mistakes, says the same inaccuracies, and

follows the same poor advice repeatedly. Like the dog, he *"returns to his vomit"* (verse 11).

This is a sad list and one that I hope does not describe you. If you find there is some level of foolishness in your life, all is not lost. You just have to be willing to accept instruction and truly have a desire to change. As we have learned, God is waiting and willing to help us if we surrender to Him and ask for help.

One Thing Worse

We had a student who always wanted to fight with his hands down. He was a very fast and explosive fighter, so he thought he could win by using his speed. While taekwondo is a sport that relies mostly on kicking, you still need your hands to block, protect, and counter. Not only did he keep his hands down, he would taunt his opponents by leaning his head forward in a way that said, "Come on. Just try to hit me." His confidence grew as he fought in many local tournaments and won using this strategy – regardless of not heeding instruction to "guard his grill." Finally, when he attended the U.S. Open tournament in Las Vegas, he found other world-class opponents who were as quick as he was and that hands-down strategy left him beat and out of the tournament much sooner than he should have been. This student's fighting strategy was not only foolish but showed his level of conceit.

It's hard to believe after reading all of that, but verse 12 tells us there is one thing worse than being a fool and that is being conceited. Conceit means to be excessively proud of yourself or vain.

Romans 12:16 spells it out pretty clearly, *"Do not be proud, but be willing to associate with people of low position. Do not be conceited."* This is not the same as being proud of yourself for doing a good job or for passing your belt test or winning gold in the state tournament. You should be proud of the accomplishments and victories in your life. This type of pride in verse 12 ignores all humility. This person thinks so highly of himself that he won't talk to certain people, he won't associate with those he feels are beneath him, and he treats others with contempt. This type of person would not be found helping a new student who is joining class, cleaning up after others, or giving positive accolades that would give another student a higher status. This person projects an attitude that makes it obvious he thinks life is all about him.

A fool – well, they are just dumb and often have no clue about life around them, but a conceited person knows exactly what he is doing and does not care. That's why there's more hope for the fool. They sometimes act out of a lack of knowledge and comprehension, which can be taught if the fool is willing to try. Woe to the prideful who won't try to change. Proverbs 16:18 reads, *"Pride goes before destruction, and a haughty spirit before a fall."* Pride can trip you up and put you flat on your face. Pride puts stumbling blocks in your way and blinds you from seeing them. To get pride under control, if you suffer from a conceited heart, start in the dojo by simply helping another student. It's a small act that will start destroying this stronghold in your life. Constantly be on the lookout for other ways to put someone before yourself.

Lazy is the Fool

Another form of foolishness is laziness. We have seen this same teaching in Proverbs chapters 6 and 10 and here it is again in chapter 26. I would guess that if you are enrolled in a martial arts class and attend in regular fashion, you have overcome laziness to some degree. Laziness would keep you from engaging in physical activity and working to better yourself. Being a martial artist is one way to overcome the sin of laziness because you are engaging your body to exercise, your mind to think, and your spirit to flourish and develop.

Laziness can be a battle in your mind if you let it. It's easy to come up with hundreds of reasons why you should not work, exercise, or improve. Laziness that is not kept in check will grow like a cancer and the one excuse will turn into daily excuses that confine you to your bed. The more you feed laziness, the more it takes over your life. The less you do, the less you desire to do, and the more useless you will become. Laziness robs you of the life God has prepared for you. It takes away your health and your mind and reduces you to a person who sits in their house playing solitaire.

We all have days where we show up at the dojo and just don't feel productive. We are tired and don't have any energy to get the muscles pumping. We've all been there. This is not the same as being lazy. Lazy sits in a chair. Lazy won't go to work. Lazy watches TV for hours. Lazy is unmotivated, unambitious, uncreative, unenthusiastic, un - everything! Lazy has no place in the life of a martial artist. A true martial artist is daily growing, always thinking, and continually making progress in all areas of their life. Laziness keeps you from fulfilling the great commission Jesus gave us in Matthew 28 to *GO* and make disciples. You can't make disciples when you are lying in bed and not interacting with anyone. Martial arts can be your avenue to fulfill the commission God has called us to.

Laziness can be overcome. For me, I need a plan that is easy to follow, posted in a visible location, that tells me exactly what I need to do. When I am training for a marathon, I print my running schedule and put it on the fridge. I don't have to think about how many miles I am going to run because the plan has it all laid out for me from day one to race day.

Training for anything can be hard and thoughts of quitting are not uncommon. So, get a plan to overcome that falling-off point that takes you back to being lazy. Put one foot in front of the other with small, realistic steps that get you to a goal. Maybe your goal is within the dojo or maybe it's something like learning a new language or writing a book. Create a plan that helps you take steps forward, out of the funk of laziness. Working truly is good for the soul – it gives you purpose for the day and gives you the opportunity to be the hands and feet of Christ to those you encounter.

This does not only apply to our physical self, but also our spiritual self. We are foolish if we are too lazy to remove ourselves from the dangers of the world. We might be lazy about reading God's word, taking time to talk to Him, or going to church. Staying in relationship with God keeps us from getting spiritually lazy and falling into a life that He did not design for us. Laziness might also be a lack of effort to stop doing addictive things that hurt your body, or a lack of effort to tame your tongue – which we learned in the last chapter takes work! Work hard to not let your laziness separate you from a life of prosperity and fulfillment. Ask others for help and find an accountability partner to help you fight the good fight.

Stop Talking Trash

"Talking trash" is usually interpreted as being boastful to intimidate someone, talking about someone behind their back, or telling stories that you know are untrue. There is always a trash-talker in every crowd. We even have them in our dojo, but typically if Master Rangel hears it the person must prove it or suffer the consequences of their talk. Trash talking doesn't really benefit anyone and it's typically one person trying to make him or herself feel better. But there is one type of trash-talk that is particularly harmful and can leave a lasting impression. That talk is called gossip. Spreading gossip, like laziness, is another form of foolishness.

It's unfortunate how much people love gossip. Verse 22 in the Living Bible reads, *"Gossip is a dainty morsel eaten with great relish."* Gossip spreads like wildfire and usually gets embellished with each recounting. For some reason, when people know "the inside scoop," it makes them feel important, makes them feel better than others, or makes them feel like they can build stronger social bonds by telling secrets. While some may think spreading gossip puts them on a social pedestal, gossip can ruin the culture of a dojo by destroying trust and honesty among the students.

A person who spreads gossip should be immediately addressed and the drama stopped. Read verse 20, *"Without wood a fire goes out; without gossip a quarrel dies down."* Gossip stirs strife among teammates, but it can be stopped by a master instructor, upper belt, or truly anyone who will stand up and say, "This is not right." Stopping gossip will save relationships and could save a school from destroying itself. You can be a key person in stopping the effects of gossip. If you will make a conscious decision to not complain about another student, you will see improvements in your life when you cut the fuel line that feeds the fire. Refusing to kindle the coals of gossip will promote trust, peace, and a welcoming spirit at your dojo.

Points to Remember

- *Don't give your energy to working with a fool unless you see they truly have a heart to change. Fools will suck the life out of you if you let them.*
- *No amount of money or fame will make you better than anyone else. Don't let conceit tell you otherwise.*
- *Laziness and gossiping destroys any witness you have for Christ. It's a sign of foolishness that robs you of what God has called you to be.*

| 27 |

True Friends

Do not boast about tomorrow, or you do not know what a day may bring.

²Let someone else praise you, and not your own mouth; an outsider, and not your own lips.

³Stone is heavy and sand a burden, but a fool's provocation is heavier than both.

⁴Anger is cruel and fury overwhelming, but who can stand before jealousy?

⁵Better is open rebuke than hidden love.

⁶Wounds from a friend can be trusted, but an enemy multiplies kisses.

⁷One who is full loathes honey from the comb, but to the hungry even what is bitter tastes sweet.

⁸Like a bird that flees its nest is anyone who flees from home.

⁹Perfume and incense bring joy to the heart, and the pleasantness of a friend springs from their heartfelt advice.

¹⁰ Do not forsake your friend or a friend of your family, and do not go to your relative's house when disaster strikes you— better a neighbor nearby than a relative far away.

¹¹Be wise, my son, and bring joy to my heart; then I can answer anyone who treats me with contempt.

[12]The prudent see danger and take refuge, but the simple keep going and pay the penalty.

[13]Take the garment of one who puts up security for a stranger; hold it in pledge if it is done for an outsider.

[14]If anyone loudly blesses their neighbor early in the morning, it will be taken as a curse.

[15]A quarrelsome wife is like the dripping of a leaky roof in a rainstorm

[16]restraining her is like restraining the wind or grasping oil with the hand.

[17]As iron sharpens iron, so one person sharpens another.

[18]The one who guards a fig tree will eat its fruit, and whoever protects their master will be honored.

[19]As water reflects the face, so one's life reflects the heart.

[20]Death and Destruction are never satisfied, and neither are human eyes.

[21]The crucible for silver and the furnace for gold, but people are tested by their praise.

[22]Though you grind a fool in a mortar, grinding them like grain with a pestle, you will not remove their folly from them.

[23]Be sure you know the condition of your flocks, give careful attention to your herds;

[24]for riches do not endure forever, and a crown is not secure for all generations.

[25]When the hay is removed and new growth appears and the grass from the hills is gathered in

[26]the lambs will provide you with clothing, and the goats with the price of a field.

[27]You will have plenty of goats' milk to feed your family and to nourish your female servants.

Chapter 27: Daily Devotional

Who is your best friend? When I ask myself that question, I think of so many wonderful people in my life who I consider my best friends. But the truest example of a best friend that I think of is the friendship Chris had with Ron Ornelas. Martial arts brought these two men together and they spent countless hours at the dojo together, training, talking, and tormenting each other. Laughter was never lost and neither was deep-down, heartfelt, hard conversations. They were "thick as thieves," "like peas and carrots," and "joined at the hip" – any phrase that describes the best of friends would apply to these two. They were real with each other and could say things to each other that if said by anyone else would be offensive. Ron and Chris were the best of friends.

Friends are an amazing gift from God. True friends tell you what you need to know regardless if you like it or not and they do so because they care about you. Inviting this type of friendship into your life will bring you safety, comfort, and joy.

The Pitfall of Pride

At our martial arts school we have been privileged to work with some very talented martial artists. They had all the athletic abilities you could imagine and possessed the skills to master their art beautifully. When thinking back over this list of outstanding students, not only do I remember their physical abilities, but I remember their character.

One such student came from a broken home, but he had a grandmother who was not going to let that be a barrier in his life, and she worked hard to surround her grandson with Godly men. They showed up at our school when the boy was about 9 years old and stayed with us until he turned 17, around his junior year in high school. His attendance diminished some when he got into high school, but he was still around. The men in our school poured into the life of this boy – inviting him to their home, taking him to church and vacation bible school events, putting him on their flag football teams, coaching him in rec basketball and more. No matter how hard the grandmother and others tried to instill virtues in him, he remained an unruly, hard-headed kid. This boy was like the fool of verse 22 – *"Though you grind a fool in a mortar, grinding him like grain with a pestle, you will not remove their folly from him."*

He loved to show-off because he wanted the praise of others. This desire caused him to drift toward the praise of friends who only wanted his athletic abilities and unbridled tongue to help them cause trouble. That praise continued to lure him throughout his life and seven years after leaving our school he has found himself with multiple children from different women, a long rap sheet of trouble, and a record that includes time in the state penitentiary.

Ironically, one night at class Chris was teaching students how to perform a drill and he told the story of how this particular boy could do this drill with absolute perfection. At that very moment the boy, now a grown man, walked through the doors of our school. The timing was like something out of a movie. He was not the same vibrant, spirited boy of his youth, but rather a tired, broken man who smiled when he remembered his days as a martial artist.

Pride is such a dangerous snare and Proverbs talks about it many times. Verse 21 reads, *"The crucible for silver and the furnace for gold, but people are tested by their praise."* How does praise test you? It checks your humility like high temperature tests metals. Praise can impact you in a very negative way if you let it; however, praise in itself is not a bad thing. At the end of each class Chris routinely sits his students in a circle and praises them for one good thing they did well. This praise is necessary to help students develop confidence and overall growth, but when praise becomes your god and you use it to elevate yourself above others, it can produce a sinful nature that is destructive. If pride becomes your god, be reminded that *"Pride goes before destruction, a haughty spirit before a fall"* (Proverbs 16:18).

People with integrity are not swayed by praise. They know who they are as a martial artist and a person and they continually do the right thing regardless if they are praised for it or not. Praise does not make them work harder; a lack of praise does not make them stop working hard. The true satisfaction they receive comes from an internal compass that tells them whether they gave their best effort. Praise is merely icing on the cake for a job well done. It says, "I noticed and I appreciate your effort."

Another thing about praise is who gives it. *"Let someone else praise you, and not your own mouth; an outsider, and not your own lips"* (verse 2). This particular boy liked to tell others how great he was and praised himself in an effort to be elevated higher than his teammates. This likely stemmed from wanting to feel better about himself, but what it really did was turn others off. They got tired of his "trash-talking" and began to ignore him.

Remember the conceited person we learned about in chapter 26? Praising yourself shows the conceit in your heart and reveals your true character. Rather than telling everyone what a gifted martial artist you are, let your actions speak for themselves. If someone else praises you for your talent, accept the compliment and continue doing what you're doing.

Got your Back

As a school owner, you worry about everything and wear lots of hats. Not only do you have to think about the physical building, equipment, and utilities, you also have to consider the curriculum, class offerings, and instructors needed. You also think about collecting tuition, setting belt testing dates, choosing tournaments, getting a website... and the list goes on and on. Regardless if you operate on a full or part-time basis, the ins and outs of running the school are always in the back of your mind. With all the responsibilities of being a business owner, it can be easy to overlook the very people who help you keep the doors open – your students and families.

"The one who guards a fig tree will eat its fruit, and whoever protects their master will be honored" (verse 18). This verse refers to those students and families who help support the school. They are the ones who take care of the things that don't always get done or do the things you don't have the expertise to do. We have many wonderful families in our school, but we have one particular woman who has amazing artistic abilities. She graciously paints and designs all the artwork in the school including our logo, t-shirts, team uniforms and certificates. She is also gifted in organization and has created enrollment forms and testing flyers and put order to our payment processes. She can run any tournament without a hiccup! Her family drives 80 miles round-trip four days a week to train and are always asking what else they can do to support the school.

We have many men in our school who have amazing talents with building and construction. Chris, quite frankly, cannot hang a picture, so these men are an absolute Godsend to us. They have hung doors, built raised floors, installed new boxing rings, designed our MMA cage, laid flooring and so much more. Without their help, our school would never be where it is today.

So many people have helped us over the last 26 years that it's hard to express the gratitude for those that "tend the fig trees" of our school. For quite some time we had a small concession stand and a family in our school took it upon themselves to purchase the supplies for the concessions. They donated supplies to the school and we sold them for a small side profit. When we moved locations, we sent out an all-cry for help and had 10 trucks and trailers lined up and ready to make the move. These people stand behind us, work hard, and help get the job done without expecting anything in return – no breaks in tuition, no unearned promotion, no free t-shirt, nothing! They support the school because they are faithful students and, more importantly, faithful friends.

As we have learned over the years, it's important to not take these people for granted. They make your life easier, your school better, and your mission outreach farther. This verse should be a reminder to look at all the helpers in our lives and the daily impact they have on all we do. Take a moment and inventory all the "fig tenders" you have and think about how they support you. You don't need to own a school to have these people – all of us are blessed with people in our lives who support us in one way or another. Then take time to pray for them, asking God's blessing on their lives and thanking Him for putting them in your life.

The Benefits of a Friend

God created us to do life with other humans. We have a built-in desire for human interaction. Even the introverts of the world want to share life with others – it might just look differently than an extrovert. To fill this need, we seek out friends and build relationships. Proverbs 27 tells us there are many benefits to having friends in our lives.

One benefit is your friend can be your best critic. Think about it: who would you rather take criticism from, a friend or an enemy? In an ideal world you would probably not like to take criticism from anyone at all -- but in real life, if you need some tough love, the best person to deliver it is a friend. That might sound counterintuitive but consider the source. Your friend has your best interest at heart. while someone who does not know you or want the best for you might only tell you what you want to hear. Verses 5-6 put it this way: *"Better is open rebuke than hidden love. Wounds from a friend can be trusted, but an enemy multiplies kisses."* What this tells us is that it's better for our friend to correct us because they are doing it out of a heart of compassion as opposed to an "enemy" who could care less about you.

Another benefit is idea creation. When you share your ideas with a friend, this turns into a lively discussion. You and your friend weigh the pros and cons of the idea, discuss its strengths and weaknesses, and determine the possibilities of success or failure. This "meeting of the minds" helps redefine your idea so you see it in a new light. It brings clarity to your decisions as your friend challenges your ideas to help stimulate improved plans and thoughts. You and your friend bounce an idea off each other until it becomes a new version or gets pitched. When you are doing this idea creation, there are no egos involved. It's just you and your friend talking, planning, dreaming, thinking, creating and attacking the idea – not the idea maker. Friends help bring clarity to your situation because they are good people to be around, not because they are there to steal your idea. Why do you need to be around friends like this? Because *"As iron sharpens iron, so one person sharpens another"* (verse 17). True friends simply make you better.

A third benefit is sound advice. Verse 9 tells us that a friend's advice is as pleasant as perfume. Perfume makes you feel good and so does well-grounded advice from a friend. This advice can spur you on to great things, change your course, or comfort you in a time of need. There's nothing like the advice you get from a trusted, faithful friend. Proverbs 17:17 describes this type of friend as one that *"loves at all times."*

Do you feel a sense of "friendship" at your dojo? Friendships begin by making an acquaintance, having conversation, and sharing stories. A mom in our school recently posted this statement:

"Ultimate Martial Arts, this training center we call home, has brought our family so many blessings, not only learning martial arts but the friendships we've gained. I just needed a moment to show appreciation of the good people at UMA. Starting with Chris Rangel and following his lead and example, many MANY others are leading the way of kindness."

Martial arts might be the common connection that you have, but through conversation and kindness a deeper friendship can develop. Look at how martial arts can open the door to new friendships in your life.

Points to Remember

- *Check your stance. If your stance is built on pride, you can be sure that your legs will not support you and you'll fall every time.*
- *Don't take the people in your life for granted who are always there to support you. Tell them how much you appreciate them.*
- *Find a good friend you can rely on through thick and thin, who makes you a better you.*

| 28 |

Do the Right Thing

The wicked flee though no one pursues, but the righteous are as bold as a lion.

²When a country is rebellious, it has many rulers, but a ruler with discernment and knowledge maintains order.

³A rulerwho oppresses the poor is like a driving rain that leaves no crops.

⁴Those who forsake instruction praise the wicked, but those who heed it resist them.

⁵Evildoers do not understand what is right, but those who seek the Lord understand it fully.

⁶Better the poor whose walk is blameless than the rich whose ways are perverse.

⁷A discerning son heeds instruction, but a companion of gluttons disgraces his father.

⁸Whoever increases wealth by taking interest or profit from the poor amasses it for another, who will be kind to the poor.

⁹If anyone turns a deaf ear to my instruction, even their prayers are detestable.

¹⁰Whoever leads the upright along an evil path will fall into their own trap, but the blameless will receive a good inheritance.

[11]The rich are wise in their own eyes; one who is poor and discerning sees how deluded they are.

[12]When the righteous triumph, there is great elation; but when the wicked rise to power, people go into hiding.

[13]Whoever conceals their sins does not prosper, but the one who confesses and renounces them finds mercy.

[14]Blessed is the one who always trembles before God, but whoever hardens their heart falls into trouble.

[15]Like a roaring lion or a charging bear is a wicked ruler over a helpless people.

[16]A tyrannical ruler practices extortion, but one who hates ill-gotten gain will enjoy a long reign.

[17]Anyone tormented by the guilt of murder will seek refuge in the grave; let no one hold them back.

[18]The one whose walk is blameless is kept safe, but the one whose ways are perverse will fall into the pit.

[19]Those who work their land will have abundant food, but those who chase fantasies will have their fill of poverty.

[20]A faithful person will be richly blessed, but one eager to get rich will not go unpunished.

[21]To show partiality is not good— yet a person will do wrong for a piece of bread.

[22]The stingy are eager to get rich and are unaware that poverty awaits them.

[23]Whoever rebukes a person will in the end gain favor rather than one who has a flattering tongue.

[24]Whoever robs their father or mother and says, "It's not wrong," is partner to one who destroys.

[25]The greedy stir up conflict, but those who trust in the Lord will prosper.

[26]Those who trust in themselves are fools, but those who walk in wisdom are kept safe.

[27]Those who give to the poor will lack nothing, but those who close their eyes to them receive many curses.

²⁸When the wicked rise to power, people go into hiding; but when the wicked perish, the righteous thrive.

Chapter 28: Daily Devotional

One important tenet of taekwondo is service. This tenet refers to being part of a community, and as a member of this community we are called to be of service and give to others. This tenet encourages us to be "just" in our service to others within our community. The Bible uses the word "just" periodically and it simply means to be fair, equitable, or honest. Being "just" to others is a character trait that is contrary to the world, but one we are called to be as a Christian martial artist.

Doing the right, or just, thing can come with sacrifice. It might be a sacrifice of time, money or even friendship, but the Bible tells us that God will repay our sacrifice with blessing. Doing the right thing speaks volumes about your character and sets positive consequences in motion that will open unforeseen doors of opportunity. When you do the "just" thing in what may seem like small details, God and other people will then trust you to handle the bigger issues in life.

Do the Just Thing

Over the years we have witnessed martial arts instructors who promote students when they are not ready, all in the name of profit. The philosophy is that if the student's check clears, then they too can become a black belt. This is such an injustice to the student and to martial arts itself. Martial arts is not a quick, overnight degree advancement program, but rather a journey where the student learns and develops over months and years, and is promoted on a timeline consistent with that training. Money should not be the determining factor for promotion. This practice is deceitful and unjust, but as we know, it's often the way of the world. Verse 5 confirms this thinking by saying, *"Evildoers do not understand what is right, but those who seek the Lord understand it fully."* Unearned promotion is not the only form of injustice in martial arts. So is cheating at tournaments by scoring unfairly, not showing up to instruct the class yet taking people's tuition money, lying about your certifications and rank to attract students, and more.

It's sometimes hard to understand the injustice that prevails in people, but this is what we *do* know. Satan is the ruler of this world and his mission operative is deceit, lies, trickery, and all things that lead to darkness. While we are on this earth we will continually battle against his dark forces, but we have the weapons to defeat him. Ephesians 6:10-20 outlines all the armor provided for us to withstand the attacks of the devil. Your armor has these pieces:

- belt of truth
- breastplate of righteousness
- gospel of peace
- shield of faith
- helmet of salvation
- sword of the spirit

As you put on this armor, it's important to understand who you are really fighting and Ephesians 6:12 tells us who that enemy is. *"For our struggle is not against flesh and blood, but against the rulers, against the authorities, against the powers of this dark world and against the spiritual forces of evil in the heavenly realms."*

Now, imagine the person who does not know about this armor. Matthew 13:15 tells us that people who do not know God have calloused hearts, ears that won't hear and eyes that are closed to the things of God. So, it really shouldn't surprise us when evil men say or do things that are contrary to what we know is right according to God's Word. Quite frankly, we shouldn't even expect them to understand God's ways of righteous justice because they refuse to listen and learn. God is a God of justice who is described in Deuteronomy 32:4 this way:

"He is the Rock, his works are perfect, and all his ways are just. A faithful God who does no wrong, upright and just is he." In order to walk in God's ways, we are called to a just lifestyle. We cannot claim to love God and ignore being just in our business and in our daily lives.

Payment is Coming

There is a payment coming to the unjust... and it's not the payment they are counting on! This payment is how God will repay their unjust behavior. Verse 8 reads, *"Income from exploiting the poor will end up in the hands of someone who pities them"* (Living Bible). God will take the wealth they gained by injustices and give it to those who are just. What's awesome about this is we don't have to try and keep count or worry about this transfer of wealth. The Bible tells us that God will take care of the transfer to those who do right. God makes this promise of repayment again in Deuteronomy 32:35: *"It is mine to avenge; I will repay. In due time their foot will slip; their day of disaster is near and their doom rushes upon them."*

Our charge as Christian martial artists is to not worry about what other schools are doing to gain wealth, but focus on operating with integrity and finding ways to show kindness to the poor. This is one small example, but it was a powerful statement in our school. We had a family who sacrificed a lot for their son to take martial arts lessons. It was something the boy had always wanted and the parents worked hard to give it to him. One day the family came to class and the boy was visibly upset. The bike he had been given for his birthday was stolen right off his front porch. Chris mentioned to one other instructor that it would be great if we would replace this boy's bicycle – and that's all it took. Our martial arts family rallied together, gathered donations, and Chris had the privilege of presenting this boy with a new bicycle just days after his was stolen. Our generous martial arts family has collected food donations for those in need, delivered surprise Christmas gifts to families, paid for other children's tournament fees or bought their hotel rooms, and sent flowers to hurting families.

Injustice says, "I want it and I will take it in whatever unjust ways I can." The just says, "Let me give what I have to help you." God is keeping count of the measures the unjust use to make their gains and in His time will take it from them to funnel through the just, who will pass it on to those who need it most. God is very clear that the transfer of wealth is coming for the just and he tells us in Ecclesiastes 2:26: *"To the person who pleases him, God gives wisdom, knowledge and happiness, but to the sinner he gives the task of gathering and storing up wealth to hand it over to the one who pleases God."*

Proverbs 28:27 is another guarantee of the payment coming for the person who gives to the poor. *"If you give to the poor, your needs will be supplied! But a curse upon those who close their eyes to poverty"* (Living Bible). In his book *Thou Shall Prosper*, Rabbi Daniel Lapin offers ten fundamental commandments to creating wealth based on the established principles of ancient Jewish wisdom. Commandment #9 is "Act Rich: Give Away 10% of your After-Tax Income." Now, that's contrary to the world's view! Rabbi Lapin is repeating what we read in verse 27 by telling us if we give away what we have, God will supply our every need. In fact, the Bible challenges us to try and outgive God. God's reply to that challenge is Luke 6:38 *"Give, and it will be given to you. A good measure, pressed down, shaken together and running over, will be poured into your lap. For with the measure you use, it will be measured to you."*

Don't Be Jealous

It can be easy to get jealous of the unjust person's wealth and successes, but have you ever stopped to think about what you *don't* see about this person? For example, you might see a fancy home, fast car, expensive clothes and all the luxuries that wealth can bring, but notice what is missing from this list. Peace, happiness, joy -- these are all things money cannot buy.

There are so many free, yet priceless gifts given to a child of God, but I am biased that my favorite is peace. Philippians 4:6-7 is my "peace" verse. *"Do not be anxious about anything, but in every situation, by prayer and petition, with thanksgiving, present your requests to God. And the peace of God, which transcends all understanding, will guard your hearts and your minds in Christ Jesus."* I guess peace is my favorite because I grew up in the house of a worrier. In my early days of being a parent, I prayed that I would not have that burden of worry and I don't! I would not trade my gift of peace for all the money in the world.

Wisdom is another wonderful gift that God gives His children and it's one that the unjust takes for granted. The unjust think they are special because of their wealth and they do not need to rely on anyone for wisdom. If they are so rich, they must be wise, right? Not at all. The Bible says the poor (just) man is richer in spirit. *"The rich are wise in their own eyes; one who is poor and discerning sees how deluded they are"* (Proverbs 28:11). The just man knows that he needs to depend on God, not on his own material wealth. This dependence on God will cultivate a richness that no wealth can provide. The poor man sees his need for God and works to develop a character that is pleasing to Him. The rich man may lose all his riches, but the poor man's character cannot be taken from him. Don't be jealous of the rich man – after all, temporary riches may be all he ever has. Don't let your jealousy change who you are to obtain the fleeting riches of the world.

Own Your Own Stuff

The last nugget that I want to focus on in this chapter is another act that certainly says a lot about your character. This is the idea of owning your own stuff. By that I mean if you make a mistake, own it. If you broke it, pay for it. If you told a lie, ask for forgiveness. If you did it, say you did! Own your own mistakes and don't put the blame on everyone else.

This is a problem I see in our culture all the time. People do not want to take ownership of their own stuff. It's never their fault that something happened. Blame is always put on someone or something else. I guess it's human nature to resist admitting we are wrong, but it sure hurts your character when you cannot admit to your mistakes.

The Living Bible says it very plainly in verse 13, *"A man who refuses to admit his mistakes can never be successful. But if he confesses and forsakes them, he gets another chance."* We can appreciate a person who says, "I screwed up" and are clearly remorseful for what they did. This person has a strong self-image and is someone you can with good conscience offer a second chance. In the book of James, we are told to *"confess your sins to each other and pray for each other so that you may be healed."* The first step to forgiveness is confession. Confession heals your wounds and repairs the relationship with the people you may have hurt.

Owning your own stuff and being just are both about doing the right thing. When you are faithful to make these two acts a priority in your life, verse 20 promises you *"... will be richly blessed."* That's a promise worth being "just" for!

Points to Remember

- *If a person has not surrendered to God, it should not surprise you when they do unjust things. Be the "just" witness they need to see.*
- *It may not feel like it today, but God has a payment plan already set in motion for the unjust. Don't be jealous of what you can see, but instead be thankful for the unseen gifts of God that come from being a just person.*
- *Own your stuff – especially your mistakes. People will like you and respect you for it.*

| 29 |

Trust His Vision

Whoever remains stiff-necked after many rebukes will suddenly be destroyed—without remedy.

² When the righteous thrive, the people rejoice; when the wicked rule, the people groan.

³ A man who loves wisdom brings joy to his father, but a companion of prostitutes squanders his wealth.

⁴ By justice a king gives a country stability, but those who are greedy forbribes tear it down.

⁵ Those who flatter their neighbors are spreading nets for their feet.

⁶ Evildoers are snared by their own sin, but the righteous shout for joy and are glad.

⁷ The righteous care about justice for the poor, but the wicked have no such concern.

⁸ Mockers stir up a city, but the wise turn away anger.

⁹ If a wise person goes to court with a fool, the fool rages and scoffs, and there is no peace.

¹⁰ The bloodthirsty hate a person of integrity and seek to kill the upright.

¹¹ Fools give full vent to their rage, but the wise bring calm in the end.

¹² If a ruler listens to lies, all his officials become wicked.

[13] The poor and the oppressor have this in common: The Lord gives sight to the eyes of both.

[14] If a king judges the poor with fairness, his throne will be established forever.

[15] A rod and a reprimand impart wisdom, but a child left undisciplined disgraces its mother.

[16] When the wicked thrive, so does sin, but the righteous will see their downfall.

[17] Discipline your children, and they will give you peace; they will bring you the delights you desire.

[18] Where there is no revelation, people cast off restraint; but blessed is the one who heeds wisdom's instruction.

[19] Servants cannot be corrected by mere words; though they understand, they will not respond.

[20] Do you see someone who speaks in haste? There is more hope for a fool than for them.

[21] A servant pampered from youth will turn out to be insolent.

[22] An angry person stirs up conflict, and a hot-tempered person commits many sins.

[23] Pride brings a person low, but the lowly in spirit gain honor.

[24] The accomplices of thieves are their own enemies; they are put under oath and dare not testify.

[25] Fear of man will prove to be a snare, but whoever trusts in the Lord is kept safe.

[26] Many seek an audience with a ruler, but it is from the Lord that one gets justice.

[27] The righteous detest the dishonest; the wicked detest the upright.

Chapter 29: Daily Devotional

As a parent, you will experience a period of time called "the terrible twos." This is a time when your child displays defiant behavior, throws fits and tantrums, and displays rapid mood changes. During this developmental stage of a child, it can be difficult to correct their behavior. You might try time-out, spanking, or loss of toys. You might try bribery, gifts, or fun activities. It may seem that no matter the consequence for this stubborn behavior, the child does not change. This child wants his or her own way and will not give in or give up. The child simply cannot understand this as inappropriate behavior – it's just part of their normal developmental growth.

As Christians we are often like this child, wanting things our way and throwing fits when life does not go according to our plans; however, we are called to a different standard of thinking. We are called to live a life that is dependent on God and not our own ways. God has a perfect plan for us if we will just relinquish our control and let Him guide our lives. He sees the bigger picture and we should trust His vision better than our own.

Don't be Stiff-Necked

Over the years our school has participated in many martial arts tournaments. In all of these tournaments, Chris is running from ring to ring, coaching his students and yelling out instructions. He is very good at watching opponents to find their tendencies and weaknesses, then giving commands to help his students capitalize on those flaws. He is also always correcting. If I had a dollar for every time I have heard, "Guard your grill!" or "You're dropping your left!" then I would likely be a millionaire. Our students know that when they hear Chris's voice, they need to respond because he is giving them instruction to help them be successful.

However, you always have that student who has watched too many MMA fights and thinks they know better than the master instructor.

They forget that they cannot see the whole match like the instructor can and may be overlooking key strategies to help them win the fight. Instead of listening to instruction, they decide they know better and do their own thing. There are usually no countdowns once you have been warned, and in a split second this student will find himself flat on his back or with a rocking headache due to the foot that just landed on his head gear.

Responding in a martial arts match needs to be instantaneous. The match is fast and you have to make split-second decisions about your opponent and your own game. If you don't respond right when you hear your instructor's voice, it could be over and done before you know it, and you missed a winning opportunity. As with any competitor in life, you must learn to listen to your instructor, take criticism when it's needed, and make corrections to your performance. This is vital in developing yourself as a martial artist.

The Bible has a term for that student who will not listen: "stiff-necked." Have you ever slept on your neck wrong and woke to a sore, stiff neck that is painful to move? A stiff neck makes you inflexible, rigid, and limited in your movement. Compare this condition to a stiff-necked person – a person who won't move, change direction, and is painfully stubborn.

Verse 1 talks about the stiff-necked person. *"Whoever remains stiff-necked after many rebukes will suddenly be destroyed – without remedy."* Not only does this sound like that student, but it sounds like many of us in our own lives and in our Christian walk with the Lord. When we refuse to listen to criticism or wise advice, we leave ourselves open to disaster. Instead of waiting until it's too late, the moment to change is *now*. Don't hang on to a lifestyle that is contrary to the Word of God. As believers we know that Christ will return again to take us to heaven and that return will happen in *"in a flash, in the twinkling of an eye"* (I Corinthians 15:52). Waiting around for "the right time" or "when I get older" or "when I have kids" or "whenever" is the wrong time.

Don't be stiff-necked about your relationship with God. He has given us many opportunities to have a life with Him and many warnings that He will come again. The longer you have the attitude that you'll wait until later to commit your life to God, the more hardened your heart becomes. Sin will become so commonplace in your life that you will either refuse to be corrected or you will have so much guilt that you won't see how God can forgive you. This of course is never true – God will always forgive your sins if you repent, even during your last breath on this earth.

Playing a waiting game with God is a dangerous choice to make. I have been in church my entire life and have heard many sermons on Christ's return. This date seems to be so near that I simply would not want to take the chance of living however I want to live in the moment and risk the chance of not living an eternity with Christ. If no other devotional in this book has struck a chord in your heart, I pray that this one does. Christ loves you and wants to be Lord of your life. Don't be stiff-necked and refuse his correction, pleas, and invitation. With no guarantee of tomorrow, today may be the last day you have an opportunity to invite Christ into your life.

Even in the Bible

The Bible is not all about people who did wonderful things and followed God with all their heart. In fact, much of the Bible is about fallen people and their daily struggles in living a righteous life. The Bible has great examples for us to learn from. Sometimes the best examples are when things go wrong – we often remember that lesson because it hurts the most.

The Israelites gave us a lesson that shows us what being stiff-necked can do. When the Israelites were captives in Egypt, God sent Moses to free them. During this transition from slavery to freedom, God performed many miracles to encourage them, feed them, and keep them safe. For example:

- He provided a pillar of cloud to lead them during the day and a pillar of fire to guide them at night. (Exodus 13:21)
- He split the Red Sea and they walked through on dry land, meanwhile destroying all the Egyptians who were chasing them. (Exodus 14:21-31)
- He provided manna and quail every morning to feed them when they were hungry. (Exodus 16:4,13-18).
- He made bitter water sweet and poured water from a rock. (Exodus 15:22-25; Exodus 17:2-6)
- He allowed them to prevail over their enemies. (Exodus 17:9-13)

These are just some of the highlights, but even this short list makes you wonder how the Israelites continued to argue with and distrust God. Simple – they were stiff-necked. The Bible even gives us a reminder to hear His voice and not be like the Israelites. *"Today, if you hear his voice, do not harden your hearts as you did in the rebellion, during the time of testing in the wilderness"* (Hebrews 3:7-8).

The scary thing about being stiff-necked is that there may come a point when God says, "Fine. I'm not that important to you. You want to live life your own way. Here you go." Staying with our Israelites, we see that this happened. In Numbers 13 the Lord commanded Moses to send ten spies to explore the land of Canaan. After exploring the land, eight of the ten returned to say there was no way that the Israelites could take the land. The people were giants and they would easily defeat the Israelite armies in their opinion. Two spies, however, had a different perspective. *"Let us go up at once and possess it,"* he said, *"for we are well able to conquer it!"* (Numbers 13:30, Living Bible). The people, however, hardened their hearts and believed the negative report over the report of Caleb and Joshua. Even though they had seen the mighty things God had done for them in their journey to this place, they still could not believe that He would be able to win this battle. Now God was fed up.

"Nevertheless, as surely as I live and as surely as the glory of the Lord fills the whole earth, not one of those who saw my glory and the

signs I performed in Egypt and in the wilderness but who disobeyed me and tested me ten times — not one of them will ever see the land I promised on oath to their ancestors. No one who has treated me with contempt will ever see it. But because my servant Caleb has a different spirit and follows me wholeheartedly, I will bring him into the land he went to, and his descendants will inherit it. ...Not one of you will enter the land I swore with uplifted hand to make your home, except Caleb son of Jephunneh and Joshua son of Nun" (Numbers 14:21-24, 30).

The Israelites were now left to stay in the land that was so much less than what God had intended for them. The teaching of Proverbs 29:1 happened to them. The Israelites were now broken without remedy.

Take a walk through the history of your life and count the many times God has intervened on your behalf and provided for you in much the same ways He did for the Israelites. But we are just like the Israelites. We have seen the hand of God move when we cried out to Him, and then we returned to our negative, sinful lifestyle. So we can't really look at them and say, "What is wrong with you people?" when we do the very same thing today!

I am the first to admit that I am guilty of second-guessing God. He has provided for our martial arts school so many times over the last 26 years, yet even now I sometimes wonder how we are going to stay open during the next month. (As I write this, we are facing the shut-down of our business due to the Covid-19 pandemic.) Should you ever start to become stiff-necked, ask God to give you the will to be like Joshua and Caleb.

Live in Integrity

Recently I was on one of my social media accounts and read a post from a famous Christian athlete about his faith in God. The post went viral when it was marked as having "sensitive content." Part of the post read, "You never know what God is doing with your life. You never know what he is preparing you for. So many times in the Bible when we look at the heroes, there were times in their life where — if they stopped, if they quit, if they said, 'No, God, I've had enough' — then they would have missed out on the impactful, most influential times of their life" (Tim Tebow Twitter post, July 2020). The article said it was not known what part was marked as "sensitive," so I read the post in its entirety. I know I have a biased Christian worldview, but there did not seem to be anything offensive in this post – especially compared to many of the other things that are put online.

This post brought me to Proverbs 29:10: *"The bloodthirsty hate a person of integrity and seek to kill the upright."* Jesus tells us in Matthew 10:22, *"You will be hated by everyone because of me, but the one who stands firm to the end will be saved."* Have you ever noticed that when you make a positive change, find success, speak truth, or do just about anything good, there is always someone who wants to destroy you? This is because as we learned in the last chapter, Satan is the ruler of this world and he lives to destroy God's people. When you live in the integrity God has called us to, it's important to remember who the attacks are really from. Even after all the blows the world will give people of integrity, Ephesians 6:13 promises they will still be standing!

Seek to live this life of integrity every day. When you enter the dojo consider your words, actions, and thoughts so that they are reflective of strong moral uprightness and principles. Consider ways you can continually build yourself physically, mentally, and spiritually with great character. You are setting an example that will carry to the world outside the dojo doors.

Points to Remember

- *It's a dangerous gamble when you are resistant to living a life dedicated to Christ. Don't play the waiting game of making a decision for Christ.*
- *God will provide for you. Don't try to navigate this world without Him or get your eyes off Him. Desire to be a Caleb or Joshua.*
- *Be ready for the attack. Have a firm stance. The blow will come when you stand for integrity.*

| 30 |

Be A Nobody

The sayings of Agur son of Jakeh—an inspired utterance. This man's utterance to Ithiel:"I am weary, God, but I can prevail.

² Surely I am only a brute, not a man; I do not have human understanding.

³ I have not learned wisdom, nor have I attained to the knowledge of the Holy One.

⁴ Who has gone up to heaven and come down? Whose hands have gathered up the wind? Who has wrapped up the waters in a cloak? Who has established all the ends of the earth? What is his name, and what is the name of his son? Surely you know!

⁵ "Every word of God is flawless; he is a shield to those who take refuge in him.

⁶ Do not add to his words, or he will rebuke you and prove you a liar.

⁷ "Two things I ask of you, Lord; do not refuse me before I die:

⁸ Keep falsehood and lies far from me; give me neither poverty nor riches, but give me only my daily bread.

⁹ Otherwise, I may have too much and disown you and say, 'Who is the Lord?' Or I may become poor and steal, and so dishonor the name of my God.

[10] "Do not slander a servant to their master, or they will curse you, and you will pay for it.

[11] "There are those who curse their fathers and do not bless their mothers;

[12] those who are pure in their own eyes and yet are not cleansed of their filth;

[13] those whose eyes are ever so haughty, whose glances are so disdainful

[14] those whose teeth are swords and whose jaws are set with knives to devour the poor from the earth and the needy from among mankind.

[15] "The leech has two daughters. 'Give! Give!' they cry.

"There are three things that are never satisfied, four that never say, 'Enough!'

[16] the grave, the barren womb, land, which is never satisfied with water, and fire, which never says, 'Enough!'

[17] "The eye that mocks a father, that scorns an aged mother, will be pecked out by the ravens of the valley, will be eaten by the vultures.

[18] "There are three things that are too amazing for me, four that I do not understand:

[19] the way of an eagle in the sky, the way of a snake on a rock, the way of a ship on the high seas, and the way of a man with a young woman.

[20] "This is the way of an adulterous woman: She eats and wipes her mouth and says, 'I've done nothing wrong.'

[21] "Under three things the earth trembles, under four it cannot bear up:

[22] a servant who becomes king, a godless fool who gets plenty to eat,

[23] a contemptible woman who gets married, and a servant who displaces her mistress.

[24] "Four things on earth are small, yet they are extremely wise:

[25] Ants are creatures of little strength, yet they store up their food in the summer;

²⁶ hyraxes are creatures of little power, yet they make their home in the crags;

²⁷ locusts have no king, yet they advance together in ranks;

²⁸ a lizard can be caught with the hand, yet it is found in kings' palaces.

²⁹ "There are three things that are stately in their stride, four that move with stately bearing:

³⁰ a lion, mighty among beasts, who retreats before nothing;

³¹ a strutting rooster, a he-goat, and a king secure against revolt.

³² "If you play the fool and exalt yourself, or if you plan evil, clap your hand over your mouth!

³³ For as churning cream produces butter, and as twisting the nose produces blood, so stirring up anger produces strife."

Chapter 30: Daily Devotional

"What do you want to be when you grow up?" That's a question we ask nearly every elementary-aged student. At that age the answer is likely, "An NBA star!" or "A famous singer!" It's fun to dream of fame and all the accolades it brings, the lifestyle it affords, and the notoriety it offers. But what would you think if that school-aged child said, "I want to be a nobody!"? That would certainly catch anyone off guard and make you question what they mean. No child or adult would typically say that, so we have to dig a little deeper to understand. When we think of this answer in a spiritual realm, it is exactly what God is calling you to be – a nobody.

Can you believe God enough to call yourself a "nobody?" That sounds like such a negative word, but it's all in your perspective. Being a nobody says, "I give it all to God. I am nothing without Him in my life." Being a nobody doesn't mean you are worthless. It means you trust God with it all.

Be a Nobody

There's a song by a popular Christian band that gives a powerful message about the impact anyone can have when they share Jesus Christ with others. The lyrics of the chorus describe the everyday man as a "nobody." This nobody has the power to share God with everybody, thus living a life that is reflective of Christ.

As we begin reading Proverbs 30, we meet a man who is only mentioned in the Bible here in verse 1, Agur. Little is known about Agur, but scholars believe he was a wise teacher and that assumption is pretty much all that is known about him. So, most readers might find him a "nobody." Agur gives good reason, however, for scholars to make their claim of wisdom because he comes out with strong words to show his submission to God's authority.

Agur begins his writing by declaring how stupid he is. He writes, *"Surely I am only a brute, not a man; I do not have human understanding."* The Living Bible says, *"I am too stupid even to call myself a human being!"* Agur is being pretty hard on himself, but what he's saying is that, like in the lyrics of the Christian song, he's just a nobody. He's not an eloquent speaker, gifted musician, or famous writer. He's just a nobody. But what this nobody realizes is his need for God. Agur is showing humility, which is a characteristic God has instructed us to walk in.

In today's world, being a nobody is not an attractive description. Most people want to be somebody famous or recognized. They network with influencers to get their name in the right circles and elevate to a higher social status. Making a name for yourself is not a bad thing, but you have to be honest about the intent of your heart. There are many great preachers, writers and singers who use their talents for God and not personal gain as their motivating factor, and we might call them "famous." As long as they are living for the right reasons, their fame is not a detriment to their spirit.

A beautiful thing with God is that we don't have to be somebody in the eyes of man to share Christ with others. In fact, just being a normal, ordinary person who shares what God has done in his or her life is equally as powerful as the "somebody's" story. A "nobody's" story about God's provision shows that He cares for each of us the same and is no respecter of persons. Peter tells us this in Acts 10:34 *"...I now realize how true it is that God does not show favoritism."* God has an equal playing field and that should excite us to come to the table and rub elbows with the best of them.

Being a nobody requires us to leave our notion that we are better than others at the door. When you walk in the dojo, don't think of yourself as superior to others because the color of your belt shows a higher rank. Here's an example. We have a 15-year-old black belt in our school who demonstrates this understanding of being a nobody. "E", as we affectionately call him, has many reasons why he might think of himself as better than others. Outside of the dojo, he is an honor student, gifted musician and speaks both English and Japanese. He has a family that loves him and a solid support system in his life. E is a handsome young man, has an infectious smile and demonstrates the highest level of respect by addressing adults with "sir" or "ma'am." E stands at 6'3" and about 140 pounds and has superior athletic abilities. Inside the dojo, E has earned the rank of black belt and has won many tournaments in fighting, forms, and weapons. He also gained the attention of many elite competitors in martial arts and has been asked to compete in some accomplished arenas. He teaches at our sister school in a nearby town, helps run classes at our local studio, and gives independent lessons to students seeking one-on-one instruction. E is confident yet compassionate and everyone who knows him, loves him. This is the description of a teenager who has much going for him – so much that he might feel arrogant or better than others. Most boys his age would take all this and get a big head. (In fact, many adults would do the same!)

But E remains friendly, hard-working, and down-to-earth; he does not think of himself as a "somebody."

When it boils right down to it, people want to see your character, not your best technique, and those are the traits that they remember, brag about, and use to define you. Agur recognizes his complete lack of anything without the help of God in his life and says, "I'm a nobody." As a martial artist, you too should desire to be a nobody in such a way that you have ears willing to listen, a mind ready to learn, and eyes to see that you have abilities, but only by the grace of God.

Just Enough

In the book of I Timothy, Paul teaches us about balance in our life. He writes:

"Do you want to be truly rich? You already are if you are happy and good. After all, we didn't bring any money with us when we came into the world, and we can't carry away a single penny when we die. So we should be well satisfied without money if we have enough food and clothing. But people who long to be rich soon begin to do all kinds of wrong things to get money, things that hurt them and make them evil-minded and finally send them to hell itself. For the love of money is the first step toward all kinds of sin. Some people have even turned away from God because of their love for it, and as a result have pierced themselves with many sorrows" (I Timothy 6:6-10, Living Bible).

Let's look at this teaching in light of Proverbs 30:7-9. Here Agur is saying that having too much money can be a dangerous thing, but so can having too little. Both Paul and Agur are saying we should have just enough. Just enough to have food and clothing and not have to resort to dishonest measures to meet our needs. Just enough so that we don't think we are "somebody" because of our wealth. Just enough to live a happy and good life. Agur writes that having too much may cause us to say, *"Who is the Lord?"* meaning we no longer need Him because we think our money is a bigger contender.

But as we see in scripture and played out daily in our world, people struggle to have "just enough." Some struggle because they live in poverty, while others fight and climb to always have more. Finding contentment in either situation can be hard, but God says he will provide both the unmet needs of the impoverished and the unsettled spirit of the person who craves for more. The key in both situations is to trust God. Trust that He is our great provider. Matthew 6:25-26 reminds us of this promise. *"Therefore I tell you, do not worry about your life, what you will eat or drink; or about your body, what you will wear. Is not life more than food, and the body more than clothes? Look at the birds of the air; they do not sow or reap or store away in barns, and yet your heavenly Father feeds them. Are you not much more valuable than they?"* Having just enough keeps us centered on the fact that God is our provider and our circumstance is not greater than He is.

Some may read this and think, "Are you saying I can't make money, want nice things, or hope to be rich?" That's not what I am saying at all. In fact, God has promised to bless us in such a way that it overtakes us. Go to Deuteronomy 28 and read verses 2-8. Look at all those blessings – blessed when you come, blessed when you go, blessed in the city, and blessed in the country. I count the word "bless" eight times in those scriptures. The thing that is so awesome about God is that He knows when we should and need to be blessed, what our capacity for blessing is, what the blessing means for our future, and how the blessing will impact our spiritual walk. God blesses each of us in different ways and at different levels, but He always blesses what we give Him with a humble heart. My blessing might look much different than yours, but that's because God tailored the blessing to meet our individual personalities.

Don't be envious of another's blessing. Instead be grateful for the customized, personalized, made-to-order blessing that is yours alone.

Only God

As we noted, Agur recognizes that he can't understand men, let alone God. Agur not only is recognizing his lack of daily knowledge, but also his lack of spiritual knowledge. In verse 3 he writes, *"I cannot understand man, let alone God"* (Living Bible). God tells us in the book of Isaiah that, *"As the heavens are higher than the earth, so are my ways higher than your ways and my thoughts than your thoughts"* (Isaiah 55:9). Agur gets that! He is trying to make it perfectly clear that he understands God is all-knowing and all-powerful and he will never be able to think on God's level. Anyone who thinks otherwise is "stupid!" This passage shows Agur's reverence to God and his submission to that authority. Nowhere does Agur try to show that he has any level of superiority, arrogance, or importance.

Agur asks several questions in verse 4 and the only answer to each one of them is GOD. Only God has done all the things Agur is asking and he knows that. He's just making a point. ONLY GOD is the point! Only God created the foundation of the earth (Isaiah 45:18), formed us in the womb (Genesis 2:7, Ecclesiastics 11:5), counts every hair on our head (Matthew 10:30), and knows the day of His return (Matthew 24:36). ONLY GOD! We are foolish to think we can be smarter than Him. Agur looks at God and says, "I am a nobody in comparison to you."

Over the course of owning and operating our martial arts school we have said many times, "Only God." Only God helped us finance that new building. Only God brought that family to our school. Only God kept us safe. There are many questions I cannot answer and events I cannot explain, but I know that it's only by the hand of God our school has weathered every storm and continues to be a place of hope for martial artists.

Points to Remember

- *Your name may never go down in history as an all-time great, but your character will be spoken of forever. A humble nobody will leave a powerful story!*
- *Consider areas you need to let go of your "somebody" thinking and realize that "ONLY GOD" is the right answer.*
- *God is good. All the time. And all the time. God is good. He is good to provide "just enough" for us to handle.*

| 31 |

The Best Version of You

The sayings of King Lemuel—an inspired utterance his mother taught him.

² Listen, my son! Listen, son of my womb! Listen, my son, the answer to my prayers!

³ Do not spend your strength on women, your vigor on those who ruin kings.

⁴ It is not for kings, Lemuel— it is not for kings to drink wine, not for rulers to crave beer,

⁵ lest they drink and forget what has been decreed, and deprive all the oppressed of their rights.

⁶ Let beer be for those who are perishing, wine for those who are in anguish!

⁷ Let them drink and forget their poverty and remember their misery no more.

⁸ Speak up for those who cannot speak for themselves, for the rights of all who are destitute.

⁹ Speak up and judge fairly; defend the rights of the poor and needy.

¹⁰ A wife of noble character who can find? She is worth far more than rubies.

¹¹ Her husband has full confidence in her and lacks nothing of value.

¹² She brings him good, not harm, all the days of her life.

¹³ She selects wool and flax and works with eager hands.

¹⁴ She is like the merchant ships, bringing her food from afar.

¹⁵ She gets up while it is still night; she provides food for her family and portions for her female servants.

¹⁶ She considers a field and buys it; out of her earnings she plants a vineyard.

¹⁷ She sets about her work vigorously; her arms are strong for her tasks.

¹⁸ She sees that her trading is profitable, and her lamp does not go out at night.

¹⁹ In her hand she holds the distaff and grasps the spindle with her fingers.

²⁰ She opens her arms to the poor and extends her hands to the needy.

²¹ When it snows, she has no fear for her household; for all of them are clothed in scarlet.

²² She makes coverings for her bed; she is clothed in fine linen and purple.

²³ Her husband is respected at the city gate, where he takes his seat among the elders of the land. ²⁴ She makes linen garments and sells them and supplies the merchants with sashes.

²⁵ She is clothed with strength and dignity; she can laugh at the days to come.

²⁶ She speaks with wisdom, and faithful instruction is on her tongue.

²⁷ She watches over the affairs of her household and does not eat the bread of idleness.

²⁸ Her children arise and call her blessed; her husband also, and he praises her:

²⁹ "Many women do noble things, but you surpass them all."

³⁰ Charm is deceptive, and beauty is fleeting; but a woman who fears the Lord is to be praised.

³¹ Honor her for all that her hands have done, and let her works bring her praise at the city gate.

Chapter 31: Daily Devotional

There are many books, sermons and ministries built on the foundation of the Proverbs 31 woman. The last chapter of Proverbs paints a description of a virtuous superwoman who can do it all. You might read this chapter and think a couple of things:

1. I'm a man and this is for women only, OR
2. I'm a woman and I could never be all that.

Regardless of your gender or lack of superhuman powers, there is something special for you in this chapter. God has designed you to be the best version of you. This chapter outlines many great character qualities, so our goal is to find the ones that best describe you and focus in on them. Let's dive in!

You Have a Voice

I have shared the story about how our school started. The mother of a bullied, young boy came to our house without anywhere else to turn. She was looking for ways to help her son defend himself against bullies. Since this first occurrence, we have worked with many families who have brought their children to martial arts lessons to help them gain confidence and have the courage to stand up against school bullies. In a round-about way our school is fulfilling the instruction found in verses 8-9. *"Speak up for those who cannot speak for themselves, for the rights of all who are destitute. Speak up and judge fairly; defend the rights of the poor and needy."* We are providing the skills to help these students speak up on their own behalf. This indirect method of help has proven beneficial and we have witnessed many students change from shy and scared to bold and brave.

A more direct approach would be closer to what the scripture is implying: that you speak up in the moment, standing right alongside the one who cannot speak. In 1984 the movie *The Karate Kid* debuted about a teenager named Daniel LaRusso who was new to his school. The martial arts bullies in his new school identified him as an easy target. Daniel did not have the skills these students did and he did not know how to defend himself. Mr. Miyagi, a local martial artist, offered the indirect approach of teaching Daniel, but he also spoke up and directly defended him in a face-to-face confrontation. He spoke for Daniel when he could not speak for himself. Miyagi had the martial arts training to back up his challenge and he was confident that Daniel would learn. Daniel so appreciated his friend's help that he trained relentlessly and grew a strong appreciation for the art Miyagi practiced. This theatrical example is one we can practically apply in our everyday lives.

We are all called to be Miyagi's when we see a need and speak up for those who are unfairly judged, abused, or neglected. This is a tough challenge sometimes. You might think, "I don't want to get involved" or "It's not my business." Speaking up for others requires that we shoulder some of the pain, lend a hand of help, give of our time, put ourselves out there for criticism, and risk retaliation from others. However, as Christian martial artists, these concerns should take a back burner to the instruction in these verses. You are not thinking of yourself; instead, you are clearly putting the needs of others before yourself.

In a quick Google search of "putting others first," Google identified 100 scriptures that might fit these parameters. One person's fight might not be your business, but the Bible is very clear that we are to help and to *"learn to do good; seek justice, defend the oppressed; take up the cause of the fatherless, plead the case of the widow"* (Isaiah 1:17). The next time you see an injustice that you have the power to intervene in, ask God for the strength to do so and overcome the concerns that might cause you to keep quiet. You have a voice –don't let belt rank, fear, or experience keep you from using it.

Strive to Be

You cannot be all things to all people and you do not possess every talent imaginable to man. After that shocking news sinks in, let's look at what you do have. You do have an unique set of talents that helps you meet the unique challenges and adventures in your life. 1 Peter 4:10 tells us, *"God has given each of you some special abilities; be sure to use them to help each other, passing on to others God's many kinds of blessings"* (Living Bible).

Let's use verses 10-31 to identify the talents you do have and find *one* to focus on that you want to develop. This is an interactive task and requires you to read, reflect and write. Take this last chapter of Proverbs as your springboard to dig into the Word of God. If the version of the Bible you are using is hard for you to understand, try another version. (You've probably noticed that I like the Living Bible). Read each verse and write down the qualities of this woman. For example, in verse 11, this woman is trustworthy and people can confide in her. Keep doing this for each verse through 31. When you are done, find one, just *one*, quality that you want to develop. Remember you likely do not possess them all and your day is not long enough to do everything she does. Don't be discouraged but rather be encouraged that God will walk right beside you and His Holy Spirit will guide you in your learning.

If this is a new, uncomfortable challenge for you, try practicing on your martial arts family. Bring your new talent to class and let your actions and words demonstrate how you are developing your noble character. Daily write in the list you just generated. Identify how you are growing and changing to obtain the virtuous qualities in Proverbs we are all called to possess.

What You Become

In our school Chris uses the phrase, "It's not what you are, it's what you become" to motivate students in their pursuit of blackbelt excellence. When class ends and students circle up for their final instructions of the practice, Chris scans the circle and speaks to each student individually about their strengths and areas for improvement. He emphasizes the fact that today they struggled with this particular technique, but with a small change and more practice, this technique can be perfected. The idea is to not stay where you are but grow and improve.

As you work on developing the trait you selected from the verses in Chapter 31, don't get discouraged in your effort to practice and improve in that area. You may take one step forward and two steps back some days, but even small steps are steps in the right direction. Keep this motto as your true north: "It's not what you are, it's what you become."

Is She Pretty?

After you read Proverbs 31:10-31, ask yourself if the woman in these verses is pretty. If you answer that based on what the world would define as beauty, the answer should be, "I don't know." This is because nowhere in these verses does it say that the woman had beautiful eyes, the perfect weight or figure, or was super attractive. This woman was, however, diligent, hard-working, compassionate, and resourceful, which are many of the same godly characteristics we have learned about in our journey through Proverbs. The world looks at the outside and sees your outwardly appearance, but the true you is the character you develop and project from your inward person. That's the person God is looking at.

There is a great story in the Bible that illustrates God's x-ray vision. The prophet Samuel was sent to anoint David as the next king of Israel. He went to the house of Jesse, David's father, and asked to see all of his sons. Jesse brought seven sons before Samuel and Samuel said that none of them were the one God had chosen. *"So he asked Jesse, 'Are these all the sons you have?' 'There is still the youngest,' Jesse answered. 'He is tending the sheep'"* (I Samuel 16:11). Before Samuel even arrived at Jesse's house, God had already prepared him for what He was looking for. *"But the Lord said to Samuel, 'Do not consider his appearance or his height, for I have rejected him. The Lord does not look at the things people look at. People look at the outward appearance, but the Lord looks at the heart'"* (I Samuel 16:7).

Your character trumps physical appearance every time in the eyes of God. That should make us jump for joy. Everyone could say that they have some limitation – even Moses complained when God called him, saying he could not do the job because of his stutter. Other great men of God had physical ailments – Isaac suffered from blindness, Jacob had a limp after wrestling with the angel, and Mephibosheth, son of Jonathan and grandson of King Saul, was lame in both feet. Even the apostle Paul suffered from "a thorn in his flesh," but that did not stop him from being one of the greatest mouthpieces of God.

Letting the devil rob you of the blessings of God because he tells you are not qualified is a lie from the pit of hell. That's why it took me nearly fourteen years to finish this devotional. The devil told me my motivation for writing was not in the right place and I believed it and quit writing. If God has called you, He has already equipped you AND guess what? You are called. Each one of us are called to the specific work He has assigned us. To know your calling, check your character because that is where He looks to determine your readiness. As every martial artist at Ultimate Martial Arts will tell you, we know that our mission is *to build ourselves physically, mentally, and spiritually with great character, Sir!*

Points to Remember

- *Stand up and be a voice when others need your help. God has called us to come alongside the ones the world rejects.*

- *Living for God requires a daily growth mindset. We should be always looking for ways to be more like Christ.*
- *Our UMA motto: Build yourself physically, mentally, and spiritually **with great character**, Sir! God is looking for people who have set their heart on things above.*

TESTIMONIALS

Testimonials from Ultimate Martial Arts students and families

Parents if you are looking for a positive environment for your kids of all ages, and environment where they learn discipline, teamwork, dedication, and lifelong skills come out to Ultimate Martial Arts in Newton. Leah and Noah went from quiet kids who would stay in the corner to team leaders confident in themselves and members of a great team. In just 6 months they were facing opponents' multiple levels/belts above them and winning. Winning was great but the fact they had the confidence to step up to the challenge was a win by itself. This is what you get at Ultimate Martial Arts.

--Josh Weiser, UMA instructor and parent

GM Chris Rangel, you just have no idea what an impact you have on our family. You have a true gift. Living life to the fullest. We appreciate your heart, demand for respect, knowledge, comic side and just being a real all-around good guy. Ultimate Martial Arts - this training center we call home has brought our family so many blessings, not only learning martial arts but the friendships we've gained. I just needed a moment to show appreciation of the good people at UMA. Started with Chris Rangel and following his lead and example, many MANY others are leading the way of kindness

May you and your family continue to be blessed beyond measure.

--Tina Baker, parent

[I] love working with students who truly want to learn and improve like yours do.

Miles Johns, UFC fighter

We have to get uncomfortable to make changes! We have to be humble to realize the growth that needs to take place.

So do hard things people! Find your strength in enduring the unknown and the uncomfortable. I promise there is massive growth on the other side!

--Katie Longhauser, student

I have always looked at the wrong way of life. God gave me the knowledge and strength to see the right way. I am so thankful for you and my Ultimate Martial Arts family. You've always been a good father figure to me in my life. ... God gave me the chance to see what was right in the life that I need and want.

--Etric Johns, student

THIS is our Grand Master at ULTIMATE MARTIAL ARTS!! He is the reason we continue to come, day after day. Our kids are successful in their martial arts because of all the time, talent, encouragement, .. and goofin around he does/ shares. No place like it.

-Jes Gri, parent

Many individuals and families, including our own have been impacted by Chris's personal excellence and ministry. We always appreciated how he encouraged good character and integrity. Each time he would bestow a belt on a student he would always highlight the growth in skill and /or character he observed in the student... child, teenager, or adult. Thank you so much for the investment you have made in the lives of so many!

--Marcella Zook, parent

Five years ago, I walked into the doors of Ultimate Martial Arts as a new student. I didn't know what I needed, but I needed something that was mine, improving me - physically and mentally. That set everything into motion. 5 years later I can say I gained back confidence I had lost, strength- both physically and mentally, and a sense of belonging, and so much more. Thank you GM Chris Rangel for your vision, your school and your instruction. For seeing in me what I couldn't.

--Fran Heddin, student and parent

You fight with us spiritually and emotionally, and even physically. I love praying before and after class. Mr. Rangel, you teach us and we are willing to follow.

--Wana Oswald, student and parent

This summer I met someone who has made a huge difference in my life. This man has helped my family and me through some really hard times. He has been an amazing instructor and a special friend. I have learned a lot of fun things in his classes and even self-defense from him, so I will be able to protect myself if I need to. Mr. Rangel also introduced me to a much closer walk with God than I have had in the past. I keep God closer to me now because of Mr. Rangel's example. I am very thankful to have met you this summer and had the chance to learn from you. I can't wait until my next practice!!

--student, age 16

Thank you for everything you have done for me. You have made such a big difference in my life that I look in the mirror and see a stronger, better me. I also thank you for being there for me when I needed you most and for building my confidence up SO much from what it used to be. I hope that if someday you need my help, you know I will be there for you.

--student, age 12

ACKNOWLEDGEMENT

As iron sharpens iron, so one man sharpens another. Proverbs 27:17

I could never have written this book without Proverbs 27:17. This verse has been the mission statement of our martial arts school for years. It stems back to a friendship that Chris had with Ron Ornelas, a man God brought into our lives through martial arts. Chris and Ron were the best of friends until his death in 2009. This verse proves that having an accountability partner in your life makes you a better person. Chris and Ron talked about everything and helped each other through some tough battles. Once a week, they attended a men's bible study at 5:00 AM and held each other accountable to get up and go. Several other men came and went, but those two never missed. They knew they were each counting on the other to help them in their walk with the Lord. Their daily conversations (and they were daily) kept them mentally sharp and spiritually focused.

I want to thank all the people who have helped me remain sharp in my walk with the Lord as well as all the martial artists, especially Ron, who have sharpened Chris's walk as we have owned Ultimate Martial Arts.

Ultimately, I thank God for the strength, energy, and passion to share the gospel through the talents He has given us.

ABOUT CHRIS

Chris Rangel followed in the footsteps of his grandfather, Guadalupe Llamas, who was his martial arts instructor from an early age. Learning the art of taekwondo in his grandfather's garage, Chris continued his training and later opened his own school in 1994. After returning from his service in Desert Storm, Chris competed in the famed All Armed Forces World Class Athlete Program and Team USA for Taekwondo.

Over the years, Ultimate Martial Arts has been blessed to have UFC fighters and Olympic athletes train at the facility as well as hundreds of families from across the United States. Chris is passionate about teaching martial arts, helping school owners develop, and impacting lives.

As a highly respected leader and innovator in the industry, Chris utilizes his excellent communication skills to help both his students and business coaching clients to AIM higher than they have ever thought possible and make their dreams a reality.

Recent Accomplishments

2020 - WAKO Team USA Level 1 Bronze Coach; U.S. Junior Development Coach-WAKO; SAFE Family Defense Strategies co-founder; International Medal of Merit; UTA Olympic Sparring National Champions

2018 - 9th degree ITF Taekwondo; Master Instructor with Presas Style Kombaton

2017 - USA Martial Arts Hall of Fame - Winningest Program of the Decade

ABOUT THE AUTHOR

Melinda Rangel is an educator at heart. After teaching high school business for 22 years, she moved into administration and served as an assistant principal, career and technical education director, and virtual school administrator. She holds Master's degrees in Business Education and School Leadership and a Doctoral degree in Educational Leadership. Melinda currently serves as an Associate Professor of Business at Tabor College. She has spoken at numerous local, regional, and national conferences for business educators and has written articles for business education publications.

Melinda and her husband, Chris, own Ultimate Martial Arts in Newton, KS. They have two beautiful children – a son, Jared, who serves as a firefighter and a daughter, Jenna, who is an ICU nurse and is married to Dr. Ben Koerner. Family vacations are a must at their house and they love to travel to the beach, explore new places, and eat lots of Mexican food.

CPSIA information can be obtained
at www.ICGtesting.com
Printed in the USA
JSHW032104240321
12765JS00001B/1